Happy Felsch

Happy Felsch

Banished Black Sox
Center Fielder

Thomas Rathkamp

McFarland & Company, Inc., Publishers
Jefferson, North Carolina

ISBN (print) 978-0-7864-9487-3 ∞
ISBN (ebook) 978-1-4766-2323-8

LIBRARY OF CONGRESS CATALOGUING DATA ARE AVAILABLE

BRITISH LIBRARY CATALOGUING DATA ARE AVAILABLE

Front cover: Chicago White Sox center fielder
Oscar "Happy" Felsch, 1920 (Library of Congress)

Printed in the United States of America

*McFarland & Company, Inc., Publishers
Box 611, Jefferson, North Carolina 28640
www.mcfarlandpub.com*

For Marilyn and Robert,
the most loving and selfless parents
an aspiring writer could ever have

Table of Contents

Acknowledgments

Labors of love are rarely solitary acts. I am profoundly indebted to several gracious, generous souls. My lead-off hitter is Stuart Shea, a Chicago Society for American Baseball Research member. He provided integral research access, without which this project would have been difficult to complete. Milwaukee-area writer Jim Nitz, who wrote the excellent SABR BioProject piece on Felsch, spawned much of my interest in this project. Thanks, Jim!

Local libraries played a crucial role. Humble gratitude goes out to Emily Laws of our local Cedarburg, Wisconsin, library. Her prompt and courteous service calmed my nerves heading down the home stretch.

How did any baseball researcher survive before Retrosheet.org? Most of the statistics in this book came from this wonderful website. My thanks go to David Smith and the countless researchers who painstakingly plow through ancient newspapers and other primary sources to gather and share individual game accounts. Your influence on baseball research is immeasurable.

As a fellow member of the Society of American Baseball Research, I would like to thank the authors of earlier works on the 1919 Black Sox scandal and related subjects. One of the first was Eliot Asinof's book *Eight Men Out*. Although that book has been intensely scrutinized in other works about the scandal, a pleasant chat with the late author's son, Martin Asinof, confirmed for me that his father's heart and love for the game was always genuine.

William Lamb, author of the more recent *Black Sox in the Courtroom*, has shed bright lights on the 1921 trial, which brought a lot of ugliness into focus. Many thanks to Gabriel Schechter at the National Baseball Hall of Fame for the materials gleaned from their treasure trove of baseball research.

My appreciation extends to Laura Laurishke, granddaughter of Oscar Felsch and daughter of Oscar Jr. The memories shared from when she was a young girl reminded me of how precious family loyalty can be.

I would like to thank the Society of American Baseball Research for the wealth of resources and support that my membership provides.

Last, but hardly least, I could not have sweated over the research, bitten nails over the computer, paced in the upstairs hallway, or anguished over where my next sentence would come from, without the loyal, loving support of my dear wife Sarah, son Andrew, and daughter Stephanie. Their patience and encouragement kept me focused and alleviated the guilt I felt when this book project made heavy demands of my time. I have much to catch up on in 2016 and beyond. You have my solemn promise.

Introduction

Happy Felsch? I remember Happy Felsch. He used to ride past our house on his bicycle. Happy Felsch, yeah he was always around.

—Dave Rathkamp (the author's uncle)

My uncle, his brother Robert (my dad) and other brother Bill lived close to Oscar Felsch when they were growing up on the predominantly German north side of Milwaukee. They even worshiped at the same church, Emmaus Lutheran on North 20th Street. Felsch was a generation older, and to my dad and his brothers, he was just another codger.

Felsch honed his baseball skills on Milwaukee playgrounds and vacant lots, preceding other of Milwaukee's baseball luminaries, including Al Simmons (born Aloysius Szymanski), Joe Hauser, Ken Keltner, Tony Kubek, Bob Uecker, and Craig Counsell. Felsch's fame hung in the balance amid the biggest debacle in baseball history, just as he was approaching stardom. As Milwaukee writer Jim Nitz penned succinctly, Felsch "rose to the pinnacle of the baseball world only to be consigned forever to the sport's hell."

He started life as most young boys of the time did: finishing his chores, staying out of trouble, and playing as much baseball as the daylight permitted. The north side of Milwaukee was a hotbed of diamond matches. The preponderance of amateur, sandlot, church, and company teams in the early twentieth century was startling. Every empty parcel was officially or unofficially reserved for baseball. Felsch plied his trade for several local teams, working his way up to AA before making his major league debut with the Chicago White Sox in 1915.

The 1919 Sox were reportedly severed into two distinct camps: the barely educated and the academically refined. In those days, a high school education was less necessary than college is today. On this team, the intellectual gap was remarkably clear-cut. On one side, you had cocky and confident Ivy Leaguer Eddie Collins, Shano Collins (no relation), Nemo Leibold, Red Faber, and Ray

Schalk. In the "school of hard knocks" camp were Felsch, Eddie Cicotte, Joe Jackson, Swede Risberg, Arnold "Chick" Gandil, Buck Weaver, and part-timer Fred McMullin (the only one of this group to finish high school). The demeanor and behavior played parts, with the latter group sinking into repeated peril.

As polarizing as the two factions were, more so was their vivacious owner, Charles Comiskey. Extensive research revealed two types of people: those who loved him and those who despised him. Felsch seemed to be on both sides, depending on who asked, what year it was, or how much liquor he had consumed. The Old Roman, as he was called, was a pivotal figure in the sport's history, both as player and owner.

The man they called Happy was a wonderfully athletic brute of a man who got sucked into a ring of greed, corruption, and stunted dreams. His cheerful, jocular personality complemented his single-minded passion for baseball, and he paid little attention to activities that involved the brain. His talents on the field earned raving endorsements by sportswriters at every level, and from the man himself, Babe Ruth. His parents were first-generation German immigrants who chose Milwaukee as their new home. The Brew City welcomed immigrants openly, particularly from the Germanic states that were collectively known as Prussia. Milwaukee's growth surge, combined with the oppression and hopelessness of their homeland, made families such as the Felsches ripe for a cultural rebirth.

With his breakout year in 1920—his final campaign—Felsch was entering the peak of his career at age 28. How good would he have become? Did he have Hall of Fame talent? These questions are examined at the end of the book. Firsthand accounts by the shamed ballplayers are rare. Felsch talked the most publicly about the scandal, in three separate interviews. The first was immediately after the scandal, with his last, and arguably most contrite, coming 40 years later, not long before he died.

The preponderance of betting during the Dead Ball Era in general, and the 1919 World Series in particular, was no secret. Baseball and gambling were blood brothers long before the Black Sox scandal. "These players were not dumb," writes Sean Deveney in his book about the 1918 Series. "Game-fixing talk on team trains was nothing new. Sometimes it was idle chatter, other times not. Gambling and baseball were intricately linked."[1] Wagering was seemingly as much a part of the game as bats, balls, and gloves, and in retrospect, 1919 should not have been a surprise. The pathological denial and systematic concealment muffled the obvious, and in many ways made it tragically easy to perpetuate.

Did the scandal run parallel, historically, with the growing tugs at the rope of labor vs. management battles? Did the stranglehold of the reserve clause perpetuate management's control?

As with any controversial, puzzling event, sometimes the truth can seem as uncertain as an infant taking her first steps. Although professional baseball was over a quarter century old, the labor vs. owner war continued to be fragile and contentious. That cannot be ignored in any historical account of the scandal. As historian William A. Klingaman wrote: "What actually happened has never been established with complete certainty. Conflicting evidence, stories that changed from day to day, confessions that were later retracted, all muddy the water sufficiently to keep many of the exact details shrouded in a fog of mystery."[2]

Now, almost 100 years later, we enjoy some benefit of hindsight, but in many ways are no less puzzled. The truth notwithstanding, collective guilt is difficult to dispute. As writer Keith Jenkins wrote in *Re-Thinking History:* "The past and history are different things."

In April of 2014, Library and Archives Canada released newsreel footage that includes nearly five minutes of the 1919 World Series. Though spotty, this footage contained some of the most controversial plays—or parts of plays—of the series. Some nuggets could be gleaned from this source, including the batting stance of Felsch.

At least as early as 1971, when Harold Seymour and Dorothy Seymour Mills published *Baseball: The Golden Age*, historians have pointed out that baseball as a business isn't just a modern phenomenon. Even though Dead Ball Era owners such as Connie Mack, Clark Griffith, Charlie Ebbets, and Barney Dreyfuss grew up in the business, it was still smaller, easier to manage, and less public than it is today. Whether this contributed to the lack of empathy towards players' rights and freedoms is debatable. But it is clear that these so-called gentlemen of the sport could be just as conniving, ruthless, and self-centered as any today.

In addition to examining Felsch's role in—and the historical context of—the Black Sox scandal, this book chronicles his sandlot baseball days in Milwaukee, six years in the big leagues, legal battles, and his return to amateur competition. This return by a player to his baseball roots is rare—and we will examine the effects of Felsch having to rewind his career.

Information on Felsch family life is scarce. His kids have all passed on and surviving family members are understandably less knowledgeable, but also unwilling to rehash distant, shameful events to which they are biologically linked. The only relative who would talk to me was a grand-daughter who was only eight years old when Felsch passed away. She romantically clings to her uncle's innocence.

In 1918, during World War I, Felsch came home to work (exercising the "work or fight" option) and play for a well-known amateur team, the Kosciuszko Reds. A part-time catcher on that club was a distant relative of mine named

Harry Rathkamp, my grandfather's cousin. The family owned a grocery store on the north side of town, near where Felsch was raised.

In the parlance of baseball's history, we can never stop remembering or imagining. That's why we're baseball fans. Oscar Felsch was one of thousands who have played this sport professionally. His brief time in the highest echelon of the sport should help us appreciate how fleeting such careers can be and the difficulty of reaching baseball's pinnacle.

According to his family, Felsch was born laughing. He laughed at jokes. He laughed with teammates. He laughed at reality. He laughed at dire circumstances. And he laughed at fate.

Statistical Notation: *When including a player's statistics, this book uses the modern "slash stats" approach. For example .250/.345/.403 represents batting average, on-base percentage, and slugging percentage, respectively.*

1

Wilkommen, Charles and Marie

Milwaukee is the only place in which I found that the Americans concern themselves with learning German.... You will find inns, beer cellars, and billiard and bowling alleys, as well as German beer, something you do not find much in this country.

—John Kerler, Jr., writing to an old friend
in Reutlingen, Germany, in 1850.

What shame supposes to conceal, it instead divulges. Temptation can turn innocence into guilt and simplicity into ostentation. Mix in a little naivety and the soul is ripe for takeover. Oscar Emil "Happy" Felsch was talented, likable, driven, uneducated, foolish, gullible, simple and, like all of us, innately flawed. The lad from Milwaukee knew what he had done, and was painfully aware of what he wasted. Baseball—it was all about *baseball*.

In the end lies the beginning.

Two college freshmen at University of Wisconsin–Milwaukee meet for the first time as roommates. Sam is from Portland, Maine, Craig from Milwaukee. Craig is at ease. Sam is in a whole new world, nervous in his new surroundings. As they begin unpacking in their cramped dorm room, Sam looks up and says: "So you're from Milwaukee, that's where—" "Wait," interrupts Craig. "I know what you're going to say." Before Sam can continue, Craig spews a litany of timeless clichés about his hometown, all of which contain references to beer and 1970s sitcoms, *Happy Days* and *Laverne & Shirley*.

Those born in one of the most Germanic cities in the United States wink at the sarcasm of Sam's response. Milwaukee (not its original spelling) meant "good land" or "gathering place" to its earliest inhabitants, the Potawatomi Indians. The Teutonic tone of Milwaukee was established soon after the first German wave emigrated from Deutschland with a renewed sense of independence, modest financial resources, and an urge to plant their feet in the new frontier that was Wisconsin, in its largest dwelling, Milwaukee.

The first wave of Germans—mostly Old Lutherans—arrived in 1839, settling primarily on the north and west sides. Long before "diversity" entered the national vernacular, Milwaukee cemented its reputation as a developing melting pot of ethnic enclaves, with the Germans leading the way. Battling Solomon Juneau for new settlers to their areas, Byron Kilbourn provided willing aid and support to the labor-hungry Germans.[1] The biggest wave of European emigration to Wisconsin came in the decade following 1845. The number of German-born residents in Milwaukee doubled in 1850 and less than a decade later became a noticeable majority in Milwaukee.

They were not shy about establishing (according to some, imposing) their cultural mores and proclivities. Flexing their identity was a consequence of the urge for religious freedom and cultural autonomy. This is important to note because their home country was not a single, unified state until 1871. It was hardly a wrenching decision to flee Germany for the promise of a brighter star. Starting anew in semi-chartered land signaled a refreshing journey into cultural redefinition.[2]

The diversity of Milwaukee's people was rivaled only by the vast array of its cultural and social activities. The first beer garden opened in 1844. The Milwaukee Turners, or Turnverein, provided physical outlets with gymnastics and calisthenics. This idea was not initiated in Milwaukee, but was brought across the ocean. Felsch became a member of the Turners, with wrestling being his chosen physical endeavor when he was younger, a warm-up for his prodigious strength later on baseball fields.

As John Gurda wrote: "It can be argued that the Germans made Milwaukee safe for ethnicity, relatively speaking, for later arrivals to resist the melting pot. The Yankees were outnumbered; it was acceptable to be something else." Gurda also pointed out that what made the Germans unique was their internal diversity. "To speak of the city's German 'community' is, in some ways, a misnomer. Its members came, first of all, from every section of a country that did not exist, in a legal sense, until 1871, when it was unified under Prussian auspices."[3]

Among the Deutsche throng were Charles and Marie Felsch, who sought to grab their piece of the barely-baked American pie, having immigrated to Milwaukee from Berlin. At the time of their exodus, Berlin was not, as now, the capital of all of Germany. From 1701–1918, it was the capital of what was known as the Kingdom of Prussia. The exact date and time of their journey to America is relegated to the Atlantic Ocean or since-destroyed documents. But like other Germans who opted to bypass such cities as Buffalo, Cincinnati, St. Louis, and Chicago (other heavy German enclaves), they found Milwaukee ripe for a Teutonic explosion.

On the working front, since about 1860, Germans in Milwaukee dominated the carpentry trades (near 54 percent in 1860). Timing was everything to immigrants, and for the Felsch clan, the combination of several young mouths to feed with plentiful employment opportunities made their arrival more palatable. Charles Felsch was a carpenter by trade, a convenient profession in a growing city that would erect buildings and other permanent structures at a hefty pace. He would eventually reach the lofty status of an official of the Milwaukee Carpenters Union.[4]

Oscar Emil Felsch was born on April 7, 1891, according to his 1943 Social Security application and 1964 death certificate. Records were loosely kept in those days, if they existed at all, and one must rely on scant historical archives and human memory.

At the turn of the century, Milwaukee was a thriving, booming manufacturing town, often called "Machine Shop to the World." Herr and Frau Felsch (nee Tietz or Tiegs)—according to a 1900 census—raised 12 children, with Oscar being one of seven who still resided at their parents' 26th Street home in 1900. Oscar was the third-youngest of those four boys and three girls. He attended school until the sixth grade and then worked for $10/week as a laborer in a local factory (all but 25 cents going directly to his father). Charles, who came from a socialist German background, was a strict authoritative figure, and talking was not on the dinner menu. "He had to be strict," said Oscar Felsch in his later years. "There were 12 kids around the table. Could you imagine the babble at the table had he allowed us to speak?"[5]

The stable family unit was paramount in those days, and being poor was as common as the sunrise. To mitigate the strain of tight quarters, the kids took to leisurely activities, chiefly baseball. Charles and three of Oscar's brothers played the game. (It was thought that Charles was quite the first baseman in his day.) Charles, Jr., was an infielder, J.W. an outfielder, and Fred a pitcher. City leagues were well under way in the latter quarter of the 19th century, and the Felsch foursome had lofty aspirations.

"Being poor was nothing in those days," said Felsch.

> Everyone I knew was poor. But a lot of us played baseball. One winter, when I was maybe fifteen, I shot up big, you know. The first day in spring, I hit one over the fence. None of us kids had ever done that, and the way they all looked at me, it was something all right. Seems like all I ever wanted to do was hit a new ball with a new bat.
>
> Half the deal was to hit the long ones when the ball was still whole. Hell, we played with one baseball so long, you could hear it whimper when you hit it. After a while, it was hardly a baseball no more. Cover all gone, we'd tape it up. It wouldn't go nowhere. If you hit it, I'd make a strange sound, like a sharp fart, you know? And the pitcher had so many things to grab hold of, he could really make it dance. 'Course, most of the bats were no better. Nailed, glued, taped ... when a bat broke, everyone'd looked up, you know, and the sound'd make you sad.[6]

Of course, life wasn't all fun and leisure. Like today, one had to pay the bills to keep the old homestead viable. Counter to the more educated and cultured among them was the vast majority of laborers, artisans, and merchants that comprised the German arrivals. Unskilled workers outnumbered skilled, but that sufficed in a time when a bevy of work welcomed the numerous warm, eager bodies. To the kids, who were among those who sweated their way at work sites, baseball became their escape. This was just as true in Milwaukee as in other immigrant-dominated locales, although early signs of baseball are more known and written about in the bigger Eastern cities. Prior to dedicating his time to baseball, Felsch developed his physical prowess through wrestling.

> At one time, my friends had me kidded into almost believing that I had a chance for the heavyweight championship. They thought I would be heavier than I am when I fully developed. Once I made an opening in the baseball profession, however, I soon lost much of my enthusiasm for head spinning. I'd sooner be batting champion of the American League than conqueror of Frank Gotch. [Gotch, also of German descent, was world heavyweight wrestling champion from 1908 to 1913].
>
> The game; that was the thing. In a ball game, nothing else matters. Now ain't that something! You wonder, am I gonna hit that guy's stuff today or ain't I? You do and sometimes you don't, but there weren't never a time when I cared about doing anything else.[7]

Soon, Felsch's singular boyhood recreation elevated to a style of baseball that became the stepping-stone to success. The cultivation of his skills began, as with most budding stars, in company and city leagues that laced the urban landscape in the early 1900s.

2

The Pride of Teutonia Avenue

For me, it was the way to get out of the factory. But I guess I'd've played ball even if it kept me working in there.

—Happy Felsch, as told to Eliot Asinof

Long before a Milwaukee baseball team caught a sniff of serious, professional affiliation, the seeds were being planted and watered. The first bud emerged around 1836, when one E. J. Edgerton presented a baseball to a club of young chaps, who were to play a game on a field at the corner of North Milwaukee and East Mason Streets. Mr. Edgerton claimed to have made the ball himself, with the cover sewn on by the wife of a local shoemaker.

In the professional ranks, Milwaukee flirted with fielding a team for nearly half a century. Early on, the closest thing to a professional team was the Cream City Baseball Club, which formed on October 10, 1865. When people first hear the term "cream city," they assume it refers to the frothy libation that made Milwaukee famous. But the phrase actually originated from the Cream City brick, made of red clay found on the western banks of Lake Michigan, mixed with generous amounts of lime and sulfur. Several buildings constructed from this brick remain today, the soft cream color darkened by weather and time.[1]

Despite the years of struggle to enter a team into the big league fraternity, for Felsch and his neighborhood baseball comrades, the concentration of amateur teams set the stage for their arrival onto the Milwaukee neighborhood baseball scene. Crowds for these games reached over a thousand. Games were played predominantly on Sundays, so participation for players and spectators fit neatly into people's schedules. The game matured as Milwaukee transitioned from separate ethnic partitions to a more unified municipality.

The conditions of the ball fields were not stellar. Quality depended on voluntary care, often by the teams and ballplayers themselves. The semi-pristine fields which amateurs enjoy today are a far cry from the rugged, barely landscaped dumps of long ago. To assume that ballplayers loved those conditions is purely

9

sentimental. They cared only about the opportunity to show their skills and hoped that each subsequent level of competition called their names.

When we think of organized amateur baseball in today's terms, we really mean organized. There are forms to be filled out, phone calls to make, fields to procure, and uniform fittings to be scheduled. Parents are heavily involved for reasons clear only to them. The levels of competition—some based on age, others on subjective evaluations of ability—dilute the talent in obscene ways.

When kids a century ago became physically mature and mentally tough, they joined teams started by everyday institutions that included businesses, churches, and neighborhood groups. It was a loose recruitment of sorts, mostly by word of mouth and small advertisements in the *Milwaukee Sentinel* (morning paper) and *Milwaukee Journal* (evening paper). As Felsch entered his teen years, his sparkling talent and frightening power would carry him down the roads of Milwaukee sandlot fame.

In the major leagues in 1911, the New York Giants were preparing for their first National League pennant since 1905. Connie Mack's A's would once again rule the Junior Circuit. A gentleman named John Franklin Baker took advantage of the new cork-centered ball, and in what would seem like a flurry of clouts at the time, smacked 11 home runs to earn the nickname "Home Run" Baker. Not until later did the real home run giant emerge; on the local scene, the players aimed at their own fences, most of which didn't exist.

One such organization was the Milwaukee City League. Several teams boasted sponsorship by local businesses and even an entire city (Watertown, WI, about 30 miles west of Milwaukee). On April 3, 1911, City League President Dick Marcan announced the opening day schedule, slated for April 9. Spring in southeastern Wisconsin doesn't always permit enjoyable outdoor activities. The chill of winter often loiters for unwelcomed durations, while the lovely but treacherous snow morphs into persistent, heavy rain showers. Rare teases of warmer weather make it acceptable, but dampness endures until the summer sun takes over.[2]

Games were played once a week, mostly on Sundays. Most of the battles occurred at two venues, South Side Park at 14th and Forrest Home Avenues, and White City Park. Matches ran from late morning to early evening. The Kosciuszkos were heavy favorites heading into 1911. Louis Fon's star-studded club boasted Milwaukee Brewers AA tryout hurler Charley McShane, local favorite Eddie Bodus, and several other notable players. Fons assessed his team to be "as strong as ever" and, even a few days short of the opener, continued to sign players to his already stacked squad. (Bodus was the gentleman who would later recommend Milwaukee native slugger Al Simmons to AA Milwaukee Brewers owner Otto Borchert.) During their run through several leagues, the

Kosciuszkos also played occasional exhibitions against out-of-towners, most notably the Chicago Union Giants, a barnstorming black team.[3]

William O. Sisson and Robert Sewell were proud owners of a Milwaukee-based clothier store for men, a time when clothing didn't just hang lifeless from racks. They sponsored a team that bore their name, Sisson and Sewell's. Ahead of the signing curve was manager Art Douglass, having the most players signed thus far of any team in the league. Their 1911 opener pitted them against the Weinbrenners in a 2:15 start on Sunday, April 9, at White City Park.[4]

With the grounds mired in heavy mud, the Sissons dispatched the Weinbrenners, 4–3, in just one hour and 35 minutes, a game observed by over 1,000 "dyed in the wool" fans. Former Canadian League hurler Joe Smith toed the mound for the Sissons and scattered 12 hits. With the game tied, 2–2, heading into the final frame, Douglass' anxious squad plated two runs in the top of the ninth; in the bottom, the Weinbrenners loaded the bases against Smith but could muster only one run, giving the Sissons their opening-day triumph.[5]

Prior to Oscar Felsch's debut with the club in July, the Sissons hovered near .500. On the Fourth of July, the Sissons lost their third one-run game of the season, falling to the English Woolen Mills, 3–2. In his first foray into semi-organized amateur baseball in Milwaukee, Felsch caught on with the clothiers, making his triumphant debut on July 17, 1911, at the tender age of 20. He was joined by another local star, Nig Abler, who was acquired to help with the pitching duties. Abler was a former Marquette University star.[6]

In his debut, Felsch started at shortstop, batted sixth in the order, and collected his first hit in a 7–3 victory over Bodus' McGreals squad. The McGreals had battled the Kosciuszkos and Watertown clubs at the top of the standings. The Sissons collected a season-high 14 hits, with Abler getting three. (It was not unusual for sandlot teams to have pitchers who were just as adept at the plate as position players.) Still a work in progress with the glove, Felsch was charged with two errors.[7]

Douglass gave Felsch the next game off but he returned to the lineup the following week. Unfortunately, the Sissons dropped another one-run game (a recurring theme of 1911), this time to the Cooneys of Watertown, 1–0. Felsch fared much better in the field, with no errors, two putouts, and five assists. Another pitcher, Big Engle of Watertown, accounted for the lone run when he cranked a double and later scored, in what the *Milwaukee Sentinel* described as the "prettiest battle of the season."[8]

With the offense mired in a prolonged slump, Douglass decided to shake up the lineup by raising Felsch into the leadoff spot. He also shifted him to third base, recognizing the versatility that others would discover in future years. Felsch delivered a breakout game with four hits as the Sissons crushed their favorite punching bag, Speer's Bonfields, 17–8. The *Milwaukee Sentinel* said, "Felsch played a swell game at third."[9]

With three games remaining, Felsch and his Sisson teammates fought to avoid the City League cellar. Their remaining foes were the Weinbrenners, the sixth-place McGreals, and the powerhouse Polish aggregation. Unfortunately, the first of those games resulted in another one-run loss, a 6–5 nipping by the Weinbrenners. In the final week of the season (there were no playoffs), the Sissons found themselves matched up against the eventual league champions, the Kosciuszkos. For the Sissons, this was pride time. In a shocker, Douglass' crew doubled up on their opponents, 4–2. Gustave Westphal, the Sissons' right fielder, hammered out three hits—including two homers—and scored a run. Felsch finished his last game without a hit, but fielded his shortstop position quite well, committing no errors and tallying four assists.

In five games, Felsch accumulated six hits and three runs scored. His defense was spotty and wonderful, an inconsistency typical of a young player (imperfect playing conditions notwithstanding). Although the Sissons finished a disappointing 7–13, they managed to relinquish the basement to Speer's Bonfields.

In 1912 Milwaukee, the rise of the labor force brought about several changes and institutional enhancements. The opening of the Milwaukee Vocational School (now MATC—Milwaukee Area Technical College) was one of the first institutions of worker training in the country. Progress often spawned conflict, and Milwaukee was no exception.[10] Several local political spats ensued between then–Socialist Mayor Emil Seidel and his adversaries. A District Attorney attempted to stamp out a prostitution ring, an estimated $5,500-a-year enterprise in Milwaukee. In the neighborhoods and on the ball fields, citizens kept juggling work and play, and the sandlot teams were welcome diversions to the hum drum worker routines.

The 1912 City League season brought several changes. The Kosciuszkos and Weinbrenners bolted to the advanced Lake Shore League. Speer's Bonfields and McGreals chose not to return. President Dick Marcan welcomed three new teams, including another Polish, South-Side club named Pritzlaff and Winks (named after a jewelry store). The Sunday, April 21, *Milwaukee Sentinel* proclaimed that year's version of City League to be one of the best ever. "Never before in the league's history have prospects appeared any brighter for the fast semi-pros than they do this year and a high class article of ball promises to predominate."[11]

Art Douglass' team returned with a few new players, a more seasoned Felsch, and a veteran twirler from one of the disbanded teams, Harvey Stock. They opened on the road against one of the new out-of-town members, Waterloo, a town that had gone "baseball crazy." While rain showers forced cancellation of the games played in Milwaukee, the contests in Watertown and Waterloo were unaffected. Poised to continue his ascent and development as a ballplayer, Felsch ripped four hits—a double and three singles—and scored a run as the Sissons walloped the newcomers, 9–5, in ten innings.[12]

In the previous season, Douglass had batted Felsch sixth and first. In this game, he inserted him into the number three position, perhaps a vote of confidence for Felsch's developing power. He remained near the top of the order for his final five games in a Sisson & Sewell's uniform. The Sissons raced out to a 3–0 start, with hurler Stock directing them from the mound each time. Why did Douglass shuffle his lineup so much? Batting order and its effects on game outcomes has been a time-honored discussion point since baseball began. In 1867, Henry Chadwick offered the following:

> In arranging the order of striking, see that the strong hitters follow the poor batsmen, and that good base runners precede them. For instance, suppose that your best outfielder, or your pitcher or catcher, is not as skilful at bat as the others, in placing them on the books as a striker put a good base runner's name down before him; by this means the chances for the first base being vacated by the time he is ready to make it, will be increased, as likewise those for two runs being obtained after he has made his base. Never put three poor hitters together, but support each, if possible, as above recommended.[13]

Felsch continued his proliferation at the plate, belting a home run in a 4–1 win over Watertown behind the four-hit pitching of Stock. Felsch sat out the game against English Woolens Mills, a 2–0 victory for the Sissons. In their fourth game of the young season, Douglass' crew got lambasted by one of the newcomers of the City League, the Bob Krockers, 12–6. Felsch managed two more hits, this time a triple and a single, and one run scored.[14]

In his final two games in the City League, Felsch collected three and four hits against M. Fryes (a 5–4 loss) and Pritzlaff and Winks (a 4–3 win), respectively. He continued to struggle in the field, committing multiple errors in a few games.[15] After a brief respite following his final game with the Sissons on June 9, Felsch was courted by Manitowoc of the popular Lake Shore League, and his ascension to greater baseball heights earned constant notice.[16]

Driving up Interstate 43 from Milwaukee to Green Bay, several lakefront towns inhabit the cheese-state landscape. Approximately two-thirds of the way between Brewers-land and Packers-land lies a city named Manitowoc, home of the Wisconsin Maritime Museum (orig. 1968). The name is rumored to mean "dwelling of the great spirit," derived from either the Anishinaabe word *manidoowaak(wag)*, meaning spirit-spawn(s), or *manidoowaak(oog)*, meaning "spirit-wood(s)." Where the Manitowoc River merges into Lake Michigan, cutting through downtown, the winds and chill offer a challenge—sans any skyscrapers to block Mother Nature's gusty cruelty.

Prior to Felsch's arrival, the team, which also featured a former St. Louis Cardinals pitcher, almost never made it onto the field. Heading into the 1912 season, expectations bounced between the team "lacking interest" from its community and "they will be stronger than ever" for the season. Their status flip-flopped from one day to the next. The *Milwaukee Sentinel* hinted that the reason for the anemic interest was that more people owned automobiles and could easily "skip town" whenever they pleased. A rumor persisted that placed their new home in Fond du Lac, 62 miles southeast.[17]

A partial culprit for Manitowoc's hesitation to stay afloat was finances. The teams that were not sponsored directly by their owners and namesakes needed help from multiple local businesses and nickel-and-dime philanthropists. The president of the Lake Shore League, Clarence Klockskin, talked about a "guarantee fund" that was used to help all teams. Just a day after a doomsday article buried the team's chances, the *Milwaukee Sentinel* reported—without stating a reason—that Manitowoc would be joining the league's other five teams.[18]

The 1912 Lake Shore League consisted of two Milwaukee-area teams, the Kosciuszkos and Weinbrenners, and four out-of-towners: Racine, Port Washington, Sheboygan, and Manitowoc. The season was scheduled to start on May 12, but the usual cluster of weather-induced cancellations greeted them. A week later, two of three openers were squeezed in (at Racine and South Side Park in Milwaukee).

Manitowoc, managed by Jack Herzog, debuted on May 26 at South Side Park against the Kosciuszkos, dropping the contest to the Poles, 3–2, before 2,400+ fans. Manitowoc carried a 3–2 record into Felsch's debut on June 23, trailing the Koscuiszkos.[19] Although his tenure with the team lasted only a few games, it introduced his transition from the infield to the outfield, where he would play his entire professional career. The conversion to the Lake Shore League from the City League proved seamless for the slugger.

Felsch's remarkable transcendence notwithstanding, the difference in competition between levels back then was sometimes fuzzy. Even at the professional level, the disparity in skill between teams was vast. As Chris Jaffe writes in his 2010 book, *Evaluating Baseball Managers*, baseball fundamentals during this time were still being worked out. He surmises that high school players of today are more versed in fundamentals than major leaguers were over a century ago. For the sandlot and amateur players, the trickle-down of fundamentals was much more gradual and disjointed than today. Jaffe writes: "Even a poor kid from the Dominican Republic has access to more knowledgeable adults and coaches than was the case for the 1890s Wisconsin farm boy."[20]

In Felsch's debut against the Racine Malted Milks, Manitowoc pounded former teammate Hugo Schliefske, 8–5. At the end of the lengthy game account, the local scribe provided a juicy hint of the tendency toward player movement around these leagues: "Rumors of changes in the Manitowoc line up and of the loss of Fletch proved ungrounded, Bill Disch being the only new man on the team."[21] Felsch cranked out two hits, scored a run, and gracefully manned third base for the local team. He would later move to shortstop for other clubs in 1912, but Manitowoc already possessed a slick-fielding shortstop. The positions Felsch occupied throughout his career shared common attributes: quickness and a strong arm.

The *Manitowoc Daily Herald* provided ample coverage of the games. But apparently, they paid little attention to spelling names correctly, including their newest player, "Fletch." In Felsch's third game with Manitowoc, the scribe in charge butchered his name three different ways, with the last one being the closest approximation to the truth, referencing him as Felch. Despite the shoddy attention to spelling, the keen observance to game detail was routinely stellar, sometimes colorful, and playfully judgmental.

Felsch played a few more games for Manitowoc before moving up to loftier pastures. With the Sissons, he did not have great success against the hometown Kosciuszkos.[22] In their next game at Sheboygan, Manitowoc found itself in a pitching duel, with a slim 2–1 lead heading into the final frame. Sheboygan blew a chance in the fifth to tie the score. For this, we yield to this colorful account from the *Manitowoc Daily Herald*:

> Sheboygan was dangerous in the fifth and there was a chance for a tie up of the score that the Chairmakers threw away by poor baserunning. With two gone, Wilke singled over third and reached second on the throw in after a hot chase from first when he was caught off the bag. Brusk dropped a throw on the play and saved Wilke from death. Braun made a gallant attempt to count Wilke with a liner to left. Koppling pegged the ball to Britz at the home station and Britz relayed to Felch at third, where Wilke was caught trying to get back to safety after a run from home.[23]

Capitalizing on the Chairmakers' miscues, Manitowoc plated four runs in the ninth inning, including a Felsch home run. Only an error in the third inning prevented McGlynn from spinning a shutout. Felsch's left-side-of-the-infield sidekick, shortstop Lee, "who had been in rapid fire double action gun in the local's defense, was again the star performer in Sunday's game and the sensational playing of the little man won his plaudits from the grandstand, an unheard of tribute in Sheboygan for a visiting player. The stick work of Felsch, Braun, and Bill Disch also featured."[24]

Felsch attempted a tryout with Eau Claire of the Wisconsin-Minnesota League. After a three-day audition, he was "given the gate"—sent home without transportation. He took the next boxcar south and spent the next few days wondering what went wrong. Luckily, Oak Hennig, a fixture in Milwaukee baseball circles, hooked on with Grand Rapids and worked tirelessly to get Felsch on that club. He sent Felsch a telegram and soon after, Happy had a new baseball address.[25]

Grand Rapids (today called Wisconsin Rapids) lay in the central part of Wisconsin. Games occurred more than once a week, and Felsch displayed a prowess for hitting home runs, smacking them far past the outfield walls, gates, and fences. If the number of positive mentions in the local press coverage correlated with success, Felsch's dominance was securely validated.

Having moved up and down the lineup card on previous teams, he settled into the cleanup spot for Grand Rapids. The league featured a dominant pitcher named Jacob Jung, satirically identified in the papers as Cy Young III, a play on the famous former major leaguer. Oblivious to his opponents' nicknames, Felsch greeted Young in cruel fashion in his Grand Rapids debut, jacking a three-run home run off the vaunted hurler and breaking Young's 94-inning scoreless streak.

From the July 25 *Stevens Point Daily Tribune*: "That gentleman, who covers the shortfield for the suburban aggregation, took one healthy swipe at the pellet, and when it was recovered he as well as the two that were anchored on the sacks, had crossed the platter."[26]

The "demon swatter's" antics were not enough as Stevens Point tripped Grand Rapids, 5–4. Having beaned the first two batters prior to Felsch's clout, Jung settled down, allowing one more run. As the season progressed, few pitchers solved the Felsch riddle. Grand Rapids' next opponent was Merrill, and Grand Rapids defeated the occasional opponents in a doubleheader, 4–2 and a whopping 17–2. He made a delightful impression on the local scribes: "The sensational feature of Sunday's game was a home run by Felch, the local shortstop, who batted the ball over the fence in center field, making the longest hit that has ever been made on the local grounds, and will probably hold the record for some time to come."[27]

As July surrendered to August, Felsch paced his team with his bat, glove, and arm. In the next outing, this time a 4–1 loss to their rivals, the team was embroiled in a small controversy, the catalyst being Felsch gunning down a runner at home plate. Stevens Point's Abe Nigbor led off the seventh inning with a double and was sacrificed to third. The next hitter, Talbot, hit a sharp grounder to Felsch at short. Instead of choosing the sure out at first, Felsch targeted Nigbor at home. The home umpire, Mosel, who called the runner out, met disagreement from one of his colleagues. As the *Stevens Point Daily Journal* reported: "As Mosel had jurisdiction over the plate, his ruling stood." Back then, the umpires jostled not only with the players but also with each other. Refinement and decorum were not staples of the time.

Felsch was a constant thorn in Jung's side, taking part in breaking another of the pitcher's streaks, 13 consecutive wins. In a 4–1 Grand Rapids triumph, he hammered a three-run blast over the left field wall, added a triple later in the game, and earned adoring praise from *Stevens Point Daily Tribune*: "Not only did Cy have an off day but Felsch, Grand Rapids' newly-acquired shortfielder, proved beyond the semblance of a doubt that he is Young's real eighteen karet jinx."[28]

The batter-pitcher battle is the center of the game. This was true in the early 1900s, but how much influence was heaped on Felsch having to face virtually the same pitcher on a given team, every game? ("Cy Young III" seemed to pitch in every game.) Teams did not play every day so maybe there was some amnesia by the hitters. But how did Young reach back into his arsenal to extract a surprise pitch, a new delivery, vary speeds, or throw off the timing of mashers such as Felsch? Did they have to fool hitters at this level more than they do today?

Despite being intense combatants on the field, the town of Grand Rapids, prior to the early August matchup against their rivals, decided to throw out the welcome wagon to their guests, holding a "social time with local members of the order." This did not occur at the ballpark, but instead at the local Elks Lodge, where a resounding band escorted their visitors to the club rooms for some pomp and circumstance.

As the old saying goes, if you can't beat them, join them. In late August, Felsch joined Grand Rapids' nemesis, Stevens Point. This wasn't an intentional climb up the competition ladder; Grand Rapids disbanded and Felsch needed a new team. Despite his consistent success against them, Jung was gleeful at the prospect of not having to pitch to Felsch any more.[29]

Felsch's debut came in a September 1 contest at Stoughton. Always willing to make an exalted entrance, he greeted the locals with a two-run triple to give his new team a victory and support Jung's three-hit pitching. Coverage of his first two games was lacking (the *Stevens Point Daily Journal* reported that the games had no score keepers). Aside from referring to Felsch as the "fence buster," the paper filled the game space with speculation about another date with Stoughton. "If the fans show sufficient enthusiasm to warrant it, Stoughton will be brought here for two return games in an attempt to settle the semi-pro championship of Wisconsin. Stoughton has an all salaried team and will not come here unless a good sized bank roll and a guarantee of expenses are given them. It is planned to have a booster's day for one of the games if they are played."[30]

Stevens Point and Stoughton played a two-game series for the symbolic championship, but it was unclear whether those games settled the league crown. The innate disorganization of the league made it fuzzy as to who the true champion was. Regardless, plenty of baseball was left and Felsch continued to bop, field, and run his way towards greater achievements.

Felsch hit safely in the first four games with his new team, and his blend of power and speed led to several extra-base hits and a few stolen bases. He followed his two-hit game in a loss to Waupaca with a triple and a base theft against Stanley, and a single and run scored in the blanking of Waupaca. All was not perfect for the Milwaukee shortstop. In the victory against Stanley, Felsch was picked off third after his triple, which wasted a subsequent triple by a teammate.

With another season in the books, several players sought auditions with higher-level teams. Jung considered a late-season call from the American League Chicago White Sox. Racine pitcher Ellis Johnson joined the Sox and saw action against the Washington Senators. Although Felsch was not quite knocking on the major league door, he could probably hear it creaking in his head. He was still more like a kid, with the childhood hourglass running out and the winds of professional baseball blowing towards him.

The transition from sandlot to professional ball filtered out hundreds of players, dooming them to less glamorous vocations. Now well-known as "Happy" for his boyish exuberance and gleeful disposition, Felsch was not ready to apply the brakes to his baseball career. Instead, he hooked up with his first professional team, the Milwaukee Mollys of the Class C Wisconsin-Illinois League. Instead of just once- or twice-a-week ball, Felsch had to adjust to a heavier schedule, playing four to six games per week.

The league, formerly known as the Wisconsin State League, changed its name in 1908. It was one of five Class C leagues in the circuit, including the Canadian League. The majority of clubs hailed from Wisconsin, with Illinois contributing teams from Aurora and Rockford for two years each (rendering the league name a misnomer). Charlie Moll, the Milwaukee team owner, manager, and namesake, issued this pre-season proclamation for 1913: "I've got a good team, one that I think will be in the running all the way through. The catching staff and outfield compare favorably with any in the circuit, and I see no reason why we should not be up with the leaders."[31]

League President Frank R. Weeks declared: "The reports I have from eight cities are an indication that financial affairs are in good shape and fans in four of the cities are preparing enthusiastic receptions for the opening day—Wednesday."[32]

With their inclusion in the National Association of Baseball Leagues, teams in Class C leagues were part of a hierarchy that included Class A, B, and D. These minor leagues were pawns in the jostling for major league superiority that had lasted since before the turn of the twentieth century. The convenient ranking with letters hardly reflected the quality of play. For example, teams and players in Class C were not necessarily inferior to those in Class B.[33]

During the league's ninth season in business, two themes dominated Felsch's tenure with the Mollys: (1) The man could tear the cover off the ball; and (2) Shortstop was not going to be his signature position. Playing every day introduced Felsch to the realities of slumps and adjustments. More games meant increased exposure by opponents to Felsch's strengths and weaknesses. No longer could he hack his way on base, instead learning the nuances that aided his development.

Earlier in the season, the league was forced to adjust to *him*. Felsch greeted his new foes with an impressive debut, going 4-for-5 with three runs scored. In his first week, the "Mayor of 35th and Center Streets" amassed ten hits, five extra-base hits, and two home runs. His arrival helped earn the Mollys a 5–0 start and nine wins in their first ten games. In their fifth straight, a 13–7 triumph over Green Bay, Felsch "added to the festivities with three singles and another home run." Paul Wachtel, the starting pitcher, abetted his own cause with two hits. The *Milwaukee Sentinel* served early notice to the rest of the league, noting "If someone does not put a brake on the Mollys pretty soon, the race in the W-I League will be over until it is fairly started."[34]

The Mollycoddles, as they were often called in the local papers, split a pair of games in Wausau and then feasted again on Green Bay, sweeping them in three games. In the series, Felsch parked another home run over the fence and held his own at shortstop. The Mollys found themselves 1½ games out of the top spot. In their first loss of the young season, 4–2 to Wausau, Felsch jacked a double and added a run scored in four plate appearances. Over 3,000 fans watched their Lumberjacks send the Mollys into a first-place tie with Oshkosh. They followed the hiccup with four consecutive victories; in that span, Felsch collected four more hits, including his second four-bagger of the season.[35]

Sitting at 15–7 on May 28, the Mollys were seeking their identity as a team. To shake things up, or rather to award Felsch for his stellar play, the young player was moved from fifth to cleanup in the lineup for the May 27 game against Rockford. The immediate result wasn't apparent, as the Mollys were blanked, 10–0. Despite some brief struggles, Felsch would lay his claim to the most potent position in the order.[36]

To help lure more fans, owner Charlie Moll announced that women would watch for free during the remaining home games at South Side Park. Meanwhile, two injured players returned to help the cause, which eventually pushed Felsch to the outfield. On May 30, a doubleheader sweep courtesy of the Racine Belles—followed by a 2–1 tripping—left Moll's crew at a respectable 15–10.[37]

The month of May did not end in celebration, as the Belles knocked off the Mollys four out of five games, including the sweep on May 30. June greeted the team just as cruelly, as they lost seven of eight games to leave their record at a mediocre 16–17 entering their June 9 game against Wausau. Felsch's hot bat turned chilly, going 5-for-29 during that stretch. This was perhaps Felsch's longest nosedive yet, but it didn't last long.[38]

An average 1-for-3 line for Felsch in another win, 2–1 over Green Bay, was piggy-backed by a complete crushing the next day, 14–0. Felsch went 3-for-5 with three runs scored and a stolen base. The local papers were beginning to recognize Happy as a special player, giving him plenty of ink during this torrid hitting stretch. The Mollys hung on to second place at 21–14, as things would get interesting both on and off the field for Charlie Moll's crew.

From the June 14 *Milwaukee Sentinel*: "Happy Felsch, even without the assistance of his gang, took off a great portion of the honors. His home run stick he left at home, but he contributed a trio of peppery singles that helped in the final count."

Before this latest batting onslaught, Felsch had already amassed eight multi-hit games. Long winning streaks eluded the Molly's, but they remained above .500 and clung to contention despite occasional whispers of an impending move to either Aurora, IL, or north to Fond du Lac.

The June 21 *Milwaukee Sentinel* included another mention of a potential new destination for the Mollys. The headline of the article appeared confident, declaring that "Moll Will Manage Aurora Ball Club," with a sub-heading of "Practically Settled that Milwaukee Franchise in W-I league would be rewarded to Illinois City." The cost of the franchise move was a paltry $500, and the body of the story was less certain than its headline.[39]

Juxtaposed against the game story that informed the public of the Molly's 3–2 loss to Oshkosh, the *Milwaukee Sentinel* reported that because Aurora had been booted before due to travel inconveniences, the league brass would likely stamp Fond du Lac as the new home. The approval of a shift was as fuzzy as the rumored destinations. Wisconsin-Illinois League president Weeks narrowed down the method of decision to either a meeting or mail-in vote of the owners.[40]

Ironically, Milwaukee had inherited its club from Fond du Lac during the 1912 off-season. Franchise shake-ups were not exclusive to sandlot teams during this time. The teams of Class C, although loosely affiliated with more advanced leagues, also felt the frequent waves of financial turbulence. The primary reason for departing Milwaukee was shaky attendance, which was curious given a couple of the big draws. Even on June 22, fresh off the heels of the rumors, the Mollys drew 1,000 fans for their 3–2 loss to Oshkosh. Shaky as well was Felsch's defense as his "wild heave" cost them the contest.[41]

On June 24, the league approved the move north. Aurora had offered $1,000 for the team but their proximity issues sank their chances in the end.

The usual enthusiasm in a town that welcomes a new team did not escape the Fond du Lac folks. This would also put the Mollys just 17 miles from Oshkosh, the team they were battling for league supremacy. As finances were almost always the kicker in such decisions, "Fondy would be able to make the team a paying proposition."[42]

On the field, Felsch was clearly turning a positive corner in his career. His relentless, jaw-dropping power had continued against superior competition, feeder teams to the upper minors and major leagues. His prodigious talents drew the ire of opposing pitchers and the glee of future suitors. Inconsistency turned into steady, predictable outcomes.

As the heart of summer greeted the season, the Mollys were scrapping to stay alive in a suddenly crowded race. Felsch carried the team on his back and they eventually climbed back over .500 on July 26 with a 2–1 win over Rockford. They won seven straight after that, and soon came the news that Milwaukee Brewers manager Harry Clark would be in the stands to take a gander at Felsch. The "Breakfast Food" section of the July 29 *Milwaukee Sentinel* sports page trumpeted the keen interest in Felsch: "So many encouraging reports have been heard about Happy Felsch, the Fond Du Lac slugger, that he will probably be given a trial by the Brewers after the close of the W-I league season. Clark (Milwaukee Brewers manager) expects to look him over in the near future."[43]

The rumblings were not empty, with Felsch's ascendance up the baseball ladder reaching another rung. While Felsch was leading the Mollys to another surge in the standings, he did not have to wait until they finished the season before switching baseball addresses again. With Harry Clark in the stands, Felsch went 2-for-4 in a 4–2 win over Wausau; the Brewers' skipper needed no more time. The August 7 *Milwaukee Sentinel* carried these sub-headlines[44]:

> *Mollys Continue to Win Beating*
> *Wausau With Manager Clark*
> *in Stands, 4–2*
>
> FELCH COMES TO BREWERS
>
> *Happy Makes Hit with Brewers Chief*
> *And He Takes Slugger Home*
> *With Him*

With Milwaukee/Fond du Lac, Felsch finished with a .319 batting average in 357 at-bats, 18 homers and six stolen bases. His glove work confirmed his future fielding position. In 58 games at shortstop, Felsch collected a ghastly 36 errors. In 34 games in the outfield, he committed only *two*. He also spent some time at third base, but his career would demonstrate that his speed and strong arm would suit him better on the outfield grass.

3

Taste of Clark's Brew

Clark Liked Happy's Play and Beer Taste
—*Milwaukee Sentinel,* March 24, 1933

Charlie Carr, former baseball player and manager, knew Felsch well. "I took one look at that kid and after the game, I spent $15 of my own money for long distance tolls to talk to Frank Navin, owner of the Detroit Tigers," said Carr, who had earlier recommended catcher and future Felsch teammate Ray Schalk to Navin. "Happy impressed me as much as Schalk," continued Carr. "Again, I called Navin. Again he told me that his scouts had seen the young upstart and had turned thumbs down."

"My men have watched Felsch," replied Navin. "They tell me he'll never make the grade. They claim he's a flat-headed Swede who can run around the bases with a tub of water on his head and not spill a drop. After I saw quite a lot of both Schalk and Felsch, Happy improved with every game. What a ball hawk he was!"[1]

On August 10, Felsch reported to the parent club and debuted the same day. His performances catapulted him over class D and A, directly to the Brewers. The Mollys were eight games above .500 after Felsch played his last game with them. They won eight of ten before Felsch was promoted, taking a 43–35 record into the remaining dog days of August. His absence spelled misfortune for the team as they eventually finished in fourth place with a 63–60 record.

During the last two decades of the nineteenth century and into the twentieth, the battle for league supremacy continued to shake up the baseball landscape, with leagues popping up and disbanding frequently. The "Beer and Whiskey League"—officially known as the American Association—was an outlaw major league that set up shop in 1882 to compete with the National League.

With its offer of cheaper admission, beer sales, and Sunday games (and God forbid, beer sales *on* Sundays), the league lasted ten seasons. But in 1891, after efforts to save the financially weaker teams and squelch the raiding of players by other leagues failed, four American Association teams agreed to join the National League, and the renegade league faded into history. Their influence on the development and maturation of major leagues lasts even today. Their demise left the door open for other diamond hopefuls who had no intention of stepping on the feet of their major league counterparts.[2]

Two years after the American Association's demise, Ban Johnson became president of the minor Western League, which he ripened into the major American League. Thomas Hickey, who had served as the president of the Western League, had spearheaded efforts to form a new American Association, this time as a minor league. (The Western League was preceded by the Northwestern League, the first minor league organized in the Midwest, and its ascendance into the major American League cleared the way for the new minor league American Association.) Ripe for baseball cities such as Kansas City, Louisville, Columbus, Indianapolis, Toledo, Minneapolis, St. Paul, and Milwaukee—the inaugural entrants in 1902—the new American Association flourished for the next 60 years.

Labeling a league *major* or *minor* is a function of clarity. Players often jumped back and forth from one to the other, as scouting meant chance viewing and random selection. The delineation of talent between the two was often murky, and legal, structured affiliation between minor and major league was non-existent until Branch Rickey founded and formalized the concept of a farm system years later.

As Neil Sullivan wrote in *The Minors:* "What the National League created (in 1876) was not so much major league baseball as monopoly baseball, a business that would be characterized by the club owners' total control of major markets, players, and competing franchises." Talents wise, many AA players were equal or better than National League players.[3] The current major league Milwaukee team was not the first "Brewers"; in fact they weren't even the second. (One year later, another team by that name participated in Ban Johnson's American League in 1901, the Milwaukee Brewers of the new American Association.)

Prior to 1913, their highest finish was second place, which they achieved three times (1905, 1906, and 1909). In the American Association's first 11 years in business, the league crowned five different champions: Columbus and Minneapolis won three pennants each, Indianapolis and St. Paul two, and Louisville one. Columbus, the smallest city in the American Association, led the league in attendance eight years in a row.[4]

The Brewers played their home games in Athletic Park, on 8th and Chambers Streets. This sentimental yet flawed park was dedicated in 1888 and kept its appellation until the team was renamed Borchert Field in 1928, in honor of

Otto Borchert, who died in 1927 of a heart attack (Borchert purchased the club in 1919). After the grandstand benches were extended, Athletic Park could withstand an overflow crowd of about 17,000. Covering an entire city block, several views were obstructed in a myriad of ways and no seat permitted observation of the entire playing field. For the batters, foul lines were nice but power alleys were cruel. Games at Athletic Park typically started at 3:00 or 3:30 to placate local businessmen and avoid darkness.

In its infancy, baseball in the American Association was dominated by pitching. In 1908 alone, eight no-hitters were pitched in the league. Pitchers would go the distance in nearly every game. Relievers were used only for absolute necessities, such as an injury or a complete pasting by the opposition. Because of the distance and the limitations in travel (which was mostly by train), teams had long home and road stretches, often two to three weeks long.[5]

In 1913, Milwaukee replaced manager Hugh Duffy with veteran third baseman Harry Clark, who had played for the Brewers since 1904. Duffy had been a player-manager for the Milwaukee Creams entrant in the Western League in 1902 and 1903. After two seasons managing the Chicago White Sox, Duffy agreed to manage the Brewers, but lasted only one year before he resigned. He was the only man to lead Milwaukee-based clubs in three different leagues, his first gig being the 1901 American League Milwaukee Brewers.[6]

What prompted Clark's interest to acquire Felsch from the Mollys? The day after Clark traveled to Fond du Lac to take a gander at Felsch, the *Milwaukee Sentinel* printed this headline:

> *Help! Help! Help!*
> *Brewers Bested*

Two columns over, another headline caught the eye:

> *Felch's Home Runs*
> *Give Mollys Game*[7]

Statistically, Felsch's promotion was merited. As of July 27, only one Brewers outfielder appeared in the top six in the team's batting average, with Larry Gilbert in seventh place on the team and a disappointing 62nd in the league.

Felsch made his Milwaukee Brewers debut in a 4–0 win over Toledo. Joining Felsch as a newcomer to the Brewers was pitcher Big Bill Powell to bolster Clark's mound corps. Felsch did not replace Gilbert; Clark inserted him into the lineup because Johnny Beall was struggling against left-handers. This "platoon advantage" recognition, although not as scrutinized and prevalent as in later years, was practiced at many levels in early twentieth century baseball.[8]

The *Milwaukee Sentinel* said of Felsch's Brewers debut: "Oscar 'Happy' Felsch, late of the Fond du Lac Schnitts, broke in as a Brewer yesterday and he

A team photograph of the 1913 Milwaukee Brewers of the American Association. Felsch, 21 years old and playing in his first professional season, appears in the second row, second from the left (author's collection).

did it without much of a splash. If you look at the box score, you may not figure that his get-away was such a real success. But if you ask those who saw him take his first dip, they will tell you that he broke in with the safest and surest road to success. He replaced John Beall in left garden and had every possible chance to show his worth, even though the game went only six innings."[9]

Although Felsch was acquired to infuse power into Milwaukee's lineup, Clark was practicing patience with his young slugger. Felsch would not play again until August 18, when he was used as a pinch hitter. During this temporary hiatus, the local papers (and probably not Clark) did not dismiss the potential impact Felsch could have on the Brewers. This appeared in the August 18, 1913, *Milwaukee Journal*: "While Felsch has played but one game since joining the Brewers, nevertheless he is considered a promising youngster, and it may be that he may break into one of the games of this series."[10] In the meantime, another injury hampered Clark, this time right-fielder Newton Randall. Instead of rushing Felsch into the lineup, Clark opted for veteran outfielder Orville "Sam" Woodruff. Old Orville was merely a stop-gap replacement for the Brewers.

On Sunday August 18, the Brewers opened a vital four-game series against the Minneapolis Millers at Athletic Park, losing 3–1 to a spitballing gentleman named Ralph Comstock. The Sylvania, OH, native had an interesting baseball career, but perhaps an even more fascinating medical saga. After being drafted by the White Sox and sent to the Millers in 1912, Comstock went 6–5 for Minneapolis but missed part of the season with malaria. Early in 1913, he was admitted to a "pest house" (an isolation hospital) for what they initially diagnosed as smallpox.[11]

In the opening game against the Saints at Lexington Field in St. Paul, another loss for the Brewers, Felsch got another nibble at the plate as a pinch hitter. A hit eluded him, but he did get solid wood on ball. The real culprit was failed scoring opportunities, the last one seeing second basemen Phil Lewis whiffing with the bases loaded in the ninth to secure the St. Paul victory. The Saints were 56–66 entering the contest; the Brewers stood at 74–52.

The chase for the pennant had become a four-team race. Luckily, the Brewers captured the final two games of the three-game set, tallying back-to-back shutouts. The bats started to unwarp in this series as they rapped out 31 hits. Writers and fans are always less patient than managers, clamoring for changes they believe can be plucked off of any old tree. Hence, a little nudge was made by Manning Vaughn in the August 23 edition of the *Milwaukee Sentinel*: "While disappointed at the showing of the Brewers in the series just closed, Manager Clark is not discouraged and expects to win a majority of the games in the next week. On account of the slump in hitting, which the team has experienced during the past two weeks, it is probable that Happy Felsch will break into the outfield as a regular. The Brewer boss is convinced that Happy is a natural hitter and if given a chance, will show that he can sting the pill."[12]

Felsch did not play much to finish the season, ending with an average of .183 in just 26 games played. However, Harry Clark's confidence in Felsch's abilities never waned from the first time he observed him with the Mollys. Spring training in 1914 would allow him to continue his evaluation of the up-and-coming star, and also prevent the entire team from resting on their laurels after the Brewers' first-ever American Association championship.

Crucial in the pre-season preparation was minimizing the number of injuries in 1913. To that end, Clark hired a former local Y.M.C.A physical director, Louis Fuhrman, to whip his boys into shape in preparation for the season opener in April. During the season, Fuhrman would be available as the "rubber in chief" to help players work out their muscular kinks. Fuhrman was the first trainer a Brewers club ever had; other teams in the circuit had already instituted such a role.

In 1914, Harry Clark's spring training regimen was no picnic. Clark, the team's third basemen, came into camp 20 pounds lighter. The work he demanded of his players did not exceed the expectations he had for himself. His drills were relentless at a time when baseball players used spring training to get in physical shape as much as to work on baseball drills. Felsch did not need to shed any pounds as he reported to spring training in excellent condition. He flung around the medicine ball with little struggle.[13]

Felsch had a propensity to enjoy himself. Baseball, after all, was a game and games were meant to be fun. This included being a bit goofy and playful at times, which led some to believe that he did not take his work seriously. This was far from the truth but some believed Felsch needed to mature in order to move to the next level in his career. From the *Milwaukee Sentinel*: "Felsch, it seems, is getting wise to himself and if he cuts out the monkey work, there is no reason why he should not be the sensation of the league this season."[14]

The Clarkmen's arrival in Owensboro, KY, was greeted by a blanket of fresh snow. This obliged them to hold workouts inside a gym at the local Y.M.C.A. Limited to non-baseball activities, the players stayed active by tossing around a medicine ball and playing basketball. Outside, they later built a makeshift mound for the pitchers, as Clark asserted that anything was better than "loafing around the [hotel] lobby."

Owensboro, KY, in the northwest part of the state, was home to the Owensboro Wagon Company and was also a wintering respite for Lewis and Clark (no relation to the Brewers' skipper), back when it was called Yellow Banks. In 1865, Owensboro was savaged by Confederate guerrillas from Tennessee. In 1914, such dangers gave way to the town welcoming their beloved guests from the north for another spring training season.

When the weather transitioned to a more typical southern spring, the players got down to real business and Felsch continued to impress his mates and superiors with impressive swings. During an outdoor practice on an alternate field near the center of town, he cranked several terrific drives over a big oak tree some 400 feet away. Days before, it was reported that the St. Paul Saints had tried to lure Felsch from the Brewers, but Clark balked.[15]

The Brewers played in several exhibition games, including a March 29 battle against scaled-down teams: the Chicago Cubs and Detroit Tigers. Felsch played center field and collected two hits against the Cubs, but Clark's bunch dropped a 7–2 decision in a game that lasted just six innings due to inclement weather.[16] Against the Tigers, Felsch cranked a two-run homer in a 4–2 loss. Playing his role of team awe-inspirer, Felsch's homer was perceived to be the longest ever seen at South Side Park in Owensboro. They defeated a team from Evansville, IN, twice, 8–0 and 2–0. Before sustaining a minor Charlie horse in the second game, Felsch robbed a hitter of a home run.[17]

Heading into his first full-time campaign in upper-level professional ball, Felsch faced a lion's share of curveballs in batting practice. Clark and his staff altered his batting style and peppered him with curveballs. "We have always believed Felsch is a slugger," said Clark. "He may have fooled us, but if he attends to his business and levels all the hops in the barrels, we think he will do some big things this season. So it is up to him."

Felsch had had little trouble with the benders in the Wisconsin-Illinois League but the pitchers in the American Association threw the ball harder, with sharper breaks, and more often. How well Felsch adjusted to the crooked pitches would measure his potential success. The following assessment in a *Milwaukee Sentinel* season preview gave little credit to his non-baseball intellect: "Felsch can field, he can throw, and can run the bases," wrote Brewers beat writer Manning Vaughn. "He is not an Aristotle, but has what are commonly known as 'baseball brains' and knows what to do on the ball field. When Hap first reported to the club, his titanic hits immediately made him the most talked of player in the association. Crowds went out to see Happy bust 'em, and his name was on the tongues of every fan. And one day, he fanned the ozone four times in a row and his great batting eye had fled."[18]

Opening Day for the Milwaukee Brewers frequently generated plenty of hoopla. An estimated 10,000 fans watched Mayor Gerhard Adolph Bading toss out the ceremonial first pitch, and later enjoyed their Brewers dispatching the St. Paul Saints. Felsch debuted with a triple, RBI, sacrifice fly, and run scored, and was also fortunate with the glove. Felsch played a "beautiful fielding game." In their Opening Day 3–0 blanking of the St. Paul Saints, starter Irv "Young Cy" Young scattered six hits. Mother Nature scared away many, but more than 2,000 fans remained and provided loyal applause. Despite the pre-season hoopla, Felsch was not named a starter until game time.[19]

The Brewers took three of four from the Saints. However, Felsch committed two errors during the series, one on an errant throw to home trying to gun down a runner. Two Saints scored on the play but the Brewers clung to a 4–3 victory. Clark's crew finished April at 8–3 as Felsch hit his first home run on April 28 in a 3–2 win over Cleveland. Felsch had seven hits in the month, and his stick would soon heat up along with the weather.

Despite his continuous adjustment at the plate, Felsch's reputation as a big slugger kept getting ink in the newspapers. In a 7–3 loss to Columbus on May 3, Felsch hit what many considered to be the longest home run ever hit at Athletic Park. When the ball cleared the fence, it was still ascending, soon out of fan view. It reportedly landed a block away near 8th and Burleigh Streets. One lucky kid scooped up the ball and "started for parts unknown."[20]

His stature as a true power hitter was exemplified even when he did not hit a home run. In a 7–0 pasting by Columbus, the *Milwaukee Sentinel* used Felsch's off-day as a gauge for how dominant the opponent's pitching was. "Happy Felsch even failed to make a home run, so you can imagine the line of pitching salve Doc Cook [Columbus pitcher] was handing out." When Felsch *didn't* awe the fans or media, it was news. Getting less press, however, were his glove and arm. Felsch represented as balanced a player as there was in the league, and if the term "five-tool player" had been around in 1914, his name would have been affixed to it.

Before the summer warmed up for good, several big league baseball men appeared at Athletic Park to target Felsch. One of them was the Old Roman himself, Charles Comiskey, owner of the Chicago White Sox. Just 90 miles south of Milwaukee, Comiskey did not find it cumbersome to scout nearby talent. Comiskey told a local sportswriter that he thought Felsch was a promising kid.

Whether Felsch knew of this sudden attention is not clear. Less ambiguous was his team's reliance on his success. The Brewers played near .500 ball in May (15–14) and June (16–14), but no other team in the league was lighting up the standings. Indianapolis insisted on making it a three-team race, but Milwaukee, Louisville, and Columbus soon wrote their own chapters to the season.

In July, Felsch and the Brewers exploded. After collecting seven, 26, and 20 hits in April, May, and June respectively, Felsch tore up the league for an astonishing 45 hits in 32 July contests. The Brewers had closed June just a half-game back of Louisville at 38–31. Felsch hoisted his team on his back and hit safely in 26 of the 32 July games. He amassed 16 multi-hit games, including 4-for-4 and 4-for-5 feats. They opened July with a doubleheader sweep of the Millers and tallied a 21–10 record for the month.

While Felsch and the Brewers were heating up on the ball field, World War I soon dominated the daily headlines. After the United States entered the war, several ballplayers—including Felsch—would be greatly affected by the conflict.

On August 7—the day after Austria-Hungary declared war on Russia and Serbia declared war on Germany—the Milwaukee Brewers played an exhibition game against Beaver Dam (65 miles northwest of Milwaukee), pasting the local city league team, 16–5. More than 1,200 fans packed the local stadium to catch a peek at the newly adorned star and were happy with the result. Felsch mauled their team with a homer, two doubles, and a single.[21]

Sitting at 58–45 to start August, a 2½-game margin over Louisville, Clark and the rest of the Brewers knew that the big leagues would be knocking on Felsch's door soon. The occasional scouting and analysis morphed into tangible negotiations. On August 8, the Chicago White Sox acquired Felsch from the Brewers for $12,000 and a player to be named later. Felsch remained with Milwaukee for the remainder of 1914 and reported to the White Sox the following season.

Felsch had obviously heard the whispers of promotion as he was all smiles after hearing the terms of the deal. For Clark and the Brewers, losing players to the big leagues was not unusual. But Clark was pleased to have his "fence breaker" for the stretch run.[22] "I'm a little nervous," said Felsch. "But just until I get up there. They are not going to be harder to hit in the league than they have been in this. But anyway, I am glad that I don't have to report there until spring. That will give me a trip west in spring and I'll be used to the company by the time the season opens."[23]

The *Milwaukee Sentinel*, not averse to championing the exploits of local stars who made the show, also pointed out that Felsch had not dropped one ball in the outfield that season and that "being a former infielder is a demon when it comes to fielding ground balls."[24] Felsch had certainly earned the accolades and endorsements. Ironically, on the day the trade was made, the Brewers were demolished by Minneapolis in the most lopsided game of the season, 26–5. Felsch collected a pair of doubles, but the Millers scored 12 runs in the first three innings and piled up 14 more. Sloppiness in the field marked the debacle, with the Brewers committing a season-high seven errors.[25]

When the calendar left August behind, the Brewers began the final month by taking two of three from Louisville. After getting drubbed in the opener, 11–2, the Brewers found their own bats with 8–6 and 11–6 victories. The Brewers went 3–4 in their next two series against Kansas City and Minneapolis, but thankfully, Louisville also played .500 ball in the first half of the month. The Brewers won five of their next seven games, with Felsch once again leading the slugging charge. During that important stretch, Felsch collected ten hits, with three home runs, two doubles, and a triple, this after missing a few games with an injury. He might have been nervous for next season, but it did not show during the 1914 AA pennant race.

After splitting a twin bill with the Saints on September 16, the Brewers capitalized on Louisville going just 8–7 down the stretch, pulling away by winning ten of their last 11 games and capturing the American Association title for the second consecutive year (besting Louisville by four games). On their final day of the season, the Brewers swept the lowly Saints in a doubleheader, 10–5 and 4–2, in front of a season record of 15,199 loyal patrons. They saved their best month for last, going 22–9, a game better than their prolific July.

The final 1914 American Association standings:

	W	L
Milwaukee	98	68
Louisville	95	73
Indianapolis	88	77
Columbus	86	77
Cleveland	82	81

	W	L
Kansas City	84	84
Minneapolis	75	93
St. Paul	56	111

Happy Felsch's final 1914 numbers were his best so far. He batted .304 with a league-leading 19 home runs, 41 doubles, 11 triples, 99 runs scored, and 19 stolen bases. He assembled an amazing 43 multi-hit games; the Brewers' record in those games was 38–5. In the red-hot July, Felsch was held hitless in only three games the entire month. After averaging 4.5, 6.7, and 6.5 runs per game in the first three months, Milwaukee catapulted to 7.6 runs per contest in July, thanks largely to Felsch's breakout. His 114 strikeouts also lead the league, but his .512 slugging percentage alleviated the negative effect of the whiffs.

As a team, the Brewers rode the steadiness of their pitching staff. Promotions to the big leagues and injuries stalled the offense for a while, but with the welcome emergence of their newly formed outfield of Beall, Randall, and Felsch (all batted over .300), the rest of the league could not outlast Clark's crew and another championship was inscribed into the American Association annals.

4

Happy Times,
Clean Sox, New Pants

*Grantland Rice, the great sportswriter once said: It's not whether
you win or lose, it's how you play the game. Well, Grantland Rice
can go to hell as far as I am concerned.*

—Gene Autry, former California Angels owner

A cork-centered ball had been introduced in 1911, causing run production
to soar from 3.6 runs per game in 1910 to 4.6 in 1911. Pitchers eventually
regained control, partially the result of scuffing the balls to their advantage,
using everything from sandpaper to coins to emery boards. Baseballs were not
replaced as frequently as they are today, making them less lively, and prodigious
hitting statistics were rarely attainable.[1]

The Chicago White Sox opened the twentieth century with two consecutive
American League pennants. Charles Comiskey managed the 1900 team, leading
them to an 82–53 record. The following year, under the tutelage of Clark Griffith, the Sox finished 83–53. The city of Chicago was buzzing with pride and
jubilation.

Their next pennant waited until 1906, but after that, a long drought for
Chicago's South-siders left the rooting cranks yearning for the sweet nectar of
renewed success. From 1907 and 1915, the Sox finished no higher than third
place. In the three seasons preceding Happy Felsch's arrival, manager Jimmy
Callahan's version of the club finished fourth, fifth, and sixth—hardly the optimum direction for a manager seeking job security.

In 1915, memories of past success faded as fans anticipated the upcoming
season. Contributing, perhaps, was Comiskey's willingness to act swiftly and
confidently, which soothed the fan base. Enter Clarence "Pants" Rowland.[2]

Rowland was a fellow Wisconsin native of Felsch's, born in the southwest-
ern city of Platteville, where his father was a railroad engineer. Their major league

Pants Rowland, right, lends an ear to pitcher Eddie Cicotte, 1917. Rowland would manage the White Sox from 1915 through 1918, compiling a .578 winning percentage over that time (George Grantham Bain Collection, Library of Congress).

debuts came in the same year. The biggest knock on Rowland was his lack of major league experience, but his primary asset was his knack for treating ballplayers like human beings.[3]

Earning the nickname "Pants" after wearing his father's overalls while playing for the Dubuque (Iowa) Ninth Street Blues, Rowland leap-frogged three minor league levels from the Class B Three-I League, where he managed the Peoria Distillers, to the lead man for Comiskey's Sox. The move made many sneer, including the local press. "If you call me a minor league manager in 1916 after I served a year with the Sox, I probably will regard it as a reflection," responded Rowland.

After nine seasons at the 39th Street Grounds, a new venue, White Sox Park (later changed to Comiskey Park), was erected in 1910. Designed by architect Zachary Taylor Davis with help from Comiskey and pitcher Ed Walsh, the park featured spacious dimensions (362 feet down each line and 420 feet to straight-away center field) on the site of a former city dump. The foul lines consisted of old water hoses that were painted white and flattened.[4] Before the 1927 season, the park was enclosed by a double-decked outfield grandstand. Expansive proportions were not uncommon during this period, which contributed to the Dead Ball Era moniker.

Paso Robles, California, was the site of the White Sox's training camp. On February 26, 1915, Felsch legged out a hit and two runs scored in the first intra-squad game of spring training. Felsch became a charter member of the "first" team, even though the second team was mostly full of fellow rookies (called "yannigans" in those days). Another new member of the Sox was a wily veteran second baseman named Eddie Collins, who had been purchased in the off-season from the Philadelphia A's.[5]

In 1915, the White Sox played a bulk of their spring training games against teams from the AA Pacific Coast League. Rowland's club enjoyed moderate success, but the AA teams of that era were not worlds away in ability from the majors. Felsch enjoyed his spring-time apprenticeship, greeting the Los Angeles Angels with three hits in a 7–5 victory. The day after, Felsch hit a game-winning triple that plated fellow outfielder Shano Collins, his second three-bagger of the game.[6]

Youth and speed were attributes that Rowland craved and Felsch owned. Triples became Happy's best friend, as he wacked two more in an 8–2 win over Los Angeles. A lack of left-handed hitters concerned Rowland, although he now had five. Offense had not been the White Sox's forte in recent years, relying instead on pitching and defense. Rowland also sought a dependable leadoff hitter and waited well into the season before he settled on a reliable candidate.[7]

In 1914, the outfield was particularly sub-par, mostly occupied by Shano

Collins, Ping Bodie, and Ray Demmitt. Only Collins remained in 1915; he and Felsch were expected to form a menacing hitting and fielding duo. As spring training progressed, Felsch enjoyed frequent success at the plate and in the field. He collected several multi-hit games and moved between left and center fields while Rowland assessed his settled lineup.

On March 28, the White Sox began the customary trek back east in preparation for their season opener. With stops in Arizona, Texas, Arkansas, Kansas City, and St. Louis (visiting the Browns on Opening Day), Rowland was looking to fine-tune his squad. Despite Comiskey acquiring a few more veterans, Rowland did not believe in employing a team captain.

"I never have had a captain on any ball club that I managed," claimed Rowland. "I see no need for a captain. If one is appointed this year, it will be a departure from an old custom of mine. I will be responsible for the mistakes made by the boys. They should be well acquainted with my methods long before the first game of the season takes place."[8]

The games played during the trip back north were largely loose, fun exhibition affairs. Rowland preferred that his team "jazz up the effort" and play to win. Of course, the field conditions that greeted them were hardly conducive to top-notch baseball. In Abilene, Texas, the Sox had to battle sand burrs on the infield. These pesky little balls of dust clung to the baseball and made throwing a painful proposition.[9]

To alleviate the tedious routines, harmless pranks often occurred. This time, an April Fools hoax was played on Felsch. His teammates elicited the help of umpire Kane ("in plain life a member of the El Paso detective force"). The plan was for Kane to purposely miss-call balls and strikes, preferably patently obvious ones. This spawned swift and righteous vulgarities from Felsch, which in turn caused Kane to whip out a six-shooter (empty cartridges, of course). After one such call, the crowd responded and the joke dissolved.[10]

In his major league debut on April 14, 1915, Felsch went 1-for-6 in a 13-inning win over the St. Louis Browns, who were managed by Branch Rickey. Sox starter Jim Scott lasted seven innings, giving up three earned runs, striking out four and walking four. The White Sox out-hit the Browns, 15–8, but left nine runners stranded in the 7–6 victory.

Felsch and fellow outfielder Shano Collins were principal actors in Pants Rowland's rendition of musical chairs, swapping spots between center and right field a couple times in the game. On one play, the sun proved detrimental to the scampering Felsch, who almost caught a long fly ball on the noggin. The opener for both clubs was a diverse mixture of baseball events, fraught with blunders, double steals, and mental miscues.[11]

Felsch struggled in April with a paltry .129 batting average and sustained an ankle injury that shelved him for the second St. Louis series. Jacques Fournier replaced Felsch and the team reversed their fortunes with a seven-game winning streak, sweeping the Browns in four games and taking three of four from the Cleveland Indians. Felsch returned in the middle of that Indians series. Rowland inserted him into the cleanup spot as the Sox pounded the Tribe, 12–1. Felsch contributed one hit in four at-bats and scored two runs. "Every day, the Sox are looking more like top liners," said the *Chicago Tribune*.

With the 1915 season under way, behind the scenes, peace between the established leagues and the upstart Federal League was a constant challenge. According to *The Sporting News*, scribes across the country had declared the so-called war to be over but the weekly baseball magazine was not entirely convinced. However, one *TSN* writer proclaimed that Charles Comiskey had always been truthful in his encounters with the writer and had always engaged in friendly conversation. Meanwhile, battles on the field raged on.[12]

In back-to-back wins over Cleveland in early May, Felsch was moved to the leadoff spot for Rowland, delivering 2-for-6 and 2-for-5 outings. He manned the leadoff spot for the next two months. Felsch hit safely in five consecutive games with three multi-hit efforts, raising his average over .200. On the surface, the Sox bats were the core ingredients to victory, but the Indians' sloppy fielding extended several rallies. As the summer progressed, no token charity was turned down as the White Sox became embroiled in a pennant battle with the Detroit Tigers and New York Yankees.

Felsch's mini-surge propelled him and the White Sox through May. His power had not yet surfaced, but he was becoming more patient at the plate. Up until May 17, Felsch had drawn just five walks. During a five-game stretch soon after, Felsch coaxed seven free passes. In his first 105 at-bats, he collected only seven extra-base hits out of 28 total hits. The old adage that a walk is as good as a hit certainly applied to him. This promising rise marched lock-step with the team's success.

While young pups, including Felsch, were contributing handsomely to the White Sox's effort, the dependable veterans were the glue to Rowland's club, with the bat and glove and as mentors. Eddie Collins, in particular, became invaluable by his influence; the key benefactor was young shortstop Buck Weaver, Collins' double-play mate. Collins also helped the young hitters work on their patience at the plate, something Felsch needed to improve.[13]

The White Sox exploded to close out May, winning nine straight and grabbing the American League lead over Detroit and New York. The Yankees were stuck in a six-game rut and the Tigers were searching for consistency. In perhaps his best game of the season so far, Felsch reached based in all five of his plate appearances (three singles and two walks), helping Faber and the team

Buck Weaver, 1917. Moving to third base to make room for rookie Swede Risberg, the well-liked Weaver adapted well to his new position and stepped up his offensive performance (George Grantham Bain Collection, Library of Congress).

dispatch the Philadelphia A's, 11–6, amidst an "ice blast" from nearby Lake Michigan. Felsch even found his name in the *Chicago Tribune* headline for the first time the next day, but it was "unfortunate for him that only a few fans were there to look on," the frigid Midwestern temperatures scaring the usual plentiful throng away.[14]

Felsch finished the second month of his young career with a flurry, hitting safely in 11 of 13 games, including seven in a row. Most hits were singles, but they propelled the White Sox to a season-high nine-game winning streak, sweeping the Athletics, Red Sox, and Yankees with relative ease. In an 11–3 laugher over Boston, Felsch had two hits and scored three runs from the leadoff spot. Braggo Roth, who followed Felsch in the two-spot, went 3-for-5, allowing the opportunistic Eddie Collins to knock in five runs.

Overseas in World War I, the Germans were quasi-apologizing to the Americans after their submarines struck United States steamers *Cushing* and *Gulflight* in an apparent case of misidentification. Meanwhile, the White Sox manager had to identify a replacement for Felsch. On the day the Sox's winning streak was halted, Felsch turned his ankle while trying to beat out a hit. Rowland replaced him with outfielder Finners Quinlan, a smallish gent reaching about

5'8" and a compact 158 pounds. This was Quinlan's first action in the big leagues since his 50 at-bat cup of coffee with the National League's St. Louis Cardinals in 1913.[15] The speedy Quinlan held his own as the Sox went 3–4 in Happy's absence. On June 8, Quinlan's latest flirtation with stardom gave way to Felsch's return. He re-introduced himself to his teammates with a 2-for-5 showing in a 4–3 victory over the Boston Red Sox.

Rowland had a penchant for averting complacency in his club, even as they padded the win column. To the chagrin of some, this meant more lineup tinkering. On June 8, trailing the first-place Tigers by one game, Rowland replaced Bunny Brief (IB) and Jim Breton (3B) with Braggo Roth and Felsch's former Brewers teammate, Lena Blackburne. Jack Fournier switched from left field to first base. Blackburne took over at third and the mighty slugger Roth occupied left field.

In that game, Felsch smashed a single to left with two outs. Weaver followed with a line drive to the wall in left-center, scoring Felsch easily. In the sixth inning, with the Sox trailing the Red Sox, 2–1, Felsch's lame ankle contributed to another Boston tally, this time a home run. Dick Hoblitzel drove a ball to left-center, but Felsch was too gimpy to chase it down before it reached the wall. Right fielder Shano Collins raced over, retrieved the pill, and fired it to the cutoff man, Buck Weaver. By the time Buck fired it home, Hoblitzel had already crossed home plate.[16]

New starter Braggo Roth was a fellow rookie and a Burlington, Wisconsin, native who, like Felsch, joined the rookie ranks with future valedictorian, George Herman "Babe" Ruth. Roth was later traded from the White Sox, but he eventually became the first rookie ever to win the AL home run title. (Roth actually debuted in 1914 but did not have enough at-bats—minimum 130—or days of service—minimum 45—to qualify as a rookie.)

In a 13–0 drubbing of the New York Yankees on June 9, Rowland found himself the recipient of "lack of sportsmanship" accusations by Yankees manager Billy Donovan. The Bronx leader claimed that Rowland had stopped a runner from proceeding home when Pants was coaching third base. A not-so-friendly dialogue ensued across dugouts during the game. Donovan called Rowland a bush leaguer and Pants chided Donovan over the latter's other complaint that the White Sox were stealing signs. After the crowd took notice, umpire O'Louglin told Rowland to "cut it out" and Donovan to "get in his game."[17]

On June 18, Felsch hit his first major league home run, getting his money's worth with a grand slam in an 11–4 triumph over Connie Mack's A's. Philly outfielders Rube Oldring and Jimmy Walsh stood motionless as they watched Happy's two-out clout clear the concrete wall at Shibe Park. His bomb to the left field bleachers gave the White Sox a commanding 7–2 margin they refused to surrender. Once again, Felsch's bat wasn't the only sore spot for the opponent. In the fifth inning, Felsch sprinted in and made a one-handed, shoestring catch on a Walsh line drive. Not settling for one out, Felsch gunned the ball to first to double up Chick Davies. The Sox turned four double plays in the game.[18]

Fewer than 200 plate appearances into his career, Felsch showed flashes of belonging in the major leagues. Following his April struggles with a .324/ .412/.405 month gave ample indication of his well-earned arrival. It was not uncommon back then for on-base percentages to be near or higher than slugging percentages. In 1914, the American League on-base percentage was .319; the slugging percentage was .324.[19] Only seven of his first 28 hits went for extra bases. The power would eventually materialize for Felsch, but consistency was the immediate goal.

Heading into July, the White Sox had won 14 of 20 games and were primed to contend for their first AL pennant in nine seasons. However, after feasting on bottom-feeders Cleveland, Philadelphia, and St. Louis, Chicago lost three of four games to fellow contender Detroit and went through July without being able to string together more than three wins in a row. Felsch was nursing his sore ankle but would not yield to his ailments. Parking his backside on the bench never crossed his mind, although it hampered his mobility while patrolling center field.

During a 5–3 stretch for the team in mid–July, Rowland moved Felsch from his leadoff spot down to sixth. This switch appeared to have a positive effect on him, as he had four two-hit games during that stretch. On defense, he also moved from center to left, with Nemo Leibold taking over the anchor spot in center. Leibold had been claimed on waivers from the Cleveland Indians on July 7. Felsch remained in the run-producing sector of the lineup the rest of his career, but eventually returned to center field for good.

On July 15, the White Sox acquired outfielder Eddie Murphy from the Philadelphia Athletics for $11,500. Connie Mack continued his roster purge and did not care for players in return. This was strictly a salary dump as he needed to build up his bank account to assure the chances of another pennant run someday. Several owners were more than willing to accommodate Mack's wishes. In Murphy, the White Sox gained a capable leadoff hitter who stayed in that role for the rest of 1915.

The season became a three-dog race between Boston, Detroit, and Chicago. In a two-day span, the White Sox fell from first to third. The red-hot Red Sox won 22 of 28 games; the Tigers had not lost more than one consecutive game since mid–June. After winning five of seven games to close out July, the White Sox got within one game of the lead. Felsch was pedestrian at the plate in late July, but showed improvement, ending the month with a .258/.361/.387 line.

The spike in on-base percentage was encouraging for Felsch's development as a complete baseball player. The injury had hampered his fielding more than his hitting. In the midst of an intense pennant race, Felsch and the White Sox opened a rough stretch that carried into the late summer and early fall. During a six-game losing streak that started on July 31, the Sox scraped together just four runs in the first four losses. Since leaving home for their road trip, I. E. Sanborn of the *Chicago Tribune* wrote that the White Sox were "trying to locate the jinx in their bat bag" and that the "real sluggers of the team, Eddie and Shano Collins and Felsch have done almost nothing to bring home the bacon so far."[20]

The White Sox strung together three four-game winning streaks in August and kept themselves at least in the pennant discussion. The Boston Red Sox were torrid in August, winning 11 of their first 13 games. For good measure, they added a seven-game winning streak near the end of the month. The Detroit Tigers assembled a nine-game winning streak in August, and it was clear that the White Sox were not going to catch up by playing .500 ball.

Felsch fared pretty well during those streaks. In a doubleheader against the St. Louis Browns. Felsch went 3-for-5, including his ninth triple of the season in a Sox sweep, 8–4 and 5–1. The sweep came with a cost. Both White Sox catchers, Ray Schalk and Wally Mayer, sustained injuries. The weather was sweltering in St. Louis, not a shock in mid–August. They collected two-thirds as many hits as the Browns in the sweep, but made them count, compliments of several St. Louis miscues.

To mix things up and find an edge, on August 21 Comiskey engineered a big trade, sending Braggo Roth, Ed Klepfer, $31,500, and a player to be named later to the Cleveland Indians for Shoeless Joe Jackson. Roth had performed decently for the White Sox, but their outfield was vastly outslugged by their infield, and perhaps Rowland was looking to balance that out. Comiskey, who always admired Jackson, sent his team secretary, Harry Grabiner, to Cleveland, telling him to "watch the bidding for Jackson, raise the highest one made by any club until they all drop out." In financial terms, the deal was the biggest to date.

On August 21–22, the White Sox took three of four against the Yankees in back-to-back doubleheaders. Felsch started slowly in the series, but went 2-for-4 with a double and RBI in the final game, a 5–0 shutout. He also switched to left field in the series, relinquishing center to Jackson, who made his White Sox debut on August 21. The man who would, like Felsch, become infamous for questionable judgment later, greeted his new teammates with a walk in eight plate appearances.[21]

Cleveland owner Charles Somers was strapped with the prospect of bankruptcy in 1915 and was compelled to jettison his best player, Jackson. Obtaining the 28-year-old Jackson was a risk for Comiskey. His batting average had

A playful Joe Jackson takes the catcher's mitt, 1917. Jackson was by anyone's definition an all-time great hitter, and he was the heart of the White Sox lineup throughout his six seasons with the club (George Grantham Bain Collection, Library of Congress).

decreased nearly 50 points since 1913, and some believed his career was permanently on the downward slope.[22]

Jackson was reunited with ex-Athletics teammate Eddie Collins, who was elated at the White Sox's most recent acquisition. "I have seen the best players the last 20 years, and no one has been better than Joe Jackson, who instinctively does everything right on the playing field," said Collins. "I can't recall Jackson missing a signal from the bench or coach, when he was at bat or on the bases. And he always threw the ball from the outfield to the right spot. And how he could throw."[23]

The uneducated, somber chap from Pickens County, South Carolina, was famous for his tool of the trade, a baseball bat named Black Betsy, a 48-ounce behemoth made for him by a local lumberman. Ingredients were "the north side of a hickory tree" and multiple coats of Jackson's tobacco juice.[24]

When he signed with his first major league team, Connie Mack's Athletics, Jackson was a trite timid and seemingly anxious to graduate to the big leagues. "I hardly know as how I'd like it in those big Northern cities," Jackson told Tom Stouch, a fellow mill town player. Stouch was the man who called his friend Mack to steer Jackson and other young prospects towards Philadelphia. In *My 66 Years in the Big Leagues*, Mack recounts how he paired up the illiterate Jackson with a more learned player, to help Shoeless Joe with reading menus and game reports.[25]

Jackson assumed the starting spot in center field, relegating Felsch to spot duty for the remainder of the season. Happy was not so hot in September, hitting just .154 while logging a meager 39 at-bats. There were now five outfielders for three spots. Rowland kept right fielder Eddie Murphy in the leadoff spot. Shano Collins moved to first base for most of the remainder of the season. In mid–September, Jackson moved to left field while Felsch played left and right, and had several pinch-hitting assignments.

Why the move to diminish Felsch's role? Following the twin bills with the Yankees, his numbers sat at .255/.337/.367. Jackson's with the Indians: .327/.389/.469. Murphy's numbers did not dwarf Felsch's but Rowland preferred Murphy's speed and experience. Shano Collins was a steadier performer than Felsch at this stage in their careers. Felsch was, after all, a rookie, and his time to shine was still on the horizon.

Seven games back of the Red Sox on September 8, Rowland's club did not make a magical run. They lost four of five to the front-runners, and the top of the 1915 American League standings would not budge the rest of the way. In one game, Babe Ruth struck out Felsch in three of his plate appearances, allowing just two White Sox hits in a 2–1 nail-biter. In all fairness to Felsch, he had pretty good success against Ruth in his career, hitting .313/.353/.406 against the big hurler. Despite being virtually out of the pennant race, the White Sox finished the season with 11 consecutive victories over Washington (one win), Philadelphia (five), Cleveland (one), and St. Louis (four).

Rowland inserted Felsch into the leadoff spot three times in the last two weeks of the season, which Happy had not seen in quite a while. He had struggled mightily in September, with a 1-for-19 stretch, dipping below the .250 mark for good. Felsch waved a happy goodbye in the season finale, smashing a two-run home run in a 6–2 Sox victory, this time from the cleanup spot.

The White Sox completed 1915 with a 93–61 record, 9½ games behind the eventual World Series champion Boston Red Sox, who defeated the Philadelphia Phillies for the title. Their bats picked it up in September, but their ERA was a season-worst 3.13. They recorded 91 strikeouts as a staff in September, ten fewer than they did in April, despite playing 12 more games. Injuries, inconsistent offense from the outfielders, and shoddy defense doomed Rowland's inaugural campaign as Charles Comiskey's field general.

Felsch's rookie campaign ushered in a decent, but not transcending, start to his major league career. After a torrid April, his season brought hitting streaks, slumps, and struggles in the outfield. Because he moved up and down the lineup and saw action in all outfield spots, it was not clear what his permanent role would be. Here are some batting splits for Felsch by: (A) place in the batting order; and (B) outfield position.

First:	.267/.342/.386 (202 at-bats)
Fifth:	.184/.266/.280 (125 at-bats)
Sixth:	.310/.420/.429 (84 at-bats)
Left:	.243/.333/.350 (103 at-bats)
Center:	.260/.349/.386 (285 at-bats)

On the brighter side, Felsch's 51 walks remained the most of his career in a single season. Although he devoured Philadelphia A's pitchers at a .299/.393/.416 clip (a not so difficult feat), he also enjoyed success against the Red Sox. He did not hit well at Fenway Park, but his .298/.403/.368 season line was impressive.

An annual off-season ritual in Chicago was a "battle for the best" in the City Series between the White Sox and the Cubs. In recent years, this delightful exhibition was not hindered by either team advancing to the post-season, as the White Sox had not reached the World Series since 1906, and the Cubs since 1910. In 1915, the south-siders prevailed in the five-game series. Felsch began his busy off-season by going 6-for-16 in the series while batting mostly cleanup.

In mid–September, the bible of baseball reporting, *The Sporting News*, wrote that Pants Rowland's job was likely safe going into next season. Comiskey stated that if Pants had one flaw, it was relying on his players' judgments instead of his own. But after digging him out of the bushes to manage at the highest level, perhaps being given a chance to develop his managerial acumen was warranted.[26]

Soon after the season ended, Felsch dove into the pool of marital bliss, marrying Marie Wagner, a 22-year-old, fellow north-side Milwaukeean and homemaker, on October 27, 1915. After a brief honeymoon, Felsch was summoned to testify in Cy Slapnicka's lawsuit against the Milwaukee Brewers for back pay. After the case was postponed, Felsch, Slapnicka, and friend Fred Luderus scampered off to Little Chute, WI, for a Sunday exhibition game.[27]

5

The .300 Club

Carrots might be good for my eyes, but they won't straighten out the curveball.

—Carl Furillo, Brooklyn Dodgers outfielder

Common sense dictates that the lower a team finishes, the more likely they are to exert more effort to improve in the off-season. In his 1983 *Bill James Baseball Abstract*, author/sabermetrician Bill James attributes this to the Law of Competitive Balance, which states that the balance between the strategies of winners and losers usually favors the losers. Finishing 32 games above .500 as the White Sox did in 1915, they hoped that only a few fillers and tweaks would catapult them higher in the first division and avoid regression.[1]

The convenience of such success—despite their third-place finish in 1915—resided in the comfort that few improvements were necessary. The rotation was sound, the outfield full of depth, and apart from a couple of holes and pending decisions at third and first, last year's club remained largely intact. The 1916 team included a nice bonus: Rowland would have Shoeless Joe Jackson for an entire season, which boded well for a climb in the American League standings.

Because there were only a couple of undecided positions, players trying to sneak into the lineup probably did not mind how hard they worked to get there. Jackson and Felsch were locked into two of the outfield positions. With Jack Fournier moving to first, that left Shano Collins and Eddie Murphy for the final spot. The main concern for Rowland was third base, where he was flirting with moving Weaver from the shortstop position, with Zeb Terry sliding into short. The 5'9" Terry's glove was tremendous, which afforded him some slack with the stick.

Heading into 1916, the usual contenders provided the chief roadblocks to a White Sox pennant run: the Boston Red Sox and Detroit Tigers. Three days before the regular season started, the Red Sox dealt Tris Speaker to the Cleveland Indians for Sad Sam Jones, Fred Thomas, and $55,000. After his batting average dipped from .336 in 1914 to .322, the team brass insisted on a pay cut. Speaker balked and the team said goodbye. Three days earlier, Boston had acquired outfielder Tillie Walker from the lowly St. Louis Browns for $3,500.

Felsch hoped to put his rookie struggles, including a bum foot and ankle, behind him. In a pre-season warm-up against a decent nine in Wichita, he helped the Sox destroy the locals, 15–1. He smacked three hits, leaving 15 more for his teammates. He and fellow outfield chucker Joe Jackson gunned down runners at the plate. The *Chicago Tribune* seemed convinced that Felsch's 1915 version of May (where he batted .324/.412/.405) was a sign of things to come, writing that "Felsch has regained the batting stride out of which he was thrown last summer by an injured foot." Perhaps the dreaded sophomore jinx would not visit the young slugger.

By the time the White Sox broke camp, a little surprise was waiting for them at Comiskey Park. The Old Roman, never averse to improving his team's pennant odds, had decided to make some practical and aesthetic improvements to the ball yard. In addition to a new infield, the park got a new scoreboard, a fresh coat of Irish green paint on the seats, and a few other articles of beautification to entice more paying customers. The only enhancement Rowland cared about was the new infield, as he was determined to maximize his team speed and avoid the dust that would often greet his infielders' eyes.[2] For the betting types, the early line on the White Sox chances was 3 to 1.

The Sox opened the 1916 season with a 4–0 loss to the "jinx" Detroit Tigers, getting just three hits off Stanley Coveleski. Felsch opened with an 0-for-3 donut. He was slotted in the sixth spot of the order, behind Joe Jackson and in front of catcher Ray Schalk. Center field became his permanent fielding home.

Felsch hit .254/.312/.380 in April and the White Sox as a team did not echo the pre-season hope and hype, going 9–9 in the opening month. After the opening loss, Chicago took the next three from the Tigers and hit the ball well, scoring 24 runs. The performance remained solid for Rowland's hill men, but the bats tapered off considerably. Felsch received as many compliments for his glove as for his stick, even when the White Sox lost. In a 5–3 loss to the Cleveland Indians, the *Chicago Tribune* wrote: "Felsch made several nice running catches, in addition to his swats."[3]

Only a week into the season, Chicago embarked on an 11-game road trip that started east and moved gradually back west. The termites ate away at their bats in Detroit, as they dropped three of four and scored only eight runs. Felsch went 3-for-4 in the series opener and 6-for-12 in the four games. The White Sox recovered somewhat before returning home, sweeping the lowly St. Louis

Browns in three games. Felsch hit .333 on the trip and amassed five multi-hit games in April. Was he ready to turn a corner towards stardom?

In early May, rumors began swirling about Rowland's job security, despite the dreaded vote of confidence from Charles Comiskey. 'Rowland is doing all he can do," claimed Comiskey. "No man wished more for a pennant then he. He will stay. The poor showing of the team can be attributed directly to the batting slump of some of the stars." The Old Roman also proved that enhancing the club was never out of the question. "Changes will be made when the team returns," added Comiskey. "I will look around and see if we can secure some men that the team can use."[4] Some veterans were not playing up to snuff, and Rowland was called a "busher" repeatedly.[5]

Felsch was battling to reach the .260 mark. He fared better in May, hitting .260/.325/.356 for the month; this bested the paltry team mark of .221/.279/.301. Rowland believed that this prolonged slump would not persist and hoped that the upcoming home tilts—which included daily batting drills in the morning—would eradicate the termites from their bats. On the road, the Sox received only 15 minutes before each game. Regardless, it was time for Eddie Collins, Joe Jackson, and Jack Fournier to perform more closely to their customary levels.[6]

In the second game of their four-game split with the Yankees, the Sox found themselves in the middle of a tussle, a brief moment of controversy that fueled their fire. On June 4, with Chicago winning 5–4 in the sixth and Felsch on second following his seventh two-bagger of the season, catcher Ray Schalk attempted to sacrifice him to third. His bunt popped up into the air, Yankees pitcher Ray Fisher dashed in, lunged for the ball, and hit the ground (apparently having caught the ball). He then turned and fired to second to double up Felsch. The umpire, however, saw it differently and ruled that a catch was not made and the runners were safe. Fisher threw a mild tantrum, to no avail of course, and the brief conflict seemed to have sparked the White Sox. They added three runs in their half of the sixth, two in the seventh, and two more in the eighth for good measure.[7]

The Dead Ball Era was the feistiest ever, with players doing everything they could to glean an advantage. Although Ban Johnson prided himself on good, clean, non-cheating baseball compared to baseball in the nineteenth century, he couldn't dispose of all the rowdiness by wishing it away.[8] The game was played by cheaters, con men, drunks, and outright thieves, according to writer Bill James, who also aptly pointed out that it was the aforementioned gentlemen who provided the game's color in that era.[9]

One familiar target was the poster child for hooliganism, Detroit's Ty Cobb. In a game against the White Sox on July 2, Cobb angrily threw his bat into the Comiskey Park stands after striking out. He and his manager, Hughie Jennings, got tossed out. Earlier that week, Cobb had attempted to inflict bodily harm on a heckling fan in St. Louis. In addition to suspending Cobb, Johnson, at various stages during the season, disposed of other misbehaving players and even a couple of managers.[10]

On June 25, the White Sox crawled over the .500 mark for the first time since May 2, courtesy of a 4–3 victory over the Indians. Claude "Lefty" Williams went the distance, relinquishing six hits, walking none, and striking out seven. Shoeless Joe provided the lumber, going 3 for 4 with three runs scored and a run driven in. His solo blast over the right field fence in the second tied the score. Felsch, who singled, now found himself in the leadoff spot; Rowland put him there in their 2–0 blanking of St Louis on June 22.

Felsch hit safely in 11 consecutive games in late June and started to display steadier play both at the plate and in the field. When the calendar turned to July, Felsch had already collected 14 multi-hit games and his batting average sat at .266. In concert with his success, the White Sox were now at 33–29, in third place, and had their eyes on the second-place surprise, the Cleveland Indians.

Shoeless Joe Jackson had paced the White Sox hitting corps all season. Almost immediately after starting his professional career, Jackson earned a reputation as a fearsome, hard-swinging hitter, not unlike Ty Cobb. More later on Jackson the person; as a player, he had few equals in either league and helped keep Rowland and his teammates afloat in 1916 and within striking distance of first place. On July 1, Jackson's numbers were a gaudy .382/.442/.562 and an OPS (on-base percentage plus slugging percentage) of 1.004, not exactly Dead Ball Era metrics. In his first full-time campaign in 1911 with Cleveland, Jackson batted .408/.468/590—mind-boggling for that period in baseball.

Jackson and Felsch formed a solid pair that summer as the White Sox yearned for their first pennant in a decade. They had to contend with a resurgent Yankees team, an upstart Indians club, and every other team besides the Athletics. On July 7, in a 12-inning, 4–3 loss to the Yankees, Felsch recorded—to date—his best game of the year at the plate. He rapped out five hits in six at-bats, including his fourth triple of the year. Sadly, his mates only plated him once, leaving eight total runners stranded. This bust out put his batting average at a solid .273 and started a tear that lasted eight games.

Team	W	L	W-L%	GB	RS	RA	pythW-L%
New York	43	29	.597	—	300	245	.592
Cleveland	42	31	.575	1.5	314	276	.559
Chicago	**40**	**32**	**.556**	**3.0**	**255**	**207**	**.594**
Boston	39	34	.534	4.5	238	239	.498
Washington	38	34	.528	5.0	254	243	.520
Detroit	38	36	.514	6.0	312	300	.518
St. Louis	31	42	.425	12.5	278	289	.482
Philadelphia	17	50	.254	23.5	195	347	.258

As you can see, the White Sox had under-achieved at this point, and if one based the standings on their pythW-L percentage, they would be in first place. For half a season or even a full season, Pythagorean numbers are questionable. For the White Sox, there was little question that they had played well below expectations for most of the 1916 season.

From mid–July to about mid–August, the Sox played over .600 baseball. In July alone, they played in *eight* extra-inning marathons, winning four of them. Because of repeated rainouts, they were forced to endure a seemingly unfair number of doubleheaders. On July 10, they started a stretch that contained *seven* doubleheaders in 11 days. The Sox went 7–7 in those games, with streaks being the operative theme. The first three twin bills were all against the Red Sox. They swept the first two games and dropped the final four.

Felsch started this arduous stretch with a bang, hitting safely in the first six contests. He went 10-for-26 in those games, boosting his batting average to .283. He tapered off in their next series against the Athletics, but the Sox swept them in four games. Rowland also moved Felsch in the order from leadoff to third, then sixth, which would become his permanent slot for the remainder of the season, thanks to his extra-base abilities.

Following the bevy of twin bills, Happy Felsch got red hot. From July 21 to the end of the month, Felsch went 22 for his next 55, a blistering .400 average. He hit .315/.338/.473 in July. The biggest rise was his slugging percentage, which went from .321 in June to a staggering .473 in July, thanks to 13 extra-base hits.

Felsch was a willing contributor to the streak that catapulted the White Sox into first place. On the last day of July, he went 4-for-5 in a 4–3, 11-inning squeaker over Connie Mack's crew. He drove in two runs, on his fifth homer of the season, and also started a rally in the ninth with a one-out single. Two days prior, Felsch had begun a torrid eight-game stretch in which he collected 15 hits, hitting safely in every game. During that streak, he hiked his batting average from .274 to .291. This precipitated a remarkably consistent period in Felsch's young career.

The key to the White Sox's surge was improved hitting and reliable pitching. The team scored 148 runs in July, 59 more than any previous month. While they played 11 more games that month with the bunched-up doubleheaders, their team batting average in July was .268, up from .249 the previous month. On the mound, their team ERA hovered around 2.00, but perhaps more significant was a decrease in walks and an increase in strikeouts.

In the batter's box, their main concern was their performance against left-handed pitchers; Eddie Collins and Felsch were better than most. St. Louis Browns manager Fielder Jones, apparently not worried about spilling his own scouting report to the masses, in an interview with Ring Lardner claimed that the key for southpaws was to jam the hitters, and that Jackson, Eddie Collins, and Fournier were always looking for the high fastball and would never offer at a slow curveball on the outside.

"My pitchers are always trying to give them what they can't hit," stated Jones. "But of course, all pitchers are liable to slip up once in a while and pitch where they're not aiming. I bet there isn't a man on the Chicago club who would hit .300 if the pitchers would keep the ball down round their knees."

Jones also offered his take on why the White Sox had enjoyed success and the considerable effect that Eddie Collins had had on the team. "The boys tell me that before the White Sox got Eddie Collins, it wasn't a very difficult matter to grab off the battery signs," said Jones. "Schalk used to signal his whole infield what was going to be pitched. As soon as he had given the pitcher a sign, he'd get up, lean over and put his hand on his knees. If he kept his arms stiff, it was going to be a fastball. If he crooked them, it was going to be a curve. Collins made him cut that out and spoiled a lot of fun."

With a little over two months left, the White Sox were in a dog fight for the American League crown. After their August 2 victory over the hapless A's, they would not face them again until the last three games of the month. In the interim, they would face only fellow contenders. Happy Felsch prolonged his steady climb towards the vaunted .300 batting average plateau. In the series opener against Boston on August 7, Rowland's gang rode the back of pitcher Reb Russell, who scattered seven hits, going the distance in a 7–1 triumph. Felsch displayed a rare 0-for-4 duck, but Eddie Collins and first baseman Jack Ness paced the Sox offense. Their record stood at 61–44, 1½ games ahead of second-place Boston.

With their recent success, Pants Rowland started to get the credit he deserved after being a sacrificial goat during his team's early-season struggles. Most of the league's teams—save the Athletics—improved in 1916, and living up to the lofty pre-season aspirations took a lot of gas out of the club. After dropping three straight to the Red Sox at home, Chicago played sub-.500 ball and fell to third place heading into the last full month of the season. Felsch now hovered around the .290 mark to help his team stay in the race.

Despite Felsch's success, the White Sox suffered a crushing doubleheader sweep by rival Boston on August 16, the first two games of a four-game set. The opener lasted 16 innings with the Beantown ballplayers winning, 5–4. Fred McMullin's blunders helped the Bosox victory, but wasted rallies in regulation was the chief thorn for Rowland's crew.[11] The top five hitters in his lineup, which included Felsch in the five-hole, went 14-for-36 but scored only three runs. Felsch had three hits but the batters immediately on his tail, Fournier and Schalk, were a combined 0-for-12. The White Sox won the final two games of the series, 7–0 and 11–6, but a split merely held serve for first-place Boston in the pennant race.

In the final 11 days of the season, a Felsch onslaught at the plate raised his final batting average to an even .300. His late-season power surge seemed emblematic for the broad-shouldered former wrestler. Unfortunately, not enough winning and/or Red Sox losing transpired. The White Sox took three of four games from the Indians to close out the season, but the Red Sox clinched the pennant with two wins over the Yankees and one against the A's. They rested their men on the final two days of the season and breezed past the National League champion Brooklyn Robins, four games to one, to capture the 1916 World Series.[12]

The White Sox compiled a 19–7 record in September with non-transcendent summer months following a red-hot spring (33–29 the first three months of the season); they allowed 10 runs on the road that month. By contrast, Felsch batted .371/.409/.565 in September. In the last eight games of the season, Felsch was 14-for-32 for a blistering .438 average. He finished the season at .300/.341/.427. His seven four-baggers led the club. Inconsistency and an injury hampered Felsch late in his sophomore season. But his gradual ascent towards stardom would not cease. The *Pittsburgh Press* lauded Felsch's abilities: "Little consideration is given Happy Felsch when critics are considering the leading outfielders of the American League, yet Felsch is undoubtedly one of the most valuable outfielders in the Johnsonian Era."

Joe Tinker, manager of the Cubs, said: "If there are many better outfielders in the American League, I pity the bush leaguers trying to break in."[13]

6

100 Wins to Paydirt

*I think I have learned a great deal the last two years. I am sure I
am a much better player than when I joined the Sox.*

—Happy Felsch, prior to the 1917 season

World War I raged on, the economy began to falter, and attendance league-wide dropped an estimated 17 percent in 1917. In February, the *New York Times* proclaimed that fan interest in baseball would soon wane because of the war, but Ban Johnson, president of the American League, insisted that it would be business as usual on the field.

Coinciding with their customary baseball routine in spring training, the White Sox and other teams took part in military preparedness. Sergeant Smiley was the Sox military training gatekeeper. Following the Edmund Butts military manual, the players were subjected to company drills and formations. Johnson offered a $500 prize to the best-drilled team (won eventually by the St. Louis Browns).[1]

This military training rule was not heavily enforced by all teams, and the Cleveland Indians and Detroit Tigers had already shelved the maneuvers. Some believed that these military pseudo-maneuvers only distracted players from the baseball work and were a complete waste of time. The White Sox responded more favorably to the drills; it did not hurt that Pants Rowland and coach Kid Gleason demanded stern discipline themselves.[2]

The expectations for the White Sox in 1917 were astronomical, and Charles Comiskey's five-year rebuilding plan started to bear fruit. The gradual climb to the top, should it not reach the summit, would bring deep disappointment. *The Sporting News* proclaimed that it would be a miracle if they didn't capture the pennant. In 1914, the year before Oscar Felsch's arrival, the Sox finished a dismal sixth. Since then, they had attained third place, then second. Only the top rung remained.[3]

Felsch's late-season flurry in 1916 gave him extreme confidence heading into his third major league campaign. "I'd like to lead the league [in batting] just once," said Felsch. "That's an accomplishment that any player may be proud of with such great hitters as [Tris] Speaker, [Ty] Cobb, [Shoeless Joe] Jackson, [Eddie] Collins, [Frank "Home Run"] Baker, [George] Sisler shooting at the old alley."[4]

Defense and pitching were mantras of Charles Comiskey's St. Louis Brown Stockings teams in the American Association in the late 1800s. Pants Rowland sought to echo this emphasis with his White Sox team. *The Sporting News* commended Rowland for being "wiser" than before and wrote that his team needed to eliminate the "bad fielding elements" from their play and get them to work in harmony.[5]

Despite being later criticized (fairly or not) for his frugality in doling out petty money to keep existing players, the Old Roman did not blink an eye at acquiring them initially, even if it generated public criticism. It seems comical now, but he was even criticized for bringing in Felsch, mainly because two previous acquisitions—both teammates of Felsch in Milwaukee—were largely busts, Larry Chapelle and Lena Blackburne.

Not one to stand pat, Comiskey fortified his roster. Their 601 runs scored in 1916 were third in the American League. Their pitching was stellar with a league-best 2.36 ERA. Defense, baserunning, and overall lineup stability were areas of concern. To alleviate their concerns, Comiskey purchased shortstop Charles "Swede" Risberg from the Vernon Tigers of the AA Pacific Coast League. This allowed Rowland to move Buck Weaver back to his customary third base position. Comiskey also purchased first-sacker Arnold "Chick" Gandil from the Cleveland Indians for $3,500, after platooner Jack Ness refused a pay cut.

The White Sox began the season on fire, winning nine of their first 11 games. Opening Day was welcomed by over 27,000 fans in St. Louis, who witnessed their team get thumped by the Sox, 7–2. The game was marked by brilliant fielding and the fabulous play of newcomer Gandil, who went 3-for-4. Catcher Ray Schalk added a long blast over the left field fence to help overcome starting pitcher Lefty Williams' shaky start. Happy Felsch took a mulligan on opening day, going 0-for-4.[6]

Rowland was concerned about his pitching staff heading into the season. Williams had battled stiffness in his throwing arm in recent weeks, which he tried to loosen up during a warm-up game against the AA St. Paul Saints. Red Faber, who would turn things around to have a fine season, struggled in the second game versus the Browns, which the Sox lost, 4–3. Felsch joined the hit parade with two singles. The Sox rebounded the next day and took the rubber game. Felsch got a pair of hits as the White Sox demolished the hosts, 11–0.

The modern, media-created concept of "statement games" or "series" had

Shortstop Swede Risberg in 1917. Despite his light hitting, Risberg's strong arm and reputation for solid defense got him into all but five of pennant-winning Chicago's 154 games (George Grantham Bain Collection, Library of Congress).

not yet penetrated the vernacular in 1917. But their next trio of games at Detroit against the Tigers would certainly have qualified, since Navin Field had not been cordial to the Sox during Rowland's tenure as skipper. In 1916, the Sox won the season series from Detroit, 13–9, but were just 5–6 in their yard, an improvement over their 3–19 record there the previous two seasons. Snow flurries greeted the Motor City throng, but it didn't deter the White Sox from exorcising their Navin field demons. Pitcher Jim Scott scattered eight hits in a 6–2 victory. In a game the *Chicago Tribune* coined a "game of freeze out," Felsch, Weaver, and Schalk had two hits apiece and leadoff hitter Nemo Leibold knocked in two runs with a double.[7]

The White Sox remained near the top of the American League as April closed, one-half game behind the Boston Red Sox at 10–6. Felsch produced his best opening month to date, hitting .276. In the previous season, Felsch had employed a more aggressive approach at the plate, perhaps mimicking the proclivities of Jackson, who rarely kept his Black Betsy club on his shoulders.

Did Happy find success against some teams/pitchers over others? Against the Red Sox in 1916, Felsch scorched the champs with a .382/.405/.539 line in 76 at-bats, but played poorly against the Washington Senators, thanks largely to the best pitcher in the game, Walter Johnson. He enjoyed marvelous success against other aces such as Carl Mays, Sad Sam Jones, and Babe Ruth. In 1917, Johnson was still a tough at-bat, but Felsch enjoyed more consistency with fewer prolonged slumps.

In mid–May, the White Sox salvaged the last two games of a series against the New York Yankees. This initiated an eight-game winning streak that saw their offense crawl out of the doldrums. In that stretch, the Sox scored 46 runs, nearly six per game. Following New York, the Sox swept the Philadelphia Athletics in four games. Felsch went 2-for-3 and 2-for-4 in the final two contests.

In an incredible run that started May 12, the Chicago White Sox went 16–1–1. In most seasons, this would earn them a sizable lead in the standings. However, through May, Boston pitcher Babe Ruth was 10–1 as the Red Sox strung together their own run, winning ten of 11 in one May stretch (the other game being a tie), and the two teams would battle the remainder of the season for league supremacy. Felsch hit safely in 12 of those 18 games, including six multi-hit affairs, which yielded 20 runs batted in.

Pants Rowland, although lacking what we would call today a number one, superstar starter, was led by a duo of fairly capable hurlers, Eddie Cicotte and Lefty Williams. Cicotte began the year with an 8–2 record by the end of May. After alleviating early-season arm stiffness, Williams won his first nine decisions. They even relieved each other sometimes, a strategy that Dead Ball Era managers often employed. Teams did not have a bullpen full of relief specialists.

Eddie Cicotte loosens up his arm, 1917. Cicotte, a pivotal figure in the Black Sox scandal two years later, was perhaps the top pitcher in the American League during Chicago's final championship season of the century (George Grantham Bain Collection, Library of Congress).

Often, after a starter completed a game, he was summoned the next day to mop up another pitcher's mess. The terms "setup man" and "closer" had not invaded the game.

Eddie Cicotte, born June 19, 1884, in Springwells, Michigan (of French heritage), was the prototypical junk baller and a perfect alternative to the power pitchers of the era. It took Cicotte a while before tasting success, battling through mediocre years before hooking up with the White Sox. He was known for having a variety of pitches in his arsenal, including a nasty knuckleball. Later, in a 1952 interview, Cicotte offered these comments on the pitch's origin: "They say I invented the knuckle ball but Eddie (Kickapoo) Summers deserves a full share of the credit. We worked on it together and developed it at Indianapolis in 1906." In *The Neyer/James Guide to Pitchers*, the authors point out that Summers might have perfected certain aspects of the pitch, although both hurlers credited Cicotte with its invention.[8]

The book ranked Cicotte tenth on the all-time best knuckleballs list. But

Cicotte was not relegated to one pitch, using the screwball, spitter, emery ball, shine ball and a pitch he personally named the "sailor," a rising fastball that traveled in the manner of a flat stone being tossed in a lake. His tool box was chock full of dancing pitches that confounded hitters.

After their amazing late-May, early-June run, Chicago cooled off a bit but stayed neck and neck with Boston. How was Felsch doing during this pennant battle? Slow starts seemed to be his calling card, and this season was no different. In previous years, small streaks had rescued him from cruel slumps. On May 27, Felsch put up a donut against his nemesis, the Washington Senators. From that point on, the enthusiastic kid from the Milwaukee sandlots transformed himself into a completely different player. His batting average sat at .261 and would not dip lower than that the rest of the summer.

Lurking in the shadows was the intensifying battle overseas. On May 25, the *Chicago Tribune* reported that over 300 major leaguers had registered for the draft, including several White Sox. The "work or fight" proclamation in the United States left many with a heavy-hearted decision.[9] Men who were "proper" husbands and fathers, owned property, or worked at approved jobs, and those who participated in civic activities, received the full benefit of citizenship without fighting. This would affect the teams more in 1918, but several claimed they were in good condition either way.[10]

Felsch batted .266 in June with ten multi-hit games. His on-base percentage dipped for the month but his slugging percentage rose, thanks to 25 hits and only three walks. Now batting fifth and secured in the role of run producer, Felsch was primed to elevate all his numbers. In a four-game stretch, he drove in ten runs, including two fence-clearing clouts. Happily, the Sox won all four games.

The White Sox closed out the month with a slim 1½ game lead over Boston. Felsch, along with Eddie Collins, Buck Weaver, and Chick Gandil, picked up the hitting slack left by Shoeless Joe Jackson, who registered a rare poor month, hitting just .232. In an unwelcome diversion on June 16 in Boston, Weaver and utility infielder Fred McMullin found themselves embroiled in a fan riot. During the game, several fans rushed the field as rain started to fall. The two White Sox were accused of slugging a couple of fans, and would later have to appear in court in their own defense.

James Crusinberry of the *Chicago Tribune* suggested that the gambling crowd was responsible for the altercation. He also reported that both teams were solemn about the incident afterwards, and that "so many side features were attached to the general riot, and so much hushing was done by the management on each side, that the facts weren't available."[11] At the time the turmoil began, the White Sox were winning, 2–0. If the rowdy throng were mostly gamblers, perhaps they rushed the field in hope that the game would be postponed.[12]

The increasing presence of gamblers in and around baseball venues was partially a consequence of the government suspending all horse racing until after the war. This lured some to seek greener pastures in which to ply their trades. The rumblings of game fixing and gamblers bragging about which players they had cornered became rampant.[13]

After a 35-minute delay, play resumed, and one indisputable fact was the final score. The White Sox beat the Red Sox, 7–2, compliments of four runs in the ninth inning. The teams split the four-game set; Felsch struggled at Fenway, going just 3-for-15. The word "struggle" would cease to apply to him the rest of the way. July became the most prolific month of his career to date and ran parallel with his team's success.

In Detroit, after the White Sox dispatched the Tigers, 5–1, a fan was quoted as saying: "I don't see how any team can beat those fellows out of the pennant. They certainly looked good." Felsch contributed nicely to the fan's impressions, going 3-for-4.[14] The next day, the Sox swept a doubleheader from the Tigers by twin scores of 4–3. Felsch had ten hits in a four-game stretch. Ironically the only time he scored a run was after he was plucked by a pitch in the nightcap of the doubleheader. This clustering of hits would be Felsch's calling card in 1917.

The warm weather seemed to favor the batting exploits of Felsch. He followed an 0-for-13 slump in mid–July with an eight-game hitting streak in which he batted .352 (14-for-32). For a brief stint, Felsch batted cleanup as Joe Jackson missed nine games with an injury. Shano Collins slid into Felsch's five-spot. The *Chicago Tribune* was harsh on the suddenly reeling Sox, saying "their attack was weak, defense ragged, and there was a lack of fighting spirit."[15] Days earlier, the paper had said: "The Sox were playing in their most stylish manner when things began to happen in such rapid succession that people groaned."[16]

Rowland's crew soon put a little air between them and the Bosox, going 9–1–1 from July 17–25. Their record rose to a dominating 61–33, opening up a four-game lead. With steady pitching by Cicotte, Williams, and Faber, and the defensive efforts brought into Chicago with solid infielders, the guy who became Mr. Reliable was Felsch. His month of July was spectacular. He batted .352/.385/.500 with 45 hits. Rowland thought that many of his hitters were lapsing into "first-ball" swingers. This did not adversely affect Felsch; he walked only five times in the month, but hit three of his season total of six home runs. Making contact was the mantra of Dead Ball Era hitters, and Felsch was no different.

Felsch also timed his hits well and always appeared to be in the mix when the game was on the line. In a doubleheader sweep of the Yankees on July 12, his RBI single won the first game and he scored the tying run in the eighth inning of the second game. This prompted the local scribe to write:"Glad Hap Felsch is one for us."[17]

On July 30, the White Sox opened an important four-game series at Boston. The Red Sox took the first two, with Chicago taking the final pair. In both Red Sox wins, they jumped out to first-inning leads and hung on the rest of the way. White Sox starter Reb Russell halted the Bosox in game three, twirling a 4–0 shutout on just six hits. Red Faber and Dave Danforth combined in the finale as the White Sox breezed 7–1. Felsch carried his torrid bat into August, hitting safely in all four games. Chick Gandil, who batted behind Felsch in the order, had three hits in the final game. *The Sporting News* asserted that Pants Rowland using a consistent lineup was a good sign for the White Sox.[18]

On August 1, Buck Weaver and Fred McMullin had to appear in a Boston courtroom to answer the fans' charges during the June 17 fracas in Fenway Park. The damage suits were for $1,000 and $1,500, respectively; the players were allowed to play in that afternoon's game. Their lawyer advised them that the case would never be heard from again. Luckily, there would be no such rowdiness involving the White Sox the rest of the year.[19]

White Sox owner Charles Comiskey, who later got flooded up to his eye balls in the murky tragedy that ensued, received many kudos from adoring fans and newspapermen for his compassion and generosity. On July 23, Comiskey sent his fourth check to Orson Smith, treasurer of the Chicago chapter of the Red Cross, representing 10 percent of gate receipts at Comiskey Park. The check was for $3,702.98, which brought the generous total to $10,763.71.[20]

Staying with the hot weather theme, Felsch put together a 15-game hitting streak in the end of July and into August, going a ripping 24-for-58. The White Sox were only 7–8 in those games, but their hitting started to pick up, compensating for a few lame arms on the pitching staff. Chick Gandil and Shoeless Joe Jackson were nearly as hot as Felsch during this period. On August 19, the offense exploded for 14 runs on an efficient 14 hits in a 14–6 lashing of the A's. The White Sox played three extra-inning games in five days, two against the Indians and one against the Mackmen. Felsch hit .352/.385/.500 in July and .342/.388/.425 in August. Here are a few of his highlights:

+ July 23—Felsch went 4-for-4, with a triple, double, and two singles. Three of his hits led to runs in the 5–3 win over Boston.
+ From July 23 through August 6, Felsch amassed 27 hits.
+ August 2–6—Felsch collected two hits in five straight games, with the White Sox winning four of them.
+ September 2–3—In back-to-back doubleheaders versus Detroit, all victories by the White Sox, Felsch collected ten hits—all singles. On September 4, in the opening game of the St. Louis Browns series, he added two doubles and a single, scoring three times and knocking in two runs.

The head-to-head battles between Chicago and Boston were legendary, if only because of how incredibly even they were. Boston probably hoped for a few more dates on the schedule against the White Sox; unfortunately, that might not have mattered. From August 23 to September 18, the White Sox were a dominant 21–2. This astounding run included two nine-game winning streaks. The Red Sox would have to match this dominance, but during the same period Boston went 14–7.

Once again inspired by the bravery of our fighting men overseas, the Old Roman endorsed the idea of American League president Ban Johnson that U.S. soldiers would be supplied with issues of *The Sporting News* so that they could keep up with their favorite teams. Comiskey would become the "godfather of absent fans" to our fighting men. Comiskey also called for an annual Military Day in the American League. He got this inspiration after he hosted a special Clark Griffith Day, originated by the *Chicago Daily News*, in honor of the Old Fox's long-time dedication and contribution to professional baseball. Soon-to-be and returning soldiers were welcomed warmly at Comiskey Park and other league venues.[21]

In a Sunday twin bill on September 2 against the visiting Detroit Tigers, 35,000+ fans showed their support and could taste a pennant. "It was the greatest demonstration I have ever seen at a ball park," said Rowland. "I never saw a crowd pull for a team to win to equal the enthusiasm of the Chicago fans in the second game." It was clear that throughout the summer, the White Sox fans were still wary of Rowland's credentials as a major league manager. The mere thought was preposterous in retrospect, but back then, when a manager got such a gig seemingly out of the dark, the pressure to succeed was ten-fold in everybody's eyes.[22]

Every minute decision was dissected, from whom to pinch-hit for in a crucial stage, or when to send the runners in a possible hit-and-run situation. In the Tigers doubleheader, when Rowland summoned Shano Collins to pinch-hit for the light-hitting catcher, Ray Schalk, one fan—obviously fond of the stout receiver—yelled down from the stands: "Why didn't he send someone to bat for Jackson?" The unknown crank must not have paid attention prior; Jackson already had a homer, double, a single, and plenty of "robbing" in the outfield.[23]

The armchair quarterbacking made no difference. Rowland was focused on guiding his club to the World Series. On September 15, after a doubleheader split at Detroit, the Sox still enjoyed a 7½-game cushion with 14 games remaining for Chicago, 16 for the Red Sox. On September 21, the teams faced off for the last series, this time at Fenway Park. Now trailing by 9½ games, the Bosox required a sweep just to sniff some elusive hope.

The White Sox flexed their first-place muscles in the opener, defeating Boston 2–1 in ten innings to clinch the American League pennant for the first time in 11 seasons. Red Faber went the distance, outdueling Dutch Leonard.

Shano Collins' game-winning single in the top of the tenth scored Ray Schalk. Rowland had initially penciled in Reb Russell for the start, but during pre-game warm-ups, Faber declared himself fit and Pants made the switch. Faber got a thrilling game-ending double play in the bottom of the final frame and the celebration began.[24]

The Sporting News called the White Sox's pennant triumph a vindication for all the jeering Pants Rowland and Comiskey took for hiring the so-called "busher." The baseball weekly went so far as to say that a World Series victory would be a bonus, and a loss would not diminish the respect that Rowland has earned. With a week left in the season, the Sox had plenty of time to get ready for the National League champion New York Giants.

Felsch hit safely in the last seven games of the season, albeit meaningless matchups against Boston, Washington, and New York. He finished the season at .308/.354/.403. His six home runs led the team, along with 17 doubles and ten triples. His batting average placed fifth in the AL. He was second in RBI with 102, just one behind Detroit's Bobby Veach. With the glove, he led all American League outfielders with 14.6 fielding runs, a linear weights measure developed by Pete Palmer in the 1970s. His 3.05 range factor/game (Putouts + Assists/ Games Played) was the highest of his career. His 440 putouts were best in the American League and tied for first overall with Max Carey of the NL Pittsburgh Pirates.

The 1917 season elevated the young outfielder from high-ceiling prospect to emerging star. His friends back home in Milwaukee planned a "shower" for him. They requested Happy's hat size and his latest preference in haberdashery.[25] The White Sox finished with 100 wins and 54 losses, the best in both leagues and nine games ahead of the Boston Red Sox. The final 1917 American League standings:

	W	L	W-L%	GB
Chicago	**100**	**54**	**.649**	—
Boston	90	62	.592	9.0
Cleveland	88	66	.571	12.0
Detroit	78	75	.510	21.5
Washington	74	79	.484	25.5
New York	71	82	.464	28.5
St. Louis	57	97	.370	43.0
Philadelphia	55	98	.359	44.5

National League champion New York Giants manager John McGraw attended the White Sox's season finale, a 4–2 loss to the Yankees in New York. How much true scouting the man called "Little Napoleon" collected was anybody's guess. Shano Collins showed off with a blast over the left field bleachers, while pitcher Red Faber merely stayed loose in relief and did not focus on winning.[26]

7

White Sox Become Giants

This is not an easy game. To be champion, you have to invest a little extra.

—Pete Rose

John McGraw's glaring success with the New York Giants needed no validation. He assumed the managerial reigns from deposed skipper Heinie Smith well into the 1902 season. His portion of the record was a mere 25–38, but his wit, style, and "do whatever it takes to win" attitude earned him the full-time gig for the next three decades. An accomplished player, McGraw may be the best player ever to become a successful manager.

His 1917 Giants won 98 games, and like the White Sox did so in convincing manner, besting the second-place Philadelphia Phillies by ten games. This was McGraw's fifth appearance in the Fall Classic. The Giants went from worst to first in two years, having occupied the NL basement in 1915. Their cross-town rivals, the Brooklyn Robins, went in the opposite direction in just one season, dropping from first in 1916 to seventh in 1917, a 24-win dip.

The Giants rode the season with a balanced offense, solid starting pitching, and no real superstar. Right fielder David Robertson tied for the major league lead in home runs with 12, sharing the honors with Gavvy Cravath of the Phillies. Robertson and third baseman Heinie Zimmerman were McGraw's power sources.

The consensus dictated that the Giants possessed the edge in the dugout. McGraw's experience told its own tale, while Rowland was new to October baseball. Despite his regular season achievements, McGraw had captured only one title, back in 1905 over Connie Mack's Philadelphia Athletics. Since then, he had lost three times, two more times to the A's and once to the Red Sox.

When McGraw broke into the majors, the manager was seen more as a strict task master and the players were more self-reliant. To say he was a tough manager is a gross understatement. According to Rogers Hornsby, McGraw would fine players for speaking to somebody on the other team. He would also walk up and down the dugout and yell: "Wipe those damn smiles off your face."[1] While his style leaned towards "in your face" with unbending rules, Rowland's was much more passive, giving orders in the form of suggestions, delivered with a milder disposition.[2]

Felsch and other White Sox right-handed batters were probably salivating at facing the Giants' starters, as three were southpaws (Ferdie Schupp, Slim Sallee, and Rube Benton) with just one right-hander (Pol Perritt). Against left-handed starters in 1917, Felsch batted .347/.394/.435; against right-handers, a lesser but not too shabby .288/.333/.387. Ferdie Schupp, the ace of McGraw's staff, mixed in a steady fastball with a sharp curve and occasional slow ball; the latter pitch was an old term for what we now call a change-up. His quick, "half-kick" motion kept base-runners close to the bag. Felsch and the other Sox scamperers could not afford to be careless.[3]

Felsch *could* afford personal rewards. Before arriving in Chicago for the Series opener, he purchased a Packard chummy roadster. "Hap is a great believer in outdoor life," said the *Milwaukee Journal.* "All my sons were big, strong fellows like Happy," said his father, Charles, "but it remained for Hap to be the only one that ever blossomed out into a major leaguer and we sure are proud of him." Happy's wife, Marie, not much of a baseball fan, did not make the trip south.[4]

The Giants arrived in Chicago early and played a warm-up game against the Chicago Cubs, losing 9–5. Several White Sox players attended but left in the third inning, perhaps bored by the affair or unconvinced that the matchup had any bearing on learning about their enemies. The White Sox had no such exhibition. In fact, Comiskey Park was drenched in rain and mud, and Rowland limited activity to the pitchers and catchers.[5]

The Giants beamed with confidence but there was some apprehension that their pitchers did not have sufficient time to study the White Sox batters. Still not clear as to who McGraw would send to the mound in Game One, one of the candidates, young Ferdinand "Ferdie" Schupp, may have had the best stuff to overcome the short notice. Was this indecision a cat-and-mouse dance by McGraw to confuse the Sox, or mere contemplation to select the best man to open the Series?[6]

Rowland felt little angst over his starter, Eddie Cicotte. With his array of pitches, a 28–12 record, and years of experience, he was an obvious selection. His calm temperament and cool efficiency were paramount in facing the pesky Giants hitters. After considerable deliberation, McGraw opted for southpaw Slim Sallee to try to deliver the first game to the senior circuit.[7]

Due to a rising demand for tickets, Charles Comiskey was less than gleeful at having to turn away some fans, roughly estimated at 283,000. The price of a ticket at Comiskey Park was .50 to $1.00. Ticket people were besieged by requests almost immediately after the regular season ended. The National Commission issued a stern warning about counterfeit tickets, and any perpetrators would be identified and dealt with.[8] The 1917 World Series commenced on Saturday, October 6 at Comiskey Park. Cicotte had finished the regular season with a 28–12 record and a 1.53 ERA. Slim Sallee finished 18–7 with a 2.17 ERA. Commensurate with their solid regular seasons, a fierce mound battle was expected to grace the Fall Classic opener.

Giants left fielder George Burns led off the Series with a single, but Cicotte coaxed the next three batters to fly out. Burns stole second with two out but moved no further. In the bottom of the first, Shano Collins, who had replaced Nemo Leibold towards the end of the season in right field, singled for the Sox. Fred McMullin, playing for the ailing Swede Risberg, sacrificed; Eddie Collins grounded out and Joe Jackson popped out to end the inning. Only one batter reached base in the second inning, with Giants first sacker Walter Holke singling off Cicotte with two outs. Holke's time on the bag did not last long, as Cicotte caught him leaning and picked him off.

Felsch led off the White Sox half of the second, popping up to shortstop in his World Series debut. Gandil followed with a lineout to third and Weaver grounded to short to end the frame. A true pitchers' duel was percolating, action growing scarce. The throng of fans were well-behaved, perhaps too docile, leaving *Chicago Tribune* writer James Crusinberry longing for years past. "Away back in 1911, there were 4,500 more than saw the big show this time. It was the quietest and most orderly crowd that ever sat in at such a big event. Eleven years ago, there were fog horns and organized bands of rooters and brigades of songsters and cheer leaders."[9]

Perhaps the impetus for the mellow patrons was the lack of offensive action. The Sox got to a 1–0 advantage on Fred McMullin's RBI double. In the Sox half of the fourth inning, Joe Jackson hit a hard liner to left for the first out. Up came Felsch for his second crack. He hammered the first pitch to deep left field. Giants outfielders George Burns and Benny Kauff watched the ball sail far over their heads and into the bleachers for a home run. Sallee's fastball had plenty of juice to help Felsch give it a ride and provide a new souvenir for a lucky fan.[10] Felsch swung so hard that, as Crusinberry wrote: "he would have broken his bat."[11] The towering blast gave the White Sox a 2–0 advantage.

"It was a loud and vicious clout from the trusty bludgeon of Felsch that really upset the pride of the National League," reported the *Milwaukee Journal*. Milwaukee's famous "beef and brawn" came through for the White Sox.[12]

With runs at a premium, McGraw's crew fought back in the fifth, getting a tally on Lew McCarty's triple and a Slim Sallee bloop single, but would not score again that day.[13] The White Sox quickly disposed of the Giants 1–2–3 in the ninth, giving them a 1–0 lead in the Series. Cicotte went the distance, giving up seven hits. Sallee's numbers were nearly identical but the Giants' offense could not string together any threats. McGraw and his men were not discouraged by the loss and figured that their next mound opponent, either Red Faber or Reb Russell, posed less of a danger than the sneaky Cicotte. The Little Napoleon's hit-and-run strategy failed miserably.[14]

In honor of Felsch's Game One performance, singer Al Jolson, who attended the game, pledged to give Felsch a $50 Liberty Bond. He also received a new suit of clothes, a new hat, a new pair of shoes, and several other items.[15] Milwaukee fans who attended the game conveyed great pride in their hometown hero. One fan even opined that he would rather have Felsch over Tris Speaker, offering that Felsch "is coming while Speaker is going." When Felsch stepped up to the plate for his first at-bat in Game Two, Deputy Commissioner of Public Works Percy Braman presented Felsch with a diamond stick-pin in the shape of a baseball.[16]

There was no time for the Giants to wallow, as the following day pitted Ferdie Schupp against Red Faber. No pitchers' duel this time as the White Sox hitters teed off in startling fashion, amassing 14 hits in a 7–2 rout. Shano Collins was the only player in the lineup who failed to register a hit, although he was replaced by Nemo Leibold after one at-bat when McGraw brought in a right-handed pitcher. Felsch, fresh off his game-winner in the opener, went 1-for-4 with a run scored.

John McGraw was forced to use four pitchers in the game. Schupp lasted just 1⅓ innings, giving up two runs in the bottom of the second after the Giants tagged Faber for two of their own in the top half. Lew McCarty's two-run single spotted the Giants a brief 2–0 lead, scoring Dave Robertson and Walter Holke, who had also singled. The White Sox stormed right back, with Shoeless Joe Jackson, Felsch, Chick Gandil, and Buck Weaver hitting successive singles to even the score at 2–2.

Andy Anderson relieved Schupp and struck out Leibold and retired McMullin to squelch the Sox rally. A couple innings later, Anderson made Schupp's struggles look minuscule, thanks to a disastrous fourth inning. The Sox hammered him for four runs and extended the lead to 7–2. The Sox sent eight batters to the plate, hitting six singles in the inning. Felsch ended the carnage by lining into an inning-ending double play.

Although irrelevant to the game's outcome, Faber entertained the happy throng with a comical move on the bases. With two retired in the fifth, Faber attempted to race to third base on a hit. He might have succeeded had the base not already been occupied. Teammate Buck Weaver stood still and watched helplessly as Faber was tagged out. The *New York Times* called Faber's folly "stupid,"[17] though there was nothing shameful about Faber's true vocation, pitching.

Faber set down the Giants in order in the sixth. He wasn't perfect that day, but was rescued by three double plays. One of those was started by Felsch. After Art Fletcher led off the Giants' seventh with a single, Dave Robertson poked a ball in front of Schalk, who threw him out at first. When Walter Holke lined a smash to center. Felsch sprinted in to make a running catch. He was close enough to second to double up Fletcher, flipping the ball to Eddie Collins to end the inning.[18]

Faber made quick work of the Giants in the ninth and the White Sox enjoyed a 2–0 series lead. Joe Jackson paced the White Sox batters, going 3-for-4. Weaver also had three hits, with Eddie Collins rapping two singles. After the game, Rowland injured himself, albeit not in a celebratory manner. When he turned on the shower, "steam gushed out" and burned his hand. Apparently in those days, the initial reaction was to soak the wound in oil to minimize the burn.[19]

The White Sox's confidence was oozing. Rowland and Comiskey believed their club could sweep the Giants in four games. Comiskey conveyed his jubilation to *Chicago Tribune* writer James Crusinberry: "I never felt happier in my life than I did in that fourth inning, when the boys went out and knocked in those five runs," said Comiskey. "That clinched the ball game for us, and I figure it just as good as clinched the world's championship. The Sox proved their mettle in that attack and it seems now that nothing can beat us."[20]

Rowland's comments to Crusinberry were a tad more humble: "I'm afraid to say for publication just how I feel about the series now," said Rowland. "However, I can't help but feel absolute confidence in the final result, and I really am hoping to take four straight."[21]

Out east, the New York press was soundly critical of the Giants' performance, writing that they failed to fight back against the scrappy Sox and approached the game with indifference. Their performance was certainly uncharacteristic of a McGraw team, which was "thrashed into a limpid, lifeless ruin," according to the *New York Times*.[22]

The series moved east to the Polo Grounds in New York. Game Three was scheduled for October 9, but the weathermen had other ideas. Rains had deluged the New York area for days and after careful inspection of the field by the umpires, they decided to postpone the game. Fans who had gathered outside scowled when the announcement came. Food vendors and umbrella salesmen made out like bandits.[23]

For non-game participants, the trip from Chicago to New York almost ended in disaster. The Pennsylvania Limited train that was carrying members of the

National Commission collided with a freight train near Beaver Falls, Pennsylvania. Thankfully, no serious injuries occurred though members August Herrmann and John K. Tener were shaken up. A replacement train was summoned and the men were ushered safely to New York.[24]

The unanticipated break allowed Rowland to feel comfortable with trotting out Eddie Cicotte again. Comiskey's confidence was genuine. His prediction of a four-game sweep rang false, however, as the Giants recovered by blanking the White Sox, 2–0, behind pitcher Rube Benton. Rowland's boppers mustered only five hits off Benton. Felsch rapped a single to left field in the fourth inning, but all six White Sox base runners that day failed to reach home plate.

Despite holding a one-game edge, the favored White Sox were mired in a scoring slump, not tallying a run in their last 13 innings. Granted, this was the Dead Ball Era, but getting shut out delivered the same result in any era; in Game Four, the Giants' pitchers made sure this dearth would persist.

Rowland continued his two-pitcher rotation, sending out Red Faber to face Schupp. Faber did not pitch terribly, but Schupp was superb as the Giants evened the series with another shutout, this time 5–0. Young Ferdinand, who hailed from Louisville, Kentucky, went the distance, giving up seven hits and striking out as many. Faber relinquished three runs on seven hits in seven innings. Dave Danforth pitched the eighth and validated Rowland's strategy of going primarily with two pitchers, surrendering three hits and two more runs. Felsch misplayed a ball in the crucial fourth inning. Benny Kauff hit a long fly towards Happy, who, while playing deep, misjudged the ball and watched it sail over his head. The ball stuck at the base of the fence and by the time Felsch retrieved it, Kauff scored on an inside-the-park home run.[25]

This was shaping into a suddenly competitive World Series. Since the first Series in 1903 between the Pittsburgh Pirates and Boston Pilgrims, eight of the Fall Classics had resulted in the losing team winning no games or one game, including the three that immediately preceded 1917. The White Sox needed to marry their pitching with timely hitting and fewer mistakes. Felsch was not happy with his failures in the fourth inning of Game Four, and the team was perceived to be the victims of their own over-confidence.[26]

Returning to the comforts of home, albeit cold, shivering Chicago, the White Sox faced the familiar Slim Sallee. Rowland chose to experiment with southpaw Reb Russell as his Game Five starter. Russell had posted a solid 15–5 record during the regular season, and perhaps his penchant for fastballs would provide enough of a contrast to Eddie Cicotte's junk array to secure a White Sox victory. Rowland's trial failed miserably as Russell was replaced by Cicotte after just three batters, but the damage was tempered and the White Sox bats later awakened in grand style.

Trailing 2–0, the White Sox got on the scoreboard in the third inning. With one out, Eddie Collins walked and later scored on a Felsch double to left, his second extra-base hit of the Series. The Giants responded with two more in the fourth, with Slim Sallee in reasonable control on the mound. In the sixth, however, the Sox hitters began to rattle the veteran hurler. Weaver smashed a one-out single and Schalk followed up with another. Swede Risberg, still nursing leg soreness, pinch-hit for Cicotte and ripped a single to right, scoring Weaver. Though they managed only one run and left two runners stranded, the little rally was a precursor to an offensive onslaught in the seventh.

At certain junctures in the game, McGraw's players resorted to taunting tactics in an attempt to rattle the White Sox's cages. Replete in their verbal arsenal was a litany of name-calling and merciless insults. In the field, McGraw's directives reeked of his old-school ways. Shortstop Art Fletcher and Pants Rowland nearly came to blows over the Sox skipper's objections to Fletcher blocking the base paths. Luckily, home plate umpire Silk O'Laughlin slid in between the two willing combatants and forestalled an ugly incident.[27] Soon after, the White Sox replied with grace and calm. They decided to use legal tools of their trade, most notably their baseball bats.

The Giants took a 5–2 lead in the top of the seventh with another run. The remainder of Game Five belonged to the White Sox. In their half of the seventh, they plated three runs to even the score at 5–5. After Eddie Collins opened with a pop fly to short, Joe Jackson and Felsch singled. Chick Gandil doubled home both runners. Even though he made the next out, Buck Weaver might have done as much to drain the life of Slim Sallee's arm as anybody. The persistent shortstop fouled off numerous pitches before he finally grounded out to short, advancing Gandil to third.[28] Schalk walked.

To the shock of the Giants, Schalk and Gandil started a double steal. The Giants' catcher, Bill Rariden, bluffed a throw to second and threw to Sallee instead. Ignoring Gandil, Slim zipped the ball to second baseman Buck Herzog, who let the elusive sphere slither under his legs into center, scoring Gandil.[29] McGraw's decision to trot out Sallee in the seventh after his sixth-inning struggles might have cost his team the game. "When Sallee went to pieces, the Giants went with him and their defense crumpled up like tissue paper," reported the *New York Times*.[30]

The White Sox provided the dagger in the eighth inning, scoring three more times. Felsch displayed the same run-producing ability he had throughout the 1917 summer. Shano Collins opened with a single, once again the catalyst for Rowland. McMullin sacrificed him over and the batting feast was on. Eddie Collins, Jackson, and Felsch—the meat of the order—all singled and the White Sox climbed in front for good. After Jackson's hit, McGraw finally replaced

Sallee with Pol Perritt, who was greeted by Felsch with a lofty Texas Leaguer. Felsch was caught trying to swipe second, but the damage was already in the books and the Sox won, 8–5.[31]

Game Six returned the teams to New York in a do-or-die game for the Giants. A Chicago delegation from Cornell University, in Ithaca, NY, staged a celebratory parade for their favorite team, supplemented by bonfires and fireworks.[32] Rube Benton faced Red Faber on the mound. Starting Faber after pitching two innings in relief two days earlier might look curious to the contemporary fan.

Would his arm wear out? Did pitch counts matter? These were queries for today's minds; this brave handling of pitchers was not unusual for the time. Furthermore, it was clear that the White Sox skipper had full trust in only two of his flingers: Faber and Cicotte. On the flip side, John McGraw teams did not throw in the towel under any circumstances. The *New York Times* referred to their loss in Chicago as tumultuous and tempestuous, but assured its faithful readers that it would not douse the Giants' confidence going forward.[33]

New Yorkers called the White Sox whiners for complaining about the physical, intimidating playing style of Giants infielders Buck Herzog and Art Fletcher. They also chided Rowland and coach Kid Gleason for riding the psyches of Fletcher and Heinie Zimmerman. Trash talking is a modern term but hardly a modern concept. Winning was winning and managers employed whatever tools they possessed. Constant jabbering aside, the Chicago White Sox had to find a way to win at the Polo Grounds. In addition, a coin flip a few days before put a potential Game Seven in New York.[34]

The battle to end the season or keep it alive started with three scoreless innings by both clubs. Red Faber and Rube Benton set the pace for their respective teams. Eddie Collins, Chick Gandil, Buck Herzog and Walter Holke were the only players in the first three frames to get hits. This changed starting in the Chicago fourth. Collins scampered all the way to second after a throwing error by Zimmerman. The next batter, Jackson, hit a popup that neither Herzog (2b) nor Robertson (RF) wanted to catch, with the latter getting an error.[35]

With runners on first and third with nobody out, Felsch's grounder to Zimmerman scored Collins on a fielder's choice on which the Giants failed to record an out. Zimmerman and Benton forced Collins into a rundown, but as Collins switched gears towards home, Zimmerman had to chase him all the way as the catcher Bill Rariden, was nowhere near home plate. Gandil followed with a clutch single to score Jackson and Felsch. The White Sox were spotted a 3–0 lead and were 18 outs from a title.[36]

Starting the bottom of the ninth, leading 4–2, Faber plunked Robertson with a pitch, putting the tying run at the plate in the person of Walter Holke. The stocky first baseman grounded out, but moved Robertson to second. Faber struck out Rariden, and the White Sox throng was rift with anticipation. They were one out away. The next batter, Lew McCarty, grounded to Collins, who tossed it to Gandil for the final out. The bush league manager, Clarence "Pants" Rowland, and his Chicago White Sox were World Champions! When the victorious team returned to the Windy City, two brass bands greeted them and "tooted vigorously" as the train rolled into the station.[37]

Giants manager John McGraw, known for his intensity and unfettered devotion to the game, walked from his first base coach's box and congratulated Gandil and Collins, then sought out Rowland to offer him equally gracious accolades.[38] Urban "Red" Faber was the winning pitcher in three of the four White Sox victories. Eddie Cicotte won one and lost one, but registered a solid 1.96 ERA. He and Faber accounted for 50 of the 52 innings pitched in the Series for the White Sox.

Felsch hit .273 in the six games, including the game-winning clout in Game One (the lone round-tripper for the White Sox in the Series). He scored four runs, struck out five times, and walked once. Veteran leader Eddie Collins paced the hitters with a whopping .409 average, nine hits and several defensive and base-running gems. Joe Jackson hit .304 and avoided striking out in 25 plate appearances. The White Sox hit .274 as a team, which bested the Giants' .256 clip.[39]

In selecting Rowland, Charles Comiskey now looked like the smartest man in the game. The only thing Comiskey did wrong was call the wrong side of the coin when the two teams flipped for a chance to host a now theoretical Game Seven. After he wrongly guessed heads, his Giants counterpart, Harry Hempstead, called the Old Roman "unlucky." Comiskey laughed and responded with this boast of assuredness: "There won't be a seventh game, so it doesn't matter. I'll see my boys grab the fifth game before the day is over and then they'll win the sixth."

The prophecy of the man known as an eternal optimist came true.

Comiskey had promised his players a bonus if they won the flag. This "bonus" came in the form of free champagne that Ring Lardner said "tasted like stale piss."[40] The Old Roman's reputation for being "frugal" would be scrutinized much more a few years later. This impression from the *Milwaukee Journal* following Felsch's Game One heroics did more than hint in the affirmative, although the adulation for Felsch was equally evident: "Happy had been given credit by the Chicago writers that he deserves. They seem to be in the league to belittle his work. Perhaps the scribes are working in the interest of Comiskey, who would have to pay Felsch more money if he is boosted as the star that he really is. Let's all get together and give Happy a big reception when he steps off the train in his arrival home."[41]

Felsch's adoring fans waited at the station for his return home to Milwaukee, but he arrived later than expected as he remained in Chicago to collect his money. Waiting for him were a host of local dignitaries, including alderman John Koerner and Secretary Oliver E. Remey.[42] Less than a week later, he was honored at a big banquet at the Hollier Pleasure Club in Milwaukee, where Felsch was a member. Local race car driver Teddy Tetzlaff gave the opening address.[43]

8

$125 a Month and Weekend Ball

I would gladly lose my whole team if the players wished to do their duty for the country, as hundreds of thousands of young men are doing.

—White Sox Owner Charles Comiskey

The 1918 season would not mirror the success and unity enjoyed during the White Sox's 1917 championship run. The entire league was flipped on its edge by the emerging involvement of the United States in World War I. Salary disputes, "work or fight" mandates, and other realities made it difficult for the White Sox to reproduce their glorious World Series triumph. This sent the pennant races into chaos. The leagues agreed to chop the regular season schedule to 140 games, with no roster limits because of the draft. Player salaries also diminished, which triggered a flurry a player evacuation and bitterness from labor *and* management.[1] *The Sports Encyclopedia of Baseball* labeled 1918 the "non-essential season."[2]

In an unexpected mishap, the train carrying the World Champion White Sox jumped the track between Fort Worth and their spring training site, Mineral Wells, Texas; the derailment delayed their initial workouts and set a tempestuous tone for the season. Felsch, Reb Russell, and coach Kid Gleason did not make the trip, all incurring various illnesses that spared them the rough train ride.[3] Swede Risberg was also tardy, having stayed behind in San Francisco to play in a benefit game with a U.S. Army outfit.[4]

Unfortunately, winning the World Series was followed by repeated, fluky misfortune. A few days after the railroad debacle, Schalk, Cicotte, Jackson, and Gandil were returning from a morning golf outing when another car emerged from a side street and rammed into them. Luckily, serious injury was limited mostly to the cars, but Cicotte sustained a sore neck that kept him inactive for several days. Gandil incurred a sore back, which did not prevent him from suiting up.

In a 16–9 Sox victory over Dallas, one of Rowland's promising young hurlers, sandlotter Ed Corey, fractured his ankle sliding into home. He started to slide, changed his mind, and his spikes stuck to the ground, folding his ankle in half. Corey was lost for the entire 1918 season. On a more pleasant note, the players were special guests of Lieutenant Colonel E. Z. Steever for dinner and entertainment at the local military camp. Looking to amplify his 1917 performance, Felsch had three hits in the exhibition game, including a home run.[5]

The White Sox entered 1918 with ample confidence. The press saw little reason not to favor them to repeat. Rowland returned all of his primary 1917 contributors and a few newcomers to take a flyer on. Having just become the first manager ever to win a World Series after never playing in the majors, Rowland did not tolerate losing spring training games. After they lost a couple to open the 1918 spring campaign, he reminded everyone that they had lost their first two the previous spring. This was not a man prone to rest on his laurels.[6]

They opened their season with a 6–1 loss to the St. Louis Browns. Felsch retained his fifth position in the batting order and his defensive parcel in center field. In the opener, he went hitless in four trips, drawing a base on balls and getting thumped by a pitch. The Browns smashed 19 hits in the game, leaving 13 runners stranded. But Browns pitcher Grover Lowdermilk made sure six runs were enough, going the distance and limiting the White Sox to four hits.

Precious little time elapsed before Felsch reprised his role as the foremost slugger in Rowland's loaded lineup. The Sox won five of their next six games, with Felsch going 8-for-26, including a three-single game in a 13- 3 victory over the Cleveland Indians. The White Sox amassed 25 total bases. Even White Sox starter and winner Joe Benz contributed at the plate with three RBI.

A week later, after the White Sox disposed of the Cleveland Indians again, Felsch did not board the train with his team. Instead, he hopped one to Brownsville, Texas, to visit his ailing brother, who was at a U.S. Army cantonment camp. According to Felsch, his brother was reportedly dying after he fell off a horse and ended up trapped underneath, where he lay unconscious.[7] Coinciding with Felsch leaving, Eddie Collins returned from a bum knee, although he was still using a cane to get around.[8]

Felsch returned on May 20 in 6–2 victory over the New York Yankees. He went 1-for-4 and resumed his trend of 1917, stringing together hits and avoiding long slumps. He soon owned a nine-game hitting streak, going 13-for-38. The team was limping along, however, and now had to withstand the loss of Shoeless Joe Jackson, who was the first to leave the team for the war industry. His last game with the White Sox in 1918 was on May 11 in a 2–1 loss to the Philadelphia Athletics. Eddie Murphy replaced Jackson in right field.

Jackson, like many other players who chose the work option, was criticized for being a slacker. In his defense, he was the sole supporter of his entire family, including his mother and brothers. Setting a curious example with a lack of decorum and class, even American League President Ban Johnson doled out his licks: "I hope that the Provost Marshall yanks Jackson and these other evaders from the shipyards and the steel works by the coat collar. I hope they are sent to cantonments to prepare for future events on the western front." The press, including the *New York Times* and *Chicago Tribune*, was equally critical of the players.[9]

Gradually, several other White Sox exercised their "work or fight" option. The fracturing of team rosters began officially towards the end of May, when the government deemed major league baseball "non-essential" to the war effort and said eligible players were required to choose between signing up to fight or working state-side in a war-support industry. This unavoidable edict had a profound effect on the pennant races and left teams scrambling to fill roster spots.

Some of the companies employing the departed professionals sponsored local teams of their own and welcomed their new "workers" with open arms. Charles Comiskey, arguably not showing patriotism, had a problem with such arrangements: "There is no room on my club for players who wish to evade the army draft by entering the employ of ship owners."[10] The first player to enlist was Boston Braves catcher Hank Gowdy, who saw considerable action overseas.

On the field, Felsch and his teammates tried to keep themselves in the race for a championship repeat. Until June, their longest winning streak was four games. On June 8, they were just 2½ games back of first-place Boston, with New York one game behind. The pitching was spectacular some days, putrid on others. Felsch picked up some of the slack after Jackson's vacancy, hitting safely in eight of the first nine games in June. The team won seven of those contests.

Felsch hit his first home run of the season on June 2 in a 6–2 win over the Yankees. Former White Sox outfielder Ping Bodie, along with his outfield cohorts, watched the ball sail clear over the fence. "Bodie recovered his wasted breath in statuesque pose against the fence," wrote I. E. Sanborn of the *Chicago Tribune*.[11] In the next game, Bodie gunned down Felsch at second when he tried to stretch a single into a double. This did not affect the outcome as the White Sox hammered the second-place Yanks, 9–2. Felsch had three of the Sox's nine hits. Eddie Cicotte, just 1–7 coming into the game, pitched brilliantly.[12]

Heading into the June 10 game at Comiskey Park vs. the Boston Red Sox, Felsch was sitting at .308/.348/.408. After that, the wheels fell off the team's momentum bus. On that day, the White Sox began a four-game home series against first-place Boston. Looking to rekindle that 1917 fortune, Rowland's boys instead bowed to the Bosox, losing three of four. They were shut out in the last two games, 7–0 and 6–0. Felsch went 2-for-13, which started a downward slide towards mediocrity. He hit safely in four straight games soon after, which was succeeded by far too many hitless tilts. After an 0-for-4 stinker against the Tigers on June 25, Felsch's line read .268/.327/.350.

What precipitated this bizarre decline? Did he face pitchers against whom he typically struggled? Was his mind preoccupied by his ailing brother? Felsch certainly was not the only player who struggled. The White Sox sat in fifth place, seven games behind the AL front-runner. Eddie Cicotte's record was 5–9. After getting blanked again by Detroit, 1–0, the Sox managed to split a doubleheader with the St. Louis Browns. Felsch went 3-for-5 in the opener, but went 0-for-11 in the next three games before he delivered a shock to his manager, teammates, friends, and Comiskey.

On July 2, the *Milwaukee Sentinel* reported that Felsch collected his payroll check and informed Rowland he was leaving the team to take a job with the Milwaukee Gas Light Company for $125 per month. He would supplement his income by playing ball on Sundays in his hometown.[13] No advance warning preceded Felsch's decision, which perplexed the Old Roman, who offered his own diagnosis. "It has been apparent Felsch has been worrying for some time, for he hasn't been playing his regular game at all," said Comiskey. "He looked like one of the greatest a year ago, but something has been on his mind for the last few weeks. At least his mind wasn't on the ball game and he wasn't doing us very much good."[14]

Felsch followed teammates Lefty Williams, Joe Jackson, and Byrd Lynn away from major league baseball towards war work. Pitcher Red Faber had left earlier to join the Navy. Upon his return to Milwaukee, Felsch kept mum about his decision. Comiskey eventually reconciled his resentment over the departure of his players, but the White Sox would not manufacture a lofty climb up the 1918 standings.

Perhaps Felsch's mind was occupied with thoughts of war or angst over his sick brother. The rumblings were sneaking into the wires about a dispute with Comiskey, who was rumored to have tendered this offer: Felsch would receive a bonus if he curtailed his drinking.[15] The *Chicago Daily Journal* suggested that the "work or fight" announcements "kept staring him in the face and preyed on his mind so that the old .100 batting mark looked like an elephant liver to a kitten."[16]

The on-field baseball reasons were less ambiguous. From June 10 to his final game on June 30, Felsch hit an abysmal .158 (12-for-76). His final batting average dipped to .252. He had not encountered many new pitchers in 1918. The usual aces, Walter Johnson, Babe Ruth, Bullet Joe Bush, and Stanley Coveleski, still tortured their adversaries.

Back home for the remainder of 1918, Felsch became content with working and playing with the local powerhouse, the Kosciuszko Reds of the Lake Shore League. There had been whispers in the local papers about Comiskey taking legal action to bar Felsch from playing with another team, but in a subsequent interview, the Old Roman took the high road and referred to Felsch as a "likeable chap."[17] Once again, Felsch would grace the pages of the local newspapers and hear the cheers of his adoring Brewtown fans.

What influence would Felsch have on a lower-level baseball team? He was already over three years removed from his sandlot days. In his first game back on July 14, Felsch greeted an old familiar teammate in pitcher Harvey Stock, saying "hello and how are you" with three hits. Stock and Manitowoc won the game, 6–4. South Side Park in Milwaukee was jammed with eager patrons who wanted to see their hometown hero once again. Despite the Reds' loss, the *Milwaukee Sentinel* wrote that "Felsch was easily the shining star of the game."[18]

Felsch did not automatically assume his center field position with the Kosciuszkos, opening instead in left. Perhaps they did not want to tinker too much with the established lineup, although adding a big-leaguer such as Felsch would seem to alter their thinking. Throughout the summer, skipper Jake Litza added more major league defectors and the lineup changed like the wind.

Over 2,200 fans crammed South Side Park and witnessed a familiar Felsch home run in a 5–3 victory. In their next game, the Reds nipped Sheboygan, 1–0. Sheboygan third baseman Miller sent a long drive towards center. Felsch, playing right field, chased down the ball and delivered a strike to the second baseman, who gunned down the potential tying run at the plate. The runner hurdled over the Reds' catcher, Eddie Stumpf, who chased and tagged him. The Sheboygan bench went ballistic, even though they did not appear to be in position to see the play clearly.[19]

In a 10–6 loss to Sheboygan on August 18, Felsch was hit on the arm by a pitch but displayed his usual toughness by staying in the game. He continued to keep his skills sharp and knock the ball all over Wisconsin parks. He closed out the season with the Reds, playing all three outfield positions, first base, and catcher. In his final game with the Reds on September 30, Felsch went 3-for-4 in an 8–0 win over the Milwaukee White Sox.[20]

Prior to Felsch's arrival, the Reds were 2–6. With Felsch, they were 8–13. Despite the additions of him and other professionals, the Kosciuszkos finished in last place. On October 14, Felsch played in an exhibition game in Chicago, pitting his Felsch's All Stars against the Albany Parks squad. He was joined by fellow local star Fred Luderus, who hit a home run in a 13–1 romp. Felsch opened the game with a nice stab from his customary center field position and added two hits.[21]

How was Felsch's former professional employer faring? The White Sox played close to .500 ball after Felsch and other players bolted. Comiskey's team finished the forgettable season in sixth place at 57–67. They played their final game of the war-shortened season on September 2, losing to the Detroit Tigers, 7–3.

The 1918 World Series was staged sans the White Sox, but the north-side Cubs captured the National League pennant by 10½ games, pitting them against the American League champion Boston Red Sox for the baseball crown. There was some trepidation that the government would not allow the Series to occur, but Secretary of War Baker gave his endorsement. The Red Sox defeated the Cubs, four games to two, and the forgettable 1918 season was a wrap. World War II ended in November, and the country and its national pastime sought to inject some normality into their daily lives.

The drama surrounding Charles Comiskey and his players was a recurring theme during this time. His criticisms of the players who did not go off to fight created some return resentment. Felsch was one of those so-called "war dodgers," and it remained to be seen whether he would be wearing a Chicago White Sox uniform in 1919. The Chicago press and *The Sporting News* seemed to fuel a lot of the drama by devoting entire articles to the supposed battles between owner and players.

On January 1, 1919, the *Chicago Tribune* reported Comiskey's side of the story regarding his conflict with Felsch. Apparently, Felsch was angered that he did not receive an $1,100 bonus, rescinded by Comiskey because Felsch did not curtail his drinking. Comiskey stated that he honored every bonus that was deserved, and emphasized that back in May, when Felsch left to tend to his sick brother, the Old Roman paid Felsch his entire salary.[22]

The biggest news entering 1919 came when Clarence "Pants" Rowland was relieved of his managerial duties, replaced with one of his coaches, Bill "Kid" Gleason. From a baseball point of view, the decision was nothing short of ridiculous. *The Sporting News* declared that "Clarence was not responsible for the world war and the leaping to service and ship yards of his leading ball players. Commy is of a revolving disposition and loves a change of scenery."[23] Comiskey's decision might look strange when viewed through today's game prism, but the Old Roman was solidly in charge.

On January 23, the *Chicago Tribune* reported that Felsch would return to the White Sox for the 1919 season. "I have a three-year contract with the Sox and do not expect any trouble when I hear from management," said Felsch. "I expect to hear from manager Gleason any day now and as soon as we get into training camp, I will be ready to crack out wallops. Everybody likes Gleason and all work to the best of their ability largely for him. He's a man all through."[24] Gleason desired to have all the primary players back from their hiatus.[25]

On the back burner of the tumultuous 1918 season were simmering disturbances and resentment between the White Sox players towards each other and management. Comiskey paid his players as he saw fit, not unlike many owners of the day. But that didn't deter the frequent objections from the lesser-paid ones, which included the bitter duo of Chick Gandil and Swede Risberg. Their anger was directed at the likes of Eddie Collins and Ray Schalk and would serve as a tension-laden antecedent to the 1919 season.

9

Prelude to Gullibility

This thing is beginning to smell. The dogs in the street know it.

—Gambler Curley Bennett,
to his roommate in Cincinnati's Sinton Hotel

The volatility of 1918 generated more questions than answers. Would all fleeing players return for 1919? Would their skills reveal decay? Would Comiskey's fickleness prevent his White Sox from a return to greatness? Was Felsch ready to put his inner turmoil and distractions behind him and forge another solid season?

The burden of alleviating these challenges fell squarely upon William "Kid" Gleason, new White Sox skipper. Born in Camden, New Jersey, in 1866, Gleason assumed his nickname from his diminutive stature, measuring in at 5'7" and 155 lbs. His family moved to the coal belt in Pennsylvania's Pocono Mountains. He skipped college to become a professional ballplayer, a career that spanned 23 years with five teams. Like many players, Gleason had a chance to leave his team for the newly-formed Players' League in 1890. But his loyalty bested his greed, which served him well when he became a White Sox coach in 1913.

Gleason appeared to be a tougher hombre than his predecessor. A stickler for punctuality and other disciplinary measures, for Gleason, "7:30 meant 7:30." The *Chicago Tribune's* short bio of Gleason in early January 1919, mentioned something about Gleason's razor strop. If that doesn't signify a man steeped in obedience and order, nothing does. After hand-picking Gleason to lead his 1919 club, Charles Comiskey shifted his attention towards procuring the prolific services of Happy Felsch, Joe Jackson, and Claude "Lefty" Williams.

A few months before the 1919 spring training season, whispers of their glorious return began to percolate. The superintendent of the war department's Bastille at Fort Leavenworth resigned amid allegations that he hung up so-called "conscientious objectors" by their thumbs, along with other questionable reprimands. None of the "work over fight" White Sox endured such castigation,

Kid Gleason ponders his next move, 1919. Named White Sox manager before the start of the season, Gleason would lead the team to a pennant in his first year. Before their inexplicable loss in the Series, he described the White Sox as a team with no weaknesses (National Photo Company Collection, Library of Congress).

but that did not spare them from Comiskey's verbal assaults. A pragmatist, the Old Roman acquiesced, lifting his personal ban and leaving open the prospect of reacquiring the three dissidents.[1] His previous contempt for the "jumpers" surrendered to thoughts of another pennant run.[2]

It was painfully certain that Gleason wanted them back, and made special note of Felsch: "It is a cinch Felsch would come back, and there is no grievance against Happy, apparently so far as the fans are concerned," said Gleason. "Despite all the things that Hap is saying when the time came, he will be back on the job."[3] Luckily, all three players returned before spring workouts commenced. Gleason acted as player procurement officer, which included some cajoling of Buck Weaver, who considered staying with his alternative club across the border, the Beloit (Wisconsin) Fairies. Swede Risberg also required careful recruitment.[4]

Felsch occupied his off-season with a lucrative Christmas tree business in

Wisconsin. A shortage of labor prompted Happy and his partner to venture off into the north woods and hack down the big evergreens themselves.[5] This physically grueling task prepared Felsch for his return, looking fit as ever and ready to demonstrate his clouting talents.

Days before the start of spring training, major league baseball decided to shorten the length of the 1919 regular season to 140 games. This led to some angst among the ballplayers, and their request for pay hikes were met by the owners citing the three fewer weeks of work. The Old Roman had earlier objected to the shortening of the season.

In his first exhibition game of the season, Felsch legged out a triple, but he and a couple of others were nursing sore ankles. Despite being in fairly good shape otherwise, he struggled through the spring campaign. He displayed signs of recovery with a string of multi-hit games, mixed in with several hitless tilts.

Felsch hardly ripped the cover off the ball but managed to squeeze in a few solid performances. During the White Sox's final spring swing, they defeated the Cincinnati Reds in back-to-back games. As was common during that era, major league clubs scheduled only a couple of exhibition contests against their professional peers. In 1919, the Sox happened to be opening the regular season in St. Louis, and a couple of games against the Reds were a regional convenience. After going hitless in the previous four games, Felsch swatted three hits in the two-game warm-up.[6]

The White Sox inaugurated the 1919 season against the St. Louis Browns, sporting brand-new uniforms of steel gray and blue trim to accompany the standard white stockings. Gleason's eager bunch might have looked pleasing to the eye in the wardrobe department, but looked better on the field, drubbing the home team, 13–4. Over 15,000 fans attended the opener in Sportsman's Park. Felsch went 1-for-4 but Buck Weaver was the hitting star by going 4-for-6 with five RBI. The Sox hammered 21 hits and starter Lefty Williams scattered ten Browns safeties to earn the victory.

Gleason entered 1919 with only three reliable starters: Cicotte, Williams, and Faber. Thankfully, the smoldering lumber of the White Sox's batsmen carried the load early on, leading the Sox to six wins in their first seven games. The team scored 47 runs in those contests, but Felsch was not a productive member of the party, going just 4-for-27. In a 9–7, slugfest triumph over the Detroit Tigers to close out April, Felsch broke out with a single and double in five at-bats.

On May 2, the White Sox welcomed the St. Louis Browns to Comiskey Park for their home opener. Mother Nature, who had thwarted a couple of games for the team early on, threatened this one as well. Although the game got in, the teams were unable to practice that morning because of deplorable field conditions. Equally dreadful was the White Sox's performance, dropping the contest, 11–4.[7]

Felsch's lone hit in the opener was a double. Sox pitchers Lefty Williams, Dave Danforth and Joe Benz were slaughtered by the Browns' hitters for 16 hits. A five-run St. Louis onslaught in the second inning spelled doom for Gleason's guys. The White Sox won their next four games, however, leaping to an impressive 10–2 record to open the 1919 campaign. Felsch was hitting a paltry .209/.292/.372, but Gleason was getting plenty of production from Joe Jackson (.479/.528/.792), Chick Gandil (.341/.383/.591), Buck Weaver (.356/.408/.422), and Eddie Collins (.311/.404/.489).

After going 2 for his first 22, Felsch recovered with a slight surge, going 8-for-25 to climb back up over the .200 mark. His best performance to date came in a 9–3 win over the Detroit Tigers, when he went 2-for-3 with two doubles and an RBI. He also stole second and scampered to third on the play after Tigers shortstop Donie Bush muffed the throw to second.[8]

The White Sox split the last two games, losing a 6–5, 11-inning thriller on Sunday, but winning the Monday make-up easily, with a 10–2 thumping of the Tribe. Felsch went 2-for-5 in the finale, including his eighth double and third base swipe of the young season. A mild controversy developed during the Indians series that revolved around the infamous Eddie Cicotte shine ball. First, a primer on the famous pitch by the pitcher himself in *Baseball Magazine* in 1918:

> Last season I was credited with the discovery of a new invention along this line known as the shine ball. The mysterious ball aroused a good deal of interest in various quarters. Ban Johnson must have a full trunk full of balls that were thrown out of various games and forwarded to him for inspection. I understand that a number of these balls were analyzed by a chemist to determine if any foreign substances were rubbed on the surface. This analysis, so I am informed, showed that the ball had been treated with tobacco juice. But a good many pitchers use the spitball occasionally, and most of them chew tobacco. None of the many investigations involved me in criminal practices with the ball and my own contention that the Shine ball was a myth was never successfully refuted.[9]

Although Cicotte only later admitted to the practice, prior to the May 10 game between the White Sox and Indians, the Cleveland players claimed that their defeat at the hands of Cicotte the game before was caused mostly by the suspicious pitch. Sox catcher Ray Schalk had an alternative explanation for his teammate's success, saying that Cicotte could have hit a half-dollar with the ball at any time during the game. Perhaps the right-hander's pinpoint control was the dagger that created the alibi-filled angst of the Indians' hitters.

Was Felsch's poor start typical of his early-season experience? In his first four seasons, Felsch had never jumped out of the gates with a flourish. His best start through May 31 came in his rookie season of 1915, when he hit .267/.353/.352. In 1919, one aspect that surpassed other early seasons was his increase in doubles, which hiked up his slugging percentage (.383 through May 31).

In today's game, a spike in doubles typically indicates an eventual increase in home runs. In the Dead Ball Era, that was not apparent given the dearth of home runs (sans "The Big Bambino"). For Felsch in 1919, his extra-base surge suggested that when he *was* belting the ball, he did so with extra muscle and distance. Perhaps chopping down Christmas trees would become his workout de jour going forward.

In late May, Felsch put together his first real hot streak of the young season. Following Lefty Williams' 1–0 blanking of the New York Yankees on May 22, Felsch's batting average sat at a not-so-happy .207. Soon after, he unleashed a 12-for-27 tear that hoisted his batting average to a respectable .263, including an eight-game hitting streak. This coincided with the White Sox winning 11 of 13 games to seize a five-game lead over second-place Cleveland. In a 6–5 squeaker over the Senators, Felsch was 2-for-4 and plated two runners. Grover Lowdermilk, auditioning to be the much-needed fourth starter, went seven strong innings, with Dickie Kerr and Dave Danforth closing the game book.[10]

Felsch refused to allow his batting inconsistencies to impinge on the rest of his game. On May 27, the White Sox captured their third consecutive one-run victory (4–3). In addition to scoring the winning run and turning an infield hit into a double, Felsch gunned down a would-be run at the plate in the third inning. *Chicago Tribune* writer I. E. Sanborn penned that a mad Felsch was a productive Felsch, and that the player's angst about his batsmanship paid dividends in other areas.[11]

In a May 30 twin-bill sweep of the Indians, Felsch went 4-for-7, including a screaming double against the left-field fence in the first game to knock in Joe Jackson, who had walked. In the nightcap, he scratched out the kind of hit that often rescued hitters from slumps, dropping a soft pop-up into short right field for a single.[12]

Entering the first full month of summer, the White Sox retained their modest lead in the American League and were fortunate that the other clubs had not assembled lengthy winning streaks of their own. This came in handy to start June, when the Sox dropped six of seven games. They relinquished the final game in a series with the Indians, got swept in three games at Detroit, then dropped two of three in New York. Their road trip lasted from June 2–22. The hitting hit a snooze that the pitching failed to overcome.

The spell of slumps and streaks continued for Felsch, who seemed to prefer the warmer months to the damp, wet, unpredictable spring. He went hitless in five games until a June 12 loss to the Boston Red Sox. He managed a single but Shano Collins had the only other two hits for Gleason as the Sox fell, 4–0. The White Sox went 8–10 on their road trip, with their best effort against the lowly Philadelphia Athletics, a three–game sweep. The White Sox bats got healthy during this trifecta, scoring 18 runs on 37 hits. Felsch was 5-for-13 with two home runs, five RBI, and three runs scored.

The treading water that permeated the White Sox's 1919 campaign continued through the month of June. On June 13, the Sox sat at 27–15, just one-half game better than second-place New York. From then until the Fourth of July, Chicago went 10–9 and relinquished the top spot to the surging Yankees, with the upstart Indians breathing down both teams' necks. After the games of June 23, New York and Cleveland were tied for first, with the Sox just one-half game behind. The Sox had suffered a four-game losing streak, including the first two games to the Indians.

Happy Felsch's motor and rudder began to work in harmony, which produced his best hitting stretch to date in the midst of his team's challenging times. From June 14 to July 2, Felsch went 20-for-74, a .270 clip, to push his season numbers to .242/.318/.395. A breakdown of this Happy time:

+ Felsch re-discovered his power stroke, cranking three home runs and driving in 11 runs.
+ In the nine White Sox wins, Felsch batted .270 (10-for-37); in the nine losses, he also hit .270 (10-for-37)
+ Cleveland Indians pitchers were Felsch's favorite, hitting .320 against them during this stretch (.316 for the season).
+ Felsch flourished in the field, making several spectacular catches.

Despite a six-game hitting streak, Felsch knocked in three runs but scored only one run. Despite the wasted efforts on offense, Gleason was still focused on shoring up his pitching staff. The feast or famine nature of the starters was tough to reconcile, and he knew that with four solid starters, the American League crown would be theirs. "Tired of seeing the staff hobble on three legs," mused Gleason. "We are scouring the bushes for a solution."[13]

The White Sox closed the books on June by winning two of their last three games. On July 1, they became embroiled in a rare slugfest, a 14–9 loss to the Indians. Felsch went 2-for-5 as he and his teammates pounded out 15 hits to no avail. The *Chicago Tribune* called this contest an awful game that reminded one of the old-fashioned college game before the days of coaches.[14]

Gleason was likely to dangle a couple of hitters to lure another arm or two. Spot-starting outfielder Eddie Murphy was a possibility, especially with current leadoff hitter Nemo Leibold holding his own as chief table-setter for the big bats, which included Felsch and Jackson. In a June 24, 2–0 loss to Cleveland, Felsch mastered his outfield space with eight fly-ball catches, a number the *Chicago Tribune* thought might be a record for an outfielder.[15]

It was reported by the *Milwaukee Sentinel* later in October that Felsch had indeed set a mark for center fielders by fielding 12 chances in a game without an error in a June 23 contest (11 catches and one assist). The major league putout record for outfielders was 12, set by Jimmy Slagle in 1897 while playing for the Chicago Nationals.[16]

Gleason drew some ire from the locals for not making a move to improve his pitching staff. Some scribes defended his inactivity by pointing out that the White Sox were still very strong, were hitting the ball at a hefty clip, and were very "hard to stop."[17] Their confidence in Gleason's bunch rang true as the south-siders embarked on a lengthy midsummer tear that spanned most of July and cemented them in a comfortable spot atop the American League.

The impetus for this mammoth surge may have come during the Sox's 6–4 victory over the Cleveland Indians on July 2. It was not the prettiest of baseball affairs as the teams combined to use seven pitchers, with the Sox sending Cleveland starter Stan Coveleski to an early shower in the second inning. In the sixth, the Indians had already scored a run and had runners on first and third with nobody out. Down 4–1, the Indians were desperate to get at least one runner home and employed a squeeze play. Bill Wambsganss raced in from third as the batter pushed the ball to Sox pitcher Dickie Kerr. Seeing that he was going to be out by a mile, Wamby (as they called him) took a flying lunge toward catcher Ray Schalk, who greeted him with a tag, gunned the ball to third, then gave the disposed-of runner a healthy lecture.[18] The umpires stepped in before any tussle could ensue, but the event seemed to catapult the team to crucial success going forward. Felsch contributed a single and two free passes to the effort.

The brash encounter propelled the White Sox to a 17–1 shellacking of the Tribe the next day. Felsch was the only player in the lineup who did not register a hit, but he coaxed a walk and reached base twice on errors. His teammates plated him three times. Chick Gandil and Joe Jackson were the hitting stars, going 4-for-4 and 3-for-6, respectively. Gleason's boys tagged five Cleveland pitchers. Out of the 17 runs, only six were earned, with the iron-gloved Indians committing four errors.

The four-game sweep of the A's jumped the White Sox back into first place at 45–25, two games ahead of the New York Yankees. Cleveland was lurking behind at five games back, with St. Louis 8½ behind the front-runners. From July 2–21, the White Sox went 18–4, with twenty of those games played in friendly Comiskey Park. When the streak began, they were 3½ games back of the Yankees in second place; after the surge, they were perched atop of the American League with a comfortable—but not insurmountable—six-game cushion.

Felsch aided the cause with several impressive performances. From July 12–21, he hit safely in nine of 11 games. His propensity to get on base in what-ever fashion he could was a solid complement to the slap hitters who preceded him in the batting order. In a 15–6 drubbing by the Boston Red Sox, the lone bright spot was provided by Felsch, who threw out four runners, three at the plate and one at third. This rare feat exemplified his powerfully accurate arm in the outfield, quite possibly the best wing in the league.

In mid–August, Felsch re-joined the lumber fray, going 6 for 13 during a three-game stretch that was part of the Sox's 10-game winning streak; they averaged 7.3 runs per game. In an 11–4 drubbing of the Washington Senators, Felsch went 3-for-4 with 3 RBI—including his 24th double—to help push Sox ace Eddie Cicotte to his 23rd win of the season. Joe Jackson matched Happy's effort with three hits and three RBI of his own. The veteran junkballer confounded the Senators hitters all day, scattering nine hits and striking out four. Felsch's season numbers were climbing steadily, sitting at .253/.314/.381 heading into the final game of the series with Washington.

The headline in the August 21, 1919, *Sporting News* encapsulated the reason for the White Sox's recent success: "White Sox Heavy Artillery Unlimbers and Saves Games for Wobbly Pitchers."

Despite the double-digit run outputs, small-ball wisdom and overall alertness by the hitters became the tools of choice in the closer contests. In a nailbiter against the Red Sox, Gleason scampered out to home plate to whisper something in batter Ray Schalk's ear. Everyone and their uncles surmised what was on the agenda. Schalk dropped down a bunt but the usually stellar thirdbaseman for the Bosox, Ossie Vitt, was caught snoozing and by the time he scooped up the ball, Felsch had crossed home plate.[19]

On September 12, reports surfaced that the upcoming World Series would shift to a best-of-nine format, returning to the extra games for the first time since 1903, the first such battle for supremacy between Ban Johnson's new American League and the well-established National League. August Herrmann, Chairman of the National Commission, stated that most of the clubs had ratified the new format. The individual votes were not revealed, but there was no secret that Charles Comiskey objected to the longer Series.[20] A Cincinnati report claimed that New York and Boston joined Chicago in opposing the format. Despite the result, a few owners, including Washington's Clark Griffith, had initially sided with the dissenters.[21]

As much as the emerging heat of early summer struck a charge into Felsch's bat, in 1919, the anticipation of falling leaves and pennant fever in the air carried the young slugger into a month-long stretch unlike any he had experienced since he broke in with Comiskey's club more than four years prior. The threat of another team catching the White Sox diminished as the final month progressed. Just in case, Felsch decided to wear out his welcome against opponents with his blistering bat. From September 1 to the end of the 1919 season, Felsch hit safely in a career-best 20 of 21 games. In the lone game in which he went

Felsch follows through on a practice swing, 1917. In a lineup that could also boast Shoeless Joe Jackson and Eddie Collins, the 25-year-old Felsch was one of the outstanding all-around players (George Grantham Bain Collection, Library of Congress).

hitless—a 7–0 shutout of the Philadelphia A's—Felsch still managed to score a run after reaching base on an error.

Entering the game on September 7 against Cleveland, Chicago maintained a 6½ game lead over the Indians. Winning the second of three games in the series that day rather easily, 8–3, the lead moved to 7½ and the White Sox never looked back as they won seven of their next eight games. On September 15, an 11–10 slugfest win over the A's, Felsch knocked in four runs while going 2-for-4 and scoring twice. Red Faber returned to the mound for the winners after a 26-day absence and gutted out the victory. Despite giving up eight earned runs and allowing 16 runners to reach base, Faber gave up three runs in the first seven frames, earning the opportunity from Gleason to complete the game, which he did.

In a 17-day span, Felsch increased his batting average from .252 to .267—not an easy feat this late in the season. This surge coincided nicely with the team's success. Their record was 86–45 with a 7½-game cushion with just nine games remaining. All that was left was to play out the schedule and get warmed up for their second World Series appearance in three seasons. Felsch did not seem to care that his team had all but clinched the American League pennant as he continued his hot stretch, with 20 hits in his final 44 at-bats—a sizzling .455 clip. His slash stats on September 1 had looked like this: .252/.321/.389. By season's end, they were .275/.336/.428.

In the Senior Circuit, Pat Moran's Cincinnati Reds battled John McGraw's New York Giants for league supremacy for a bulk of the 1919 campaign. A ten-game winning streak in mid–August created some separation between the clubs, with the Reds lengthening their lead to nine games. A month later, the Giants had not assembled a comeback of any significance and a rematch between the Giants and the White Sox would not materialize.

Up 6½ games with seven games to play, the White Sox could almost taste the pennant. One more victory by them or a defeat by Cleveland, and the American League was theirs. On September 20, the White Sox dropped a double-header to Boston, 4–3 and 5–4. On the same day, the Cleveland Indians swept a twin bill from the Washington Senators, leaving them 4½ games back with five games remaining. A 4–1 loss to Detroit a few days later doomed the Indians' chances. Kid Gleason and his White Sox were American League champions for the second time in three seasons.

Felsch finished with a flurry, hitting safely in his last 11 games. His final 1919 tallies (.275/.336/.428) finished an impressive upswing that would carry him into the Series. He batted .384 in September, raising his batting average from .252. The last time he had been above .260 was June 2—for two days. Perhaps his greatest accomplishment was a record that still stands firm today:

14 double plays for an outfielder in one season, tying Jimmy Sheckard's mark set in 1899 as a Baltimore Oriole.

Felsch was ready to partake in his second World Series battle in three seasons. His 1917 performance had been more than respectable, hitting .273/.304/.455. Compared to his 1917 regular season, Felsch improved his slugging percentage but dipped in on-base percentage. The White Sox certainly had their share of offense with Eddie Collins and Joe Jackson setting the table for the eager Felsch. Would the power make an appearance in this version of the Fall Classic? One thing was certain: The White Sox and their leader, Kid Gleason, beamed with confidence and the betting types did not disagree with them.

Rumors surfaced in the Cincinnati newspapers that perhaps some shady dealing would threaten the integrity of the Series. In 1987, the surviving member of the 1919 Reds team, Edd Roush, revealed in an interview that gamblers attempted to persuade one of their starting pitchers, Hod Eller, to participate in devious shenanigans, but the third-year right-hander snubbed the opportunity.[22] Roush had asked Eller what he said to one gambler. Eller responded: "I told him to get out of my sight. If I ever saw him again, I'd beat him up."

Two weeks before the Series began, White Sox first sacker Chick Gandil approached a bookie named Joe "Sport" Sullivan at Boston's Hotel Buckminster about the prospect of fixing the World Series, demanding $80,000 in payment of future services, or non-services at it were. (Other historical accounts have Sullivan initiating contact with Gandil.) The money came due before the Series began. Gandil and the ex-player Sullivan were not strangers, with the latter having schmoozed the big slugger years earlier in a pool room when Gandil was with the Washington Senators.

The Buckminster was hardly the usual hotel of choice for visiting clubs, but after excessive drinking and rowdiness in an earlier road trip to Boston at standard hotels such as the Somerset and Buckingham, Harry Grabiner, Comiskey's club secretary, decided to move the spirited club to a more remote place.[23] Little did he anticipate its advantages for gambling leeches and the power of vulnerability due to player resentment.

The day after he met with Sullivan, Gandil began efforts to recruit other members to this audacious plot. His first target was pitcher Eddie Cicotte, mainly because: (A) gamblers and their willing benefactors knew that pitchers held great control over a game; and (B) Cicotte would likely start three of the nine games, should the Series last that long. The primary luring agent used on Cicotte was his financial conundrum. Gandil knew that the big right-hander was having trouble keeping current with mortgage payments on his farm.[24]

Gandil, the 6'2", 197-pound alpha-male, began work on his second patsy-to-be, Swede Risberg, who wasted no time in agreeing to participate. By September 20, Gandil had filled out his conspiracy roster by adding McMullin, Jackson, Williams, Weaver, and yes, Felsch. Gandil convened a meeting on September 21 at the Ansonia Hotel in New York City, following their three-game series in Boston. Gandil explained his proposal to Sport Sullivan.[25] The "unholy eight," as sportswriter Fred Lieb called them, were set: Arnold "Chick" Gandil, Shoeless Joe Jackson, August "Swede" Risberg, Oscar Emil "Happy" Felsch, Claude "Lefty" Williams, George Daniel "Buck" Weaver, Fred McMullin, and Eddie "Talcum-Powder Ball" Cicotte.

That Chick Gandil became the ringleader of this fiasco seemed like a matter of timing and previous association. Gandil was not the sharp cookie of Eddie Collins' ilk, nor was he an owner of developed couth. The former club fighter and boilermaker possessed the drive and determination to see this through. His being near the end of his baseball career (32 years old) made it a bit less risky for him to pursue the monetary windfall. Felsch, years later in an interview with *Eight Men Out* author Eliot Asinof, summarized it rather succinctly: "Old Gandil was smart and the rest of us was dumb."

The predominant reason for these players being so willing was a collective disillusionment with their salaries. Jackson, Weaver, and Cicotte all made $6,000 per year. Gandil and Felsch netted $4,000, with McMullin, Risberg, and Williams right behind at $3,000. In addition, all players were bound by the famed reserve clause. Thus, their options were severely limited.[26]

Regardless, this historical, back-handed agreement does not mitigate the gullibility factor nor the split camps that existed within the White Sox clubhouse; these infamous eight showed resolute hatred for the likes of Eddie Collins and Ray Schalk. In addition, many conclude that it merely reflected unabridged greed and a chance at so-called easy money.[27] The various factors are dissected in other volumes and will not be tirelessly analyzed here. As Abe Attell would say years after, it was "cheaters cheating cheaters."

To bankroll this audacious venture, Sullivan supposedly elicited mobster Arnold "the Brain" Rothstein on September 26, 1919. Rothstein was the son of a wealthy Jewish immigrant racketeer and businessman, Abraham Rothstein, and his wife Esther. Arnold's gambling sidekick and bodyguard was an ex-featherweight boxing champion named Abe Attell (nicknamed "The Little Champ"); the two first met in 1905 and began hanging out after Attell retired from the ring.

Meanwhile, "Sleepy" Bill Burns, an ex-ballplayer and current gambler, contacted Eddie Cicotte to propose a competing offer. He and fellow gambler Billy Maharg also contacted Rothstein for financial assistance based on what the White Sox eight were willing to pull off.[28] Following his meeting with Sullivan, "the Brain" sent his associate, Nat Evans, to Chicago to gauge the seriousness of the players' willingness to fix the World Series.[29]

Rothstein approved Evans to give Sullivan $40,000 and arranged an additional $40,000 to be secured in a safe at the Congress Hotel in Chicago. According to some accounts, he also requested that Eddie Cicotte hit the first Reds batter as a sign that the fix was on. Sullivan apparently gave Gandil only $10,000, reportedly using $29,000 to place his own bets on the Cincinnati Reds. Not happy in the least, Gandil was forced to accept the paltry sum and stashed the loot under a pillow in Cicotte's hotel room.[30]

What you had here were two greedy gambling factions going to the same rich crook (Rothstein) for financial backing. Rothstein shunned Maharg and Burns in favor of Sullivan. On September 27, Burns and Maharg met Rothstein at New York's Astor Hotel to make their pitch. After hearing the spiel, Rothstein became livid and warned them never to lay eyes on him again. This, of course, was a ruse, a means for Rothstein to shake off one band of money-seekers in favor of another. Meanwhile, Evans grew nervous that too many people knew about the scheme and the whole darn thing would come apart. "Don't worry," said Rothstein. "If nine guys go to bed with a girl, she'll have a tough time proving the tenth is the father."[31]

Thirty-seven years later, talking to *Sports Illustrated*, Gandil recounted the meeting and overall recruitment: "They all were interested and thought we should reconnoiter to see if the dough would really be put on the line. Weaver suggested we get paid in advance; then if things got too hot, we could double-cross the gambler, keep the cash and take the big end of the Series by beating the Reds. We agreed this was a hell of a brainy plan."[32]

Baseball, basking in its naive state and pretending gambling didn't exist, soon changed for the worst.

10

Did Felsch Play to Lose?

Prior to 1919, most officials and fans considered baseball in the same class as one of the bath soaps advertising itself as 99.44 percent pure.

—Fred Lieb, *Baseball As I Have Known It*

The 1919 Fall Classic offered a clear contrast between league champions, a classic hitting (White Sox) against pitching (Reds) juicer that re-fueled long-standing debates over which aspect was most important to achieve baseball's highest honor. Not to imply the clubs were one-dimensional, but the numbers confirmed their primary strengths.

The top of the teams' rotations were fairly even. The White Sox boasted twin 20-game winners in Cicotte (29–7) and Lefty Williams (23–11). Pat Moran's Reds had one 20-game winner in Slim Sallee (21–7) and two 19-game winners in Hod Eller (19–9) and Dutch Ruether (19–6). Cicotte sported the only sub-1.00 WHIP (Walks plus Hits per Inning Pitched) of the entire bunch. The Reds displayed much more depth, however, with four regulars boasting a WHIP a shade over 1.00. In addition, their team ERA of 2.23 was nearly a run better than the White Sox.

Hitting favored the White Sox—at least on paper—as they bested the Reds in 1919 in almost every category. The Senior Circuit appeared to favor the pitching side of the ledger. Edd Roush paced the NL in batting average at .321, but *seven* AL players topped that mark. The Chicago White Sox were most prognosticators' heavy favorites to stomp all over the Cincinnati Reds. This one-sided forecast was probably based on the White Sox's recent successes, or their more boisterous, controversial star power, or plain old "they're just better." The early odds and countless articles championed the Old Roman's crew and validated what many coined a "no brainer" outcome.

Both managers offered their scouting reports before the baseball's annual gala:

Members of the White Sox outfield await the start of World Series action, 1917. From the left: Eddie Murphy, Shano Collins, Joe Jackson, Felsch and Nemo Leibold (George Grantham Bain Collection, Library of Congress).

Pat Moran:"Pitchers will figure a lot in the series. It will take great pitching to stop the White Sox. Gleason has a lot of heavy hitters. So did Connie Mack in 1914, but they didn't hit when they bumped into the Boston Braves. Good pitching by (Dick) Rudolph, (Bill) James, and (Lefty) Tyler stopped them."[1]

Kid Gleason:"My fellows are all right. You should have seen them in that workout this morning [the day before the opener]. I never saw a bunch with more pep. There isn't anything wrong with any fellow in the gang and they are keyed up to start the battle tomorrow."[2]

To loosen up his bunch and temporarily distract them, Gleason held batting and fielding practice in the morning, but gave the players the afternoon off to head over to the horse races at Latonia Track. Conversely, the Reds practiced all day, leading a *Washington Post* reporter to suggest that the Reds appeared more serious about the Series.[3]

During batting practice, Felsch ripped into the ball with the tenacity of a man on death row devouring his last meal. His jocular disposition always revealed itself during warm-ups, as he always enjoyed practice more than ball games. All this fun was neatly tucked inside of towering shots to the outfield.[4] Baseball's biggest stage was primed to witness a hitting exhibition in a live-game scenario.

For the managers, fans, sportswriters, photographers, vendors, and ushers, the 1919 World Series was like any other, pitting two strong league champions against each other in a classic battle. On the morning of Game One, the hotels were bustling with anxious gamblers looking to take advantage of the rumor of the fix and increase their own greedy nest eggs. When the ballplayers came downstairs for breakfast, they hardly noticed the eager throng, some of whom were waving bills in the air, including some of the $1,000 variety.[5] Subtle disposition was not part of their repertoire, but the blatant allure did not erase the general excitement in the air.

Felsch yearned to build on his late regular season surge. In his previous World Series appearance, Felsch hit a decent .273 with two extra-base hits and three RBI. The White Sox faced an even tougher pitching staff in the Reds and would endure the ultimate test to muster up some runs. In Game One, one tally would not suffice.

When Cicotte took the mound, Cincinnati fans uttered such welcoming jibes as "There's the bum from Chicago" and "Sore arm Cicotte" and "Old man Cicotte." In New York, Arnold Rothstein came to the Astonia Hotel to watch a telegraph system set up to replay the action in Cincinnati. Reports would be read aloud and a diamond-shaped chart was plastered to the wall, with the players moved from base to base to provide a visual effect. Not coincidently, Rothstein was only interested in the first pitch, Cicotte to leadoff man Maurice Rath. The Little Champ, Abe Attell, was parked in a nice box seat behind third base. Charles Comiskey was seated in a box behind first base.[6]

Hugh Fullerton, veteran scribe for the *Chicago Herald and Examiner*, kept a curious eye on the action as rumors of a fix swirled. Fullerton and a friend, retired pitcher Christy Mathewson, sat together in the press area, keeping separate scorecards and circling plays that looked suspicious to them. Fullerton would become the loudest—if not the sole—voice in protest of the tainted brand of baseball they witnessed. To Fullerton's credit, he was not considered a company man.

After the White Sox failed to score in the top of the first though Shano Collins led off the Series with a single, Eddie Cicotte trotted out to the mound. After a called strike one, Cicotte promptly plucked leadoff hitter Rath with the second pitch. Many might have perceived butterflies to be the culprit for his errant toss. However, it has been widely understood that the pitch was the first signal, the beanball a telegram of dark warning, that the *fix* was on. Was this hit batsman really intentional? If so, why on the second pitch and not the first?[7] The Reds took a 1–0 lead on Heinie Groh's sacrifice fly after Rath advanced to third on Jake Daubert's single.

The pitcher has ultimate control over the pace of the game. Cicotte has been the most visible character in nearly every account of this Series, dating back almost 100 years. There is little dispute that his plunking of Rath was the chief indicator that something was amiss. But what about the other participants? At the plate, the hitter can execute an intentionally feeble attempt at success. But in the field, they are at the mercy of where the ball is hit.

Unanswered questions outnumber answered ones by a mile. One such question is: Did Oscar Felsch play to lose the Series? Later, we will see that Felsch admitted to sub-par playing. But does the evidence on the field support his claim? The optimum word in the question is "play." Joe Jackson led off the second inning by reaching on a two-base throwing error by Reds shortstop Larry Kopf. Felsch sacrificed Jackson to third; Chick Gandil followed with a Texas League single to knot the score at 1–1. Did Felsch sacrifice Shoeless Joe purposely to avoid a full swing? The small-ball strategy was well in vogue and Felsch probably heeded the sign from a base coach. Heading into the fourth inning, with the score still 1–1, Felsch came up to bat again, this time grounding out to end a 1–2–3 inning.

In the bottom of the frame, the Reds busted the game wide open as the White Sox displayed questionable plays and decisions. Cicotte got Edd Roush to fly out to center to a hustling Felsch, who made a spectacular catch. Was this the work of a player trying to lose? Was there a mental disconnect between what the gamblers wanted him to do and his natural inclination to play his tail off?

Pat Duncan followed with a single. The next batter, Kopf, hit one back to the box at Cicotte, who some say took his sweet time to secure the ball before he turned and fired it high to Risberg at second to record the force out, with not enough time to complete a double play. Instead of three outs there were two outs with one on. Ugliness would soon engulf Gleason's men.[8]

In the press box, Fullerton turned a curious glance towards Mathewson, who peered back in non-verbal agreement. Fullerton circled the play in his scorebook, hence the first recording of a suspicious event in the 1919 World Series.[9] Sportswriter Fred Lieb, who along with Dan Daniel covered the game for the *New York Morning Sun*, overheard Fullerton later claim: "I don't like what I saw out there today. There is something smelly. Cicotte doesn't usually pitch like that." The reputation came with warrant, as Cicotte completed all but five of his 35 regular-season starts in 1919.[10]

The Reds exploded for five runs in the frame to take a commanding 6–1 lead. Even pitcher Dutch Ruether joined in the fun, surprising the White Sox with a two-run triple, scoring Greasy Neale and Ivey Wingo. The winded Ruether halted at third after Felsch relayed the ball quickly to the infield; by all accounts, Felsch hustled on the play. Cicotte surrendered five consecutive hits: three singles, a double, and a triple, forcing the right-hander to the bench in favor of Roy Wilkinson. With two out, the rookie coaxed Groh to fly out to a racing Felsch. The Reds breezed to a 9–1 victory on 14 hits.

Kid Gleason was rancorous after the game, questioning his players' drive and livid at his team's lackadaisical effort. In his own piece in the *Washington Post*, Gleason outlined his team's shortfalls. He thought that Cicotte's hesitation in the fourth inning to start a double play happened because he was waiting for Risberg to get to second base. Regardless, he believed it took five wins to capture the title and was confident this "punch in the jaw" by the Reds in Game One would spur them to success. It would have been better had he pitched a spitter instead of fast ball on two or three occasions in that fourth inning," said Gleason.[11]

Felsch went 0-for-3 with one sacrifice in the game. Ruether had his way with Happy and his batting mates. In the spring of 1919, Cincinnati had asked waivers on Ruether but withdrew the request, a reversal that paid dividends all season. He limited the Sox to six benign hits and pitched shutout baseball from the third inning on.[12]

Was there an on-field act by Felsch in Game One that would draw suspicion of deliberate tanking? He went hitless with three outs. But he also had a sacrifice, made a wonderful catch in center field, and showed abundant hustle in retrieving other balls hit his way. The hitless game does not by itself prove overt chicanery, neither does it *disprove* it.

During the Series, most of the newspaper reporters not named Hugh Fullerton—both locally and nationally—did not even hint that mistake-riddled plays were anything other than normal. But intention can be subtle and there are a myriad of ways to enact a devious baseball event without drawing suspicion. A common strategy with fielders at any position is placement. Was Felsch playing too shallow for some, too deep for others? Did he lean towards right when a right-handed pull hitter was up? In his well-written piece in the 1938 *Saturday Evening Post*, John Lardner (son of Ring Lardner) wrote this interesting tidbit: "Felsch played his position for Neale as though Greasy, a long hitter, were a crippled schoolgirl." Was this a mere misjudgment by Felsch?[13]

After the game, Bill Maharg was summoned by "Sleepy" Bill Burns for the two to collect the first $20,000 installment from Abe Attell in the Sinton Hotel, with the plan for Maharg to deliver the tidy sum to Gandil. Attell rebuffed their request, saying that the money was out on bets. The scent of a double-cross filled the air. After some not-so-kind words, the two shuffled off to Gandil's room to deliver the unsavory news. The big brute of a first baseman told the pair in a huff that Lefty Williams, the Game Two starter, was not liable to participate in the fix unless he got some loot. Burns temporarily calmed Gandil's fears, telling him that he would arrange a meeting with Attell the next day.[14]

Attell showed the participating players a telegram from Arnold Rothstein, which stated the money would be delivered to them the next morning. The telegram, a fake, was sent by a friend of Attell's from New York; players were royally duped.[15]

With the waft of treachery in the air, the Series continued without official qualms. Game Two pitted Lefty Williams against the Reds' Harry "Slim" Sallee. Williams had a solid season, going 23–11 with 125 strikeouts, 58 walks, and 2.64 ERA. Sallee bettered that record, going 21–7 with a 2.07 ERA, striking out just 24 batters and walking 20. Williams' wildness and the inability of White Sox hitters to capitalize on scoring opportunities doomed them in a 4–2 loss and a two-zip hole in the Series. Felsch had two wasted sacrifices in the game.

The *Chicago Tribune* suggested that perhaps Felsch would have been more effective swinging away than bunting. The Dead Ball Era was rife with "play for one run" strategy and managers thought nothing of sacrificing an out to that end. More than 50 years later, Baltimore Orioles manager Earl Weaver—a stingy fellow in regards to conventional edicts—said, "On offense, your most precious possessions are your 27 outs. If you play for one run, that's all you'll get."

Reds plated three runs in their half of the fourth. With two out and one run already in, shortstop Larry Kopf—an AL castoff—lashed a two-run triple to left-center, scoring Groh and Duncan. Felsch hustled to the fence and returned the ball back to the infield. Williams got Earle "Greasy" Neale to ground out to end the carnage.[16]

In the White Sox half of the sixth inning, a one-out double by the red-hot Weaver gave the Sox hope.[17] But Jackson struck out looking and, after Sallee balked Weaver to third, Felsch, anxious to swing away, cranked a towering shot to left-center that smelled of extra bases. To his dismay, Roush made a spectacular over-the-shoulder grab, leaving the White Sox wondering again. The ball was airborne long enough that Felsch was nearly rounding second by the time Roush caught the ball. "You would have mortgaged the farm that Eddie would never get on speaking terms with the ball,"[18] said the *New York Times*, which included this colorful description of the play:

> Hap hit it squarely on the nose and the ball sailed high and far in the general direction of the centre field battlement. Rousch took one peek at the ball, then turned and ran to the fence. As he galloped along with his back to the ball it seemed as if the little white object was going to crash against the green painted center field fence. When Weaver had crossed the plate and Felsch was rounding second base on his hilarious gallop, Rousch turned suddenly. He did this by intuition, for it was impossible for him to see where the ball was as there are no eyes in the back of his head. As he twisted quickly about, both hands reached skyward and he corralled the ball just as it was about to whistle over the roof.[19]

The Reds stretched their lead to 4–0 in their half of the sixth. Another walk, a sacrifice and a two-out RBI single plated the insurance run. So far in the Series, Felsch had been hitting the ball hard but was unable to evade the

Reds' fielders, who were the clear difference makers in this game. After the White Sox cut the Reds' lead in half in the seventh, Felsch came to bat in the eighth, and again hit the ball hard, but third baseman Heinie Groh snared the liner. Another White Sox threat was doused.[20]

In the bottom of the eighth, after Groh walked, Edd Roush lined out to Felsch in center, who alertly gunned the ball to Gandil at first to double up Groh. His signature hustle and strong arm seemed to refute the notion that he was supposed to have a hand in tanking the Series for his own benefit and the gamblers'. One of the aspects of the scandal that is unknown is whether there were additional meetings between the infamous eight over a losing strategy, maybe even specifics. On this play, Felsch must have had amnesia.

The almighty White Sox were scratching their heads, staring down the barrel at a 2–0 hole. Thus far, they had failed to execute in the pinch and had allowed potential rallies fade with little or nothing to show for them. They amassed ten hits in the second game, but the Reds halted most of the scoring threats with magnificent glove work. Lefty Williams, the White Sox starter, walked six batters. This perplexed many, especially catcher Ray Schalk, who was seething at his pitcher's performance. Schalk told Gleason that Williams was crossing him up (throwing unexpected pitches). Yet another hit in the batting cage of dishonest play.

Back in Milwaukee, Felsch's fans kept abreast of his play in an auditorium, watching games on an electric scoreboard. Although Felsch had been hitless, the *Milwaukee Sentinel* emphasized that north-side fans were proud to see Felsch "come up in a pinch," advancing Joe Jackson three times.[21] The *Milwaukee Sentinel* sub-headline read: "Hard Day for Felsch"

On the train ride back to Chicago, writer Ring Lardner sang this little ditty to the players:

> *"I'm forever blowing ball games.*
> *Pretty ball games in the air.*
> *I come from Chi. I hardly try.*
> *Just go to bat and fade and die.*
> *Fortune's coming my way,*
> *That's why I don't care.*
> *I'm forever blowing ball games,*
> *And the gamblers treat us fair."*[22]

Subtlety and Lardner were perfect strangers.

The return home offered comforting hope of redemption and legitimacy for the White Sox. Engaged for battle were Dickie Kerr (13–7, 2.88 ERA) and Cincinnati's Ray Fisher (14–5, 2.17 ERA)—a rookie against an eight-year veteran. Fisher, a noted spitballer, was later grandfathered in when the leagues banned the moistened pitch in 1921.

Kerr, not party to the fix, rescued his team from a potential 3–0 hole with a three-hit shutout. The "world's smallest southpaw" was an enigma to the Cincinnati hitters, who siphoned little off him the entire day, getting three hits and one walk. Kerr faced just 30 batters, three over the minimum. He allowed just six balls to reach the outfield.[23]

With the game scoreless in the second inning, Joe Jackson led off with a single to left. Felsch hit a grounder to Fisher, who threw wildly to second trying to force Jackson, advancing Shoeless Joe and Felsch to third and second, respectively. Gandil knocked in both runners with a single, advancing to second on a throw to home. Gandil hit a rocket to right fielder Greasy Neale, who failed to snag the fleet-footed Felsch.[24] Two force outs and a ground out later, the White Sox closed the frame with a 2–0 lead.

Kerr confounded the Reds hitters the rest of the way, stomping out benign rallies and taking the pressure off his defense. The 3–0 victory cut the Reds' Series lead in half and tempered some of the scandal talk—briefly. Ring Lardner decided not to place a bet on this game, writing that his decision provided the White Sox the necessary good luck.[25]

Felsch again failed to register his first hit in the Series. Asked to bunt several times, he had missed those chances to take a full whack at the ball. Despite his failings, he hustled on the base paths and was not exactly a non-factor. Shortstop Swede Risberg, perhaps forgetting that he was complicit in the fraud, played brilliantly in the field, handling ten chances perfectly.

Was this victory designed to throw off the suspicions and allay the fears of those who wanted to keep the sparkling shine on the game intact? That question might overrate the fraud architects' intellect and make a hasty assumption about their ability to carry this plot to fruition. By most accounts, the White Sox played a nearly flawless game, executing timely hits and gobbling up the baseball with regularity. However, the *Spalding Baseball Guide of 1920* wrote that in the third inning, after Gandil's two-run single, he later "loafed" to third on Ray Schalk's sacrifice bunt attempt.[26] Regardless, Dickie Kerr's incredible performance, by itself, might have stifled the fix.

Despite his own prevailing mistrust, Kid Gleason was gleeful about his team's performance, writing this in the *Washington Post*: "That fighting spirit that carried the White Sox through the pennant race came back to them for the third game and it didn't take long to put one over on the Reds. Kerr pitched one of the prettiest games I have ever looked at."[27]

"Sleepy" Bill Burns and Bill Maharg were not so tipsy, having lost all the money they had won from the previous two games. This merely piled onto the players' mistrust and sent the entire fix into temporary oblivion, diluted and scarred by false promises, double-crosses, and empty wallets. To the rescue came Sport Sullivan. Having lost his shirt on Game Three, he approached Gandil with a promise of $20,000 after the fourth game and $20,000 more after the fifth game. Gandil agreed and the fix, in its infinite disorganization and confusion, regained a dram of clarity.[28]

Felsch was now 0-for-7 in the Series with three sacrifices and ten putouts. Game Four would rescue his bat from the termites. Gleason decided to trot out Eddie Cicotte; Pat Moran sent 6'1" 170-pound right-hander Jimmy Ring to the mound. Born in Brooklyn, New York, in 1895, Ring debuted in 1917 and had become a regular cog in the rotation. Of all the Reds starters, Ring suffered from the worst run support from his hitters, getting 18 percent fewer runs per game than the league average.[29] On this day, the temperature was a comfortable 70 degrees, 34,000 fans packed the ballpark, and a bushel of runs was not essential.[30]

Ring and Cicotte dueled in a scoreless battle until the fifth inning. Felsch had extended his hitless streak to eight at-bats, executing a sacrifice bunt in the second, then grounding out to third baseman Heinie Groh in the third. On the sacrifice, Felsch missed a single by a hair, with Groh's throw narrowly beating Felsch's speed. In the top of the fifth, more Cicotte flubs allowed a couple of Reds to score. After Roush led off with a ground out, Duncan reached when the bouncer he hit grazed a leaping Cicotte's glove, veering towards third. With Weaver racing in from third, Cicotte stepped in front of him and gathered the ball, but threw wildly to first. Schalk hustled down the first-base line to recover the errant toss, but Duncan reached second base easily.[31]

Kopf followed with a single to left. Joe Jackson fielded the hit and gunned the ball home, sailing directly towards the waiting glove of Schalk. What happened next would go down in the annals as the biggest fielding gaffe of the tainted Series. Cicotte raced towards home, and tried to cut off the throw. Shoeless Joe's heave nipped the edge of Cicotte's glove and caromed towards the stands behind home plate. Duncan scored the first run of the game, and the party of rage, the wink of eyes, and the red-faced glares ensued. Neale then laced a double to left-center, scoring Kopf, who had advanced to second on the Cicotte misplay.[32]

In the press box, Hugh Fullerton drew one big fat circle around the two Cicotte transgressions. The rest of the game was calm and included no more runs. Felsch came up again in the sixth and hit a long fly out to the left field wall, caught by the back-peddling Duncan. In the bottom of the eighth and two out, Felsch lined a single over the head of third baseman Heinie Groh for his first hit of the 1919 World Series. Unfortunately, he was orphaned at first when Gandil whiffed.[33]

The Cincinnati Reds' lead was now three games to one. Ray Schalk, one of the non-plotters, was the only White Sox hitter who showed patience against Ring, walking twice, the second time with one out in the ninth inning. The next two batters swung anxiously at the first pitch and made the last two outs of the game. Although Ring pitched a solid game and deserved the victory, he had showed some stretches of wildness during the game. The White Sox batters, whether intentionally or unknowingly, did not waver from their aggressive approach and might have let the Reds' hurler off the hook.[34]

The post-game jabber concerning the questionable fielding performance of Eddie Cicotte dominated the circuit. One of the few exceptions was Tom Swope of the *Cincinnati Post,* who rationalized Cicotte's second error, claimed that perhaps he was over-hustling to make up for his previous mistake and that a taller man could have fielded the throw. He added that Cicotte was rattled from the start, although he had pitched wonderfully both before and after that treacherous inning.[35]

Cicotte dismissed his forgettable performance as pure luck, but he otherwise pitched fairly well, maybe just as good as his mound opponent, Jimmy Ring. Thus far, Cicotte was the only player who had received any money—the original $10,000 that he was given prior to the Series. But following Game Four, Sport Sullivan ponied up the additional $20,000, which Gandil distributed evenly— in $5,000 payments—to Felsch, Risberg, Williams, and Jackson.

Heavy rain showers blanketed the city, providing some reprieve from further misery on Sunday, October 5. Kid Gleason rang the desperation sirens heading into Game Five, which was scheduled for Monday, October 6. Gleason peppered his post-game column with predictable confidence and promised a surprise or two to stem the tide of the Reds' momentum. The Kid termed his thirst for altering conventional strategy "desperate baseball" and insisted that his club had not hit its stride yet.[36]

If portions of the first four games included "creme de la fix," indicators for Eddie Cicotte, Lefty Williams, and Chick Gandil, Game Five featured Happy Felsch in the "theater of the absurd" with some pretty shoddy glove work. Other than his lack of hitting, which by itself is no indictment, Felsch had displayed marvelous glove work before this game. Lefty Williams made his second start of the Series, facing the Reds' Hod Eller, who was making his Series debut.

This game was a yawner offensively until the sixth inning. Williams battled Eller pitch for pitch, holding the Reds hitless through the first four innings. His teammates started their first at-bat with a potential scoring threat. Nemo Leibold led off with a walk. Eddie Collins advanced Leibold to second with a ground out. Weaver followed with a single and an early lead seemed imminent. But Jackson and Felsch could not cash in, both registering fly outs to stave off peril for the Reds. Once again, wasted rallies haunted Gleason's men.

Both pitchers retired all six hitters in the second and third innings. Eller was extra dominant, striking out all six, a World Series record. Gandil, Risberg, Schalk, Williams, Leibold, and Eddie Collins all provided stiff breezes by keeping their bats away from pitches. After his dreadful Game Two, Williams regained his familiar control, walking just two batters in the contest. Felsch continued his offensive doldrums with another strikeout in the fourth inning.

Still scoreless heading into the sixth, Eller led off with a double to center. He was no slouch at the plate, batting .280/.287/.409 in 93 at-bats in 1919. The impressive slugging percentage was aided by seven extra-base hits, including one home run. On the double, Felsch recorded his first gaffe of the inning, throwing wildly to Risberg, advancing Eller to third. Morrie Rath followed with an RBI single, Buck Weaver retired the next batter, Daubert, on his sacrifice bunt.[37] Then Heinie Groh walked. The next play would define the entire series for Felsch—fairly or unfairly—and would be etched into baseball annals forever.

Edd Roush launched a long fly ball toward Felsch in center. On what appeared to be a sure out, given his history of making long clouts die, Felsch misjudged the ball, which bounced out of his grasp as he slipped and fell. This allowed Roush to scoot all the way to third. Rath and Groh scored and the Reds built a 3–0 lead. Eddie Collins, who took the eventual throw from Felsch, relayed the ball and almost nailed Groh. But the throw was a little short, allowing Groh to sneak behind Schalk and score.[38]

Curiously, Felsch did not seem to know where the ball was hit. According to Eliot Asinof in *Eight Men Out*, Felsch seemed to hesitate as he started for the ball. After getting up to chase down the pill, he picked it up, dropped it, then scooped it up again. His throw to Collins was a vintage Felsch heave, but too much occurred prior to retire even the slowest of base-runners.[39] The *Washington Post* wrote that "Felsch, rated as the best defensive outfielder, made a sorry mess of it."[40]

The White Sox went down dutifully in the sixth and seventh. Felsch made the second out in the seventh when he hit a weak popup to the Reds' catcher, Bill Rariden, in foul territory. Williams shut down the Reds in the eighth in order, and was lifted for the pinch-hitter Eddie Murphy in the bottom of the inning. Murphy did what Williams would have had little problem doing himself, striking out to end the inning. The big lefty gave up just four hits, striking out three and walking two. Although all four runs he gave up were earned, his defense shouldered much of the blame. A feeble White Sox rally in the ninth guaranteed a 5–0 Reds shutout and a 4–1 Series lead.

The teams returned to Cincinnati for Game Six. The streets of the Queen City were laden with enthusiastic fans waiting to snag the elusive World Series title. Bands accompanied them towards the ballpark in a makeshift parade, hollering out a series of tunes, before they squeezed into Redland Park, with nearly 10,000 more denied entrance.[41]

The momentum of the Series took a curious shift in the White Sox's favor. The scene morphed from half-willing, tepid provocateurs to defiant, committed, "let's play for real" professionals. When Sport Sullivan failed to deliver the remaining $20,000, several of the players agreed to call off the fix. It was clear that the eight's renewed vigor spelled trouble for the confident Reds. Gleason sent the diminutive but effective Dickie Kerr to the mound to battle the 19-game winner, Dutch Ruether. The gleeful fans would see the most competitive and perhaps the most entertaining game of the Series thus far.[42] *The Los Angeles Times* summarized the contest in this way: "It was a contest replete with thrills and heartbreaks, varied by some weird fielding, snappy base-running, mighty clouts and catches; in short, practically everything related to baseball."[43]

Over 32,000 fans jammed Redland Park for what many deemed the game to crown a new champion, their beloved Reds. The game started out with mundane familiarity, with both teams struggling to plate runs. The Reds broke through in the third inning. After Rath grounded out to Collins to open the inning, Daubert singled, and Groh whiffed while Daubert stole second. After Kerr plunked Roush with an erratic pitch, Duncan doubled home Daubert and Roush. Kopf flied out to a hustling Felsch in center to end the carnage.[44] Once again, the White Sox were looking uphill at a deficit.

With the Reds still up, 2–0, Felsch came up to bat in the fourth inning with two outs and kept the inning alive with a single to center. But Chick Gandil followed with a weak ground out. Cincinnati tacked on two more runs in the bottom of the inning, providing a bigger cushion.

The White Sox began to chip away, scoring one run in the fifth. Risberg coaxed a walk to open the frame. Schalk followed suit with his own free pass, and the South Siders were back in business. Dickie Kerr advanced both runners one station with a single. Still with nobody out, Shano Collins hit a shallow fly to center that wasn't deep enough to score Risberg. But on the next play, Eddie Collins hit one deep enough to plate the Sox's first tally. Unfortunately, Kerr also tried to tag on the play, but Reds center fielder Edd Roush gunned him down at second for an inning-ending double play. The run broke a 26-inning scoreless streak that dated back to the fourth inning of Game Three. This mighty band of slashers and bashers had been rendered inert for a curious duration.

Kerr, the little southpaw, stymied the Cincinnati offense the rest of the way. Despite the persistent sloppy play of his teammates, something recognizable occurred in the White Sox sixth: an offensive barrage that would tie the game at 4–4. Like an old friend who disappeared but later returned bearing gifts and food, the Sox re-introduced themselves to their manager, fans, and media. Buck Weaver, the steadiest member of this motley crew thus far in the Series, led off with a double to left. Weaver's hit started as a "can of corn" fly ball to short left. But Reds outfielder Pat Duncan and shortstop Larry Kopf seemed more intent on arguing than hustling, letting the ball drop for an unexpected double.

Shoeless Joe Jackson singled home Weaver and the rally was in full gear. Felsch doubled—his first multi-hit game of the Series—knocking in Jackson, and the lead was now one. Pat Moran decided that Dutch Ruether had had enough, replacing him with Jimmy Ring. It worked briefly, as Gandil popped out to first and Risberg grounded out to short, advancing Felsch to third. Ray Schalk, who had been the most vocal critic of the shoddy play of his teammates, ripped a sharp single to left, scoring Felsch and tying the game. After the catcher stole second, Kerr grounded out to end the rally.

The teams played to a draw the rest of the obligatory nine innings. Even though the game was now competitive, the sludgy play by both squads made it an unsightly event. Risberg recorded two errors and Felsch one. The Reds did not have an "official" error, but defensive misplays were sprinkled throughout. In the top of the ninth, with the score still knotted, Ring retired Schalk and Kerr, but walked Nemo Leibold, who had replaced Shano Collins in the seventh. The little fireplug stole second, but the other Collins (Eddie) flied out to snuff out the threat.

Gleason trotted out Kerr in the Reds' ninth, riding the young hurler as far as possible. Kerr had been far from perfect thus far, not retiring his opponents in order even once in eight innings while yielding ten hits. The ninth was no different, but once again, he escaped danger. With one out, Jake Daubert singled to center. Heinie Groh hit a fielder's choice and made the final out when Schalk gunned him down trying to swipe second. The 1919 World Series would feature its first extra-inning battle. The White Sox faced elimination and the Reds did not want to breathe new life into them with their commanding 4–1 Series lead.

The championship ceremony would have to wait. In the top of the tenth, Weaver led off with a double. Jackson followed with a bunt single, sending Weaver to third. After Felsch whiffed, Gandil singled home the lead run. With Jackson on second, Risberg lined a shot to the shortstop Kopf, whose throw to Duncan at second beat Jackson's retreat to the same destination.[45] In the bottom of the tenth, the Reds were no match for Kerr. Two ground outs and a pop out gave the White Sox their second victory of the Series; the teams remained in Cincy for Game Seven.

Felsch redeemed himself offensively with a 2-for-4 effort. His error on defense, however, was extremely uncharacteristic. One wonders if Happy had discarded thoughts of a fix and so-called easy money. The final box score looked pleasingly familiar, with Weaver, Jackson, and Felsch, the 3–4–5 hitters, combining to go 7-for-14 with four runs scored and two RBI. Weaver earned the biggest prize with three hits. It seemed possible that he and Jackson had played to win the entire Series. These two stars would become the moral outliers in later scandal lore.

Although his .167 batting average was nothing to write home to Milwaukee about, Felsch, along with his partners in chicanery, evinced a new mood the next morning prior to Game Seven. Even Hugh Fullerton, who had been the staunchest critic of their curious play, assessed their demeanor with: "By God. Anyone would think this is the winning ball club." To Fullerton, and perhaps others, this signified a renewed sense of vigor and cleansing of America's pastime during its darkest hour. He and Mathewson looked forward to putting down their critical pens and enjoying the critical Game Seven.[46]

The anticipation of panic should the Reds blow this Series was captured rather crudely by the *Chicago Tribune*, which under the apocalyptic headline "Busy Times for Coroner" offered this supposition: "If such a thing as that would happen, it might take weeks of dragging the scummy canal of this city to collect all those who had jumped in. Cincinnati is all set for a celebration. Too many postponements will drive the people down here crazy."[47]

Meanwhile, at the betting windows, the *New York Times* reported that some Cincinnati businessmen lost button-down shirts to the tune of $60,000 on Game Six, a contest they obviously expected the Reds to win.[48] The White Sox were just hoping that their new-found success would catapult them into locking up the Series and forcing a decisive Game Nine.

Felsch looked to conjure up back-to-back multi-hit games for the first time since the September 20 twin bill at Boston. He had hit safely in his last 11 regular season tilts. Every hitting streak halts eventually, but the precipitous drop in Felsch's hitting was certainly a vital cause of the Sox's early Series failures. With his hitters' bats greased once again to succeed, Kid Gleason had to decide who was going to toe the mound next in a do-or-die game.

Eddie Cicotte begged to be the Game Seven starter and was eager to redeem himself as a serious competitor again. Gleason was fully aware of his ace's intentions: "I don't know what pitcher will do the hurling," said the manager. "Eddie Cicotte wants to take the job, In fact, he is demanding it. He is dead sore over being licked twice, and is positive he can give the Reds a trimming if sent out once more."[49]

The preoccupation, confusion, and bitterness that infused the White Sox's psyche early in the Series gave way to another strong start. Wasting no time to show the Reds they meant business, Shano Collins led off the game with a single off starter Slim Sallee. Eddie Collins sacrificed the other Collins to second, and two batters later, Joe Jackson's single spotted the Sox a 1–0 lead. Felsch picked up where he had left off in Game Six by laying down a bunt for a single, but Chick Gandil hit into a force out.

"From the moment the Gleasons stepped into the arena for their preliminary practice, they looked like winners," wrote I. E. Sanborn of the *Chicago Tribune*. "Baseball men who have followed the game for more than a quarter of a century, either as players or writers, commented on the confidence that was evident in every move the Gleasons made."

Cicotte did a masterful job of keeping the Reds off the scoreboard. Meanwhile, Shano Collins led off again with a single in the third inning with the White Sox clinging to the one-run lead. The other Collins also singled, but Weaver lined into a double-play. Shoeless Joe Jackson charged to the rescue with a sharp single to left, scoring Shano and doubling the Sox's lead to 2–0. Jackson overran first on the throw home, but scurried back to the bag before the Reds could pick him off. Felsch followed with a force out to end the inning.[50]

Because of his fielding scuffles in center, Felsch was moved to right field for this game. Luckily for Gleason and his Sox, Felsch did not look unfamiliar in his new surroundings, fielding his position with aplomb. The *Chicago Tribune* aptly pointed out that Felsch played like a new man and helped put his team on "easy street" in this game. Was this resurgence enough to keep the White Sox afloat?[51]

Cicotte cruised along, retiring the Reds with little resistance in the third and fourth frames. His teammates struck again in the top of the fifth. With one out, Eddie Collins singled and Buck Weaver reached on an error when Heinie Groh fumbled the ball, then tossed high to first. Jackson reached on another Reds' gaffe when his batted ball struck second baseman Morrie Rath in the ankle and caromed away to load the bases. Felsch, the anxious Teuton, reprised his role as run producer, ripping a single up the middle to score Collins and Weaver.[52] The White Sox now owned a commanding 4–0 lead and sent Slim Sallee to the showers. Ray Fisher relieved him and recorded the final two outs.

The Reds introduced themselves to the run column in the sixth inning on a Groh double and a Duncan single. The shineballer, Cicotte, surrounded the small hiccup with a strikeout, ground out, and force out to minimize the damage to a solitary run. Perhaps showing his willingness to play seriously, Cicotte used his intellect while fielding a ground ball by Roush. He probably could have nailed Groh at third, but instead opted for the sure out (throwing to first to retire Roush), knowing he had enough runs in the bank to spot the Reds just one tally.[53]

To perhaps offset the many empty seats in the stands, Reds players parked themselves at the front edge of the dugout, chiding the Sox players mercilessly. To Felsch: "Hey Hap, drop one of mine, will you? I want a triple, too." To Jackson: "Hey professor, read any good books lately?" To Schalk: "Cracker, you going to play the whole game today?" And finally, to Cicotte, there were countless jibes about throwing games.[54]

Felsch and his teammates, according to the *Washington Post*, were "aided by the psychology of competition" and "had the Reds beaten before the game was fairly underway."[55] Their two-game winning streak defied recent odds and constant ribbing by the Reds' bench.[56] Perhaps the confident Cincy players exerted more vocal energy than physical vitality, having been thoroughly stymied by Cicotte for a bulk of the contest.

The resurgence by the infamous eight did not mitigate the baked-in hostility that permeated between them and the clean, educated, dedicated crowd led by Collins and Schalk. The tension (and some would say, immaturity) was often evident during pre-game warm-ups, when the other infielders refused to throw the ball to Collins.[57] This season-long strain, coupled with the atmosphere of scandal, added to the already daunting task of defeating the Reds.

The *New York Times* sensed a changing of the World Series guard: "The high nervous tension and the overconfidence which seized Moran's players and the Redland fans has completely changed the complexion of the baseball championship battle. The Sox, two days ago a badly battered ball club, sticking doggedly in the fight by sheer gameness now have the Reds on the defensive."[58]

Gleason was gleeful over his team's latest performance. "For the second day in succession, my gang played the kind of baseball they had been playing all summer and we won another game," said Gleason. "We beat the Reds in that first inning. When we slapped in another one in the third, the game was as good as over. The Reds began crabbing right there. It has been soft sailing for them in the early games of the series. They are getting the tough stuff now."[59]

Felsch was riding a mini hot streak, having gone four for his last nine and beaming with a confidence that rivaled his manager's. Gleason would leave ole Hap in right field for game eight, and Nemo Leibold replaced Shano Collins in center. Was Felsch's offensive resurgence a direct result of the famed eight deciding to spit in the gamblers' eyes and play hard? Other than Game Five, his defense was excellent and a brief offensive slump was not unusual for any player.

For the second time in the Series, Gleason chose a pitcher who had been defeated twice (Williams in games two and five; Cicotte in games one and four). Would Gleason have gone to either pitcher multiple times had he known that they were knee-deep in the fix? Or was he merely playing the percentages by going with his top two hurlers? Speculation indicated that Williams and his wife were threatened with death prior to the game if Lefty did not play poor enough to lose the game.

Whatever the strategic intent, the White Sox were pummeled from the get-go and a glorious comeback was halted in quick, crude fashion. The Reds jumped on Lefty Williams for four first-inning runs and never looked back, capturing their first World Series championship in the modern era by beating the Sox, 10–5. Pat Moran's bunch cranked out 16 hits, five of them in the fateful first frame. Starter Hod Eller, not stellar himself, went the distance, giving up ten hits and striking out six.

In his second—and last—World Series, Felsch hit the skids in the finale, going 0-for-4 with a strikeout. Despite getting jumped on so quickly, the Sox hitters did not go down quietly. Trailing 10–1 in the bottom of the eighth, the White Sox found some dormant zip in their fading arsenal, scoring four times to slice the lead to a less embarrassing five runs. Felsch popped out to first in the inning, but a single by Eddie Collins, doubles by Buck Weaver and Joe Jackson, and a triple by Chick Gandil made the game somewhat respectable. Three, count that *three*, of the infamous crooked eight hitters got hits in the inning, a sign that the scandal that was loosely planned and jaggedly executed. Regardless, the Series would etch itself into the historical scrolls forever.

Kid Gleason: "I congratulate Pat Moran. His team gave him everything they had. He deserved to win. I was terribly disappointed. I tell you, those Reds haven't any business beating a team like the White Sox. We played the worst baseball in all but a couple of games, that we have played all year. I don't know yet what was the matter. Something was wrong. I didn't like the betting odds. I wish no one had ever bet a dollar on the team."[60]

For the record, the betting odds had shifted in the White Sox's favor prior to the start of Game Eight. Momentum will do such a thing in the world of sports gambling, but rarely does it explain or quantify the heart and soul of a ballplayer. The Chicago White Sox—all of them—got serious towards the latter stages of the Series. The smell of dirty baseballs was diluted by the re-emergence of a team that was good enough to take their second championship in three seasons.

As for Felsch, we will never know what floated in his head as the Series approached. Baseball was his life, and playing without full effort was not in his DNA. His on-field performance was not his brightest, but also did not constitute a blatant attempt to embarrass the game. With scant video coverage of the Series, we are left with newspaper accounts and other works that have attempted to nail down additional morsels of evidence. None of that mattered as Felsch's life would undergo a sad shift going forward.

11

Happy Peak, Career Feats

We do not trust cashiers half as much, or diplomats, or policemen, or physicians, as we trust an outfielder or shortstop.

—*The Nation*, 1920

Two days after the Series ended, reports surfaced that Charles Comiskey had offered a $20,000 reward to anybody who had a clue that a player deliberately attempted to throw the Series. Later on, we will reveal why this was farcical. For now, the Old Roman had this to say: "There is always some scandal of some kind following a big sporting event like the World Series. These yarps [rumors] are manufactured out of whole cloth and grow out of bitterness due to losing wagers."[1]

"I believe my boys fought the battle of the recent World Series on the level, as they have always done," said the Old Roman. "And I would be the first to want information to the contrary—if there be any. I would give $20,000 to anyone unearthing information to that effect."

Nearly an entire calendar year elapsed before the proverbial "shit" hit the fan. The year 1920 was a turning point for the game of baseball as the Deadball Era waved goodbye. But a few months before the season began, reporter Hugh Fullerton continued his hunt for the truth and digging for information. This story, if not the first, was one of the most revealing collections of morsels that exposed Charles Comiskey as a pretentious player in the quest for full disclosure.

In Milwaukee, Operative #1; Chicago private detective John Hunter's investigative minion—hired by Comiskey[2]—conducted surveillance of Felsch's known hangouts, mostly North Side watering holes. Felsch had since moved from his parents' house on North 26th Street to his in-laws' on Teutonia Avenue. The eight-room residence housed Happy's in-laws, his wife Marie, her sister, and her sister's two children. While Felsch was on a duck hunting trip—one of his customary off-season pleasures—the operative gained access to

Felsch's residence, masquerading as someone who was renting one of the available rooms. Hunter concluded that Felsch's recent $1,800 Hupmobile purchase was not consistent with his meager, $22-per-month apartment dwelling.[3]

After the investigations, Comiskey had no choice but to mail the players' checks. Was this a Comiskey façade, feigning disgust over the lack of cleanliness in his sport? Did he or organized baseball try hard enough to break the seal on this secret, remaining loyal to the perception that the game was clean? Curiously, Felsch was offered a rather generous contract—a $3,000 raise—for the 1920 season, perhaps in exchange for his uninterrupted silence. If Comiskey had, as he stated, believed his players were on the "up and up" during the Series, was there really a need to launch an investigation? If he was truly angry over what allegedly occurred, would he have given those players raises?

When Fullerton approached the Chicago papers about publishing his findings, they balked, supposedly out of fears over libel laws. The *New York Evening World* agreed to buy the story but demanded that it be watered down. On December 15, his first article was published, but was true to form of the "just enough but not too hot" revelation strategy. He would write a lot more, with names, less than a year later.[4]

If there was a smidgen of doubt that much of the baseball media was sympathetic towards the baseball brass and hypercritical of the Fullerton types who attempted to shed light on this fiasco, one need look no further than the bastions of baseball coverage of the time, *The Sporting News* and *Baseball Magazine*. These respected magazines were also undeniable mouth pieces for Comiskey, the other owners, and Ban Johnson himself.[5] Faces looked the other way and Fullerton was castigated. There was a blatant dichotomy in these publications' coverage. On the one hand, they printed countless treatises on the evils of gambling. *The Sporting News* warned that the "cancer" of gambling had to be addressed. On the other hand, they stopped well short of indicting individuals within the game.[6]

The spring of 1920 brought the usual unabated hope of a pennant race, along with George "Herman" Ruth changing teams from Boston to New York in a blockbuster deal that netted the Red Sox a staggering $125,000. For Red Sox fans, this deal would rubber-stamp decades of self-pity (brought on by the absence of a World Series title), jinx talk and general whining. The Lively Ball Era made its debut, thanks in part to the A. J. Reach Company, manufacturer of the American League ball. Reach and Spalding, the maker of National League balls, dumped the American yarn for the much stronger Australian variety. This allowed for more tightly wound balls, which made them harder and more bouncy. Other changes included:

> • Umpires were instructed to replace balls more often; the days of tobacco-juiced, sweat-laden baseballs used for inning upon inning were done.

Felsch before a game, 1920. Rumors followed the Whites Sox throughout the 1920 season, and by September, two members of the team, Ciccotte and Jackson, had confessed their involvement to a grand jury (George Grantham Bain Collection, Library of Congress).

+ Trick pitches were forbidden, although some veterans were grandfathered in.
+ More fences were installed at ballparks to better separate the fans from the playing action.[7]

On March 25, during spring training, third baseman Buck Weaver left the club to meet with Charles Comiskey. The reason? He wanted a raise. Less than a year prior, he had signed a three-year deal. Demanding a boost in salary, old Buck said that if he did not get one, he would demand a trade to the New York Yankees.[8] Unfortunately, the noose formally called the "reserve clause" was at the beck-and-call of owners and the Old Roman was not going to succumb to such demands.

For Oscar Felsch, the 1920 season would become his best by far. His first slump came soon with little warning as termites ate their way through his bat and coincided with a dip in numbers. But from May 4 until the end of the season, Felsch would not fall south of .300 once; in fact, he wouldn't even come close. The sting of the 1919 season seemed to dissipate in the off-season, having little to no effect on the Milwaukee Mauler as he continued his journey towards major league stardom.

Gleason's lineup looked virtually identical to his 1919 version, save for first base. Chick Gandil, who turned 32 that January, did not return after being turned down by Comiskey when the hotheaded slugger demanded that his salary be jacked up to $6,500. Gandil remained in California and retired from baseball, playing semi-pro ball for the Elks Club and earning $75 per game. The White Sox replaced him initially with Ted Jourdan, a journeyman who had not played a lick in 1919. There were doubts about whether Jourdan could handle the stick at this level.

As a final warm-up for the regular season, the White Sox played Felsch's former team, the AA Milwaukee Brewers, in a couple of exhibition games. Teammates Nemo Leibold and Ray Schalk, former Brewers themselves, also returned. Playing in front of numerous friends and relatives, Happy the hometown boy went 2-for-4 with a double, single, run scored, and two RBI in a 6–2 White Sox victory.

The *Milwaukee Journal* wrote that Felsch "decided in the sixth round that Gleason's hopes had amassed a sufficient number of zeroes on the scoreboard. When Happy arrives at such a conclusion, something is bound to happen. And it did." After Happy's double scored Eddie Collins and Joe Jackson, new first-sacker Ted Jourdan singled Felsch home. Pitcher Red Faber stymied the Brewers until the seventh, when Milwaukee scored their first run.[9]

The Brewers bounced back the next day, blanking the White Sox, 1–0, in ten innings. After a two-out single by Dutch Hauser, Alex Gaston hit a long blast "over Happy Felsch's classic dome." Two gents named McWeeney and

Howard outdueled the famous Eddie Cicotte and the lesser-known Roy Wilkinson. Paul Smith, the 200-pound Milwaukee center fielder, smashed two hits off the Sox. "It must be said that he puts his entire weight back of his hits," said the *Milwaukee Journal*.[10]

The White Sox began the 1920 season by winning ten of their first 12 games. In those games, Felsch batted .286/.333/.393, while missing four games. On May 7, he went 3-for-4 with a home run (his second of the season) and two RBI, raising his average to .357. He continued to terrorize pitchers the rest of the summer, mostly the same ones he had faced in prior seasons.

While major league baseball entered another decade of play, Rube Foster, longtime owner of black barnstorming teams, demanded that "Jim Crow baseball" outfits learn from organized baseball and conjure up more effort into true structure, one that eliminated player raiding and instituted a saner system of player procurement and movement. Faced with the reality of exclusion, Foster encouraged self-empowerment.

> "This will be the last time I will ever try and interest Colored club owners to get together on some working basis," wrote Foster in a *Chicago Defender* editorial. "I have so often been refused the necessary capital, not desiring to give to others the chance of monopolizing Colored baseball, but they are not going to continue to wait on me with their money. They can do so and leave me where I am. I made the effort; it is now up to the ones that expect to permanently figure in baseball to get together."[11]

While the various regions sought to establish Negro Leagues circuits, Foster was successful in starting the Negro National League, which included a team he managed himself, the famed Chicago American Giants. From 1920 to the league's demise in 1931, Foster's Giants captured five championships, one better than the Kansas City Monarchs and two more than the St. Louis Stars. In 1937, the Negro American League opened and included some of the old players from its National League counterpart. This seminal "black ball" moment in 1920 still relinquished power and attention to organized baseball.

After their hot start heading into May, the White Sox cooled off, dropping seven of their next eight games. Lefty Williams shook off his disastrous performance in the World Series by winning his first six starts with a 1.26 ERA. His sixth win, 6–1 over the Cleveland Indians, included Felsch's 3-for-4 outburst. The big blast came in the second inning off of right-hander Ray Caldwell; the clout sailed so far over the left-field fence that, if split into two drives, might have equaled two homers.

In 1920, Felsch found his power stroke again, hitting homers in back-to-back games on May 18–19 against the Boston Red Sox. This rejuvenated potency fed his slugging percentage rather nicely, and it climbed into the .600+ range for a lengthy stretch heading into summer. As of May 20, he had more homers (five) than doubles (four). Not being limited to reaching first base only, Felsch sacrificed his stolen base talents, swiping only one thus far in six attempts.

The South-Siders lost four straight, two each at Cleveland and New York. Felsch did not let up, going 6-for-16 in those games, hiking his numbers to .362/ .413/.569. The entire offense heated up towards the end of May. In a five-game stretch that netted four victories, the White Sox bats amassed 45 runs, including the game they lost, in which they managed just one tally. In a 10–2 pasting of the A's that brought their record to 17–12, Felsch had his best game yet, going 3-for-5 with his sixth home run and four more RBI. The Sox cranked out 15 hits in that game, with Eddie Murphy and Buck Weaver getting four apiece.

"Hap Felsch didn't get quite as many swats [as Murphy and Weaver], but did hit for more bases, his chief wallop being a home run that landed into the bleacher seats in the seventh," wrote Irving Vaughn of the *Chicago Tribune*. "Hap now has six homers for the season. Babe Ruth boasts the same number."[12] Anytime a player could keep pace with the Big Bambino in any offensive category—at any point in a season—was an achievement gladly savored.

Felsch hit safely in 13 of his next 15 games. The White Sox found themselves battling in more slugfests than in recent seasons. In a doubleheader split at Cleveland at the end of May, the Indians hit a dozen doubles, dropping the first game to the Sox, 8–7, despite ten doubles, then routing Gleason's boys in the nightcap, 8–1. The *Chicago Tribune* called the Sox's game one performance "comical" and wrote that they were darn lucky to salvage a victory after "throwing the ball all over the field."[13]

Felsch went 3-for-9 in the two games with a double and two more RBI. The sizzling start was matched by Shoeless Joe Jackson's contact-hitting, high-average ways. After a 4-for-5 performance on June 2 in a 7–3 win over the St, Louis Browns, Jackson's batting average leaped to .371 with a .427 OBP and .538 slugging percentage. Add Buck Weaver's .349/.398/.430 line and the middle of the White Sox lineup was striking great fear into their opponents. Felsch, in his customary five-spot in the lineup, took full advantage of his RBI opportunities. In June alone, he cranked out an impressive 35 hits, with 22 runs scored, 22 RBI, and 15 extra-base hits (including two triples in one game on June 13).

With Felsch enjoying his best season to date, one cannot resist wondering whether he gave any thought of the 1919 post-season during this perpetually torrid stretch in 1920. If he harbored any lingering concerns over what transpired in the World Series, would it be probable for him to have this kind of success in 1920? Did his minimal involvement in the machinations of the scandal allow his mind to focus squarely on his baseball playing?

The White Sox confronted some struggles and fell six games back in the pennant race. Felsch extended a 14-game hitting streak on July 17 in an absolute disaster of a game for the Sox, a 20–5 drubbing by the Yankees. Felsch went 2-for-5 with four RBI but it made little difference in this whooping. An eight-run frame by the Bronx Bombers capped a dominating performance that chased starter Eddie Cicotte after the fifth inning. New York starter Carl Mays went the distance but was far from perfect, giving up 15 hits.

The *Chicago Tribune* found it ironic that the onslaught did not include a Babe Ruth home run (the Big Bambino did go 3-for-5 with three RBI). "Just how Babe Ruth can live through a ball game in which the Yankees got 21 base hits and not make a home run that would break the world's record is one of the most comical things about the alleged ball game played today between the White Sox and Yankees."[14]

Trying his best to keep his team in the race, Felsch began another 14-game hitting streak on July 23. He went 22-for-55 in that stretch (a .400 clip) with 12 RBI and seven extra-base hits. In that span, the White Sox played three ten-inning games in five days. The team went 10–4 during that streak but was still 4½ games out of first. With the Indians boosting their AL lead to four games over the Yankees, the Sox set their sights on second place.

The 1920 season did not escape the rancid smell and ire of gambling, suspicion, and occasional accusations. In late July, *Chicago Tribune* writer Jim Crusinberry joined Ring Lardner in a hotel room. Soon, the phone rang. It was Sox manager Kid Gleason. "Come over to Dinty Moore's [a popular sports hangout]," said Gleason quietly. "I'm at the bar with Abe Attell and he's talking, and I want you to hear it. I won't let on that I know you."[15]

The two scribes arrived, parked themselves at the bar, ordered drinks, and listened to Gleason deliver questions to Attell. "So it was Arnold Rothstein who had put up the dough for the fix?" asked Gleason. Attell nodded his head in affirmation, then said: "That was it, all right. You know, Kid, I hated to do that to you, but I thought that I was going to make a bundle, and I needed it." Crusinberry returned to the hotel with a goal of writing a story. After Lardner questioned him over who would run such a piece, Crusinberry wrote it anyway and submitted the piece to his editor. The story was quickly squashed amidst the familiar fears of libel. Once again, the lingering story of scandal was dealt an unfair blow, and true revelation, with names, dates, and places, would be written off for another couple of months.[16]

Before the 1920 season started, a player from the Cubs' 1919 club, Lee Magee, found a hard time hooking up with another team. Magee had been mentioned as a cohort in Hal Chase's gambling shenanigans in what developed into the first solid public revelation of gambling involving major league players.[17]

On the field, Felsch was smacking the baseball all over the confines. On August 9, now in third place, five games back of Cleveland, the White Sox played their first of three doubleheaders in less than two weeks. This presented a glorious opportunity to stack up wins in a short time, possibly enough to overtake the Tribe. In a six-game stretch in Detroit and Philadelphia, Felsch had multiple hits in five of those games, going 11-for-25.

Heading into the dog days of late summer, the White Sox portrayed as much confidence as they had in recent seasons. Kid Gleason and some of the players felt that, during a recent series in New York, the Gotham media was selling their team short, writing that it was the Cleveland Indians that scared the Yankees the most. *The Sporting News,* in its infinite quest for objectivity, called the White Sox's dominance over bottom-feeders Detroit and Washington "scandalous," as if those clubs made no effort at all to beat the South-Siders. The New York media hinted that teams played extra hard against the Yankees, but not against the Indians. This idle gossip did not deter the White Sox or Felsch down the stretch.

On August 15, in a 10–3 blowout of the Detroit Tigers, every player in the White Sox lineup managed at least one hit. Eddie Collins, Swede Risberg, and Felsch had two apiece (both of Felsch's were doubles), and pitcher Eddie Cicotte scored after driving in a run with a double. The shine-baller returned on two days' rest and tossed a gem against the hapless Tigers, who were now 41–67 on the disappointing season. Although Cicotte struggled early, he allowed no base runners after the fifth inning, earning his 17th win of the season against eight losses.[18]

One day later, on August 16, tragedy struck the game of baseball when New York starter Carl Mays' fastball struck Cleveland Indians shortstop Ray Chapman in the temple, producing a loud crack that reverberated throughout Yankee Stadium. Mays, thinking the ball hit the bat, scooped up the ball and tossed it to first. After stumbling off the field, Chapman was taken to a hospital, where surgeons operated and discovered a skull fracture. The 29-year-old, eight-year veteran died the next morning. Mays had stayed in the game and continued to pitch until being relieved in the ninth. Cleveland won the somber game, 4–3.[19]

Outcries about the fateful beanball accompanied urgent demands for Carl Mays to be ousted from the game. But there appeared to be no motive for Mays to plunk Chapman. His signature submarine pitch, along with Chapman's propensity to crowd the plate, yielded a frightful calamity in the sport's history. Mays was not averse to delivering chin music to batters who dared take part of home plate from him. This cat-and-mouse strategy was simply part of the game.[20]

All season, this was clearly a three-horse race between Cleveland, Chicago and New York. The White Sox were primed to swipe the lead away from the Indians. Next up were the last-place Athletics and the arm of rookie Eddie Rommel. The 6'2", 197-lb. hurler employed a fastball, curve, and occasional

Felsch ready for action, 1920. Despite increasingly intense media scrutiny, the White Sox played well, finishing two games behind the pennant-winning Indians, and Felsch had a career high year at the plate (George Grantham Bain Collection, Library of Congress).

knuckleball. (It was said that his short fingers gave Rommel a natural knuckleball feel.)[21] On this night, the Sox hitters had no answer to any pitch he heaved up to the plate. In a 1–0 shutout of the Chicago boppers, Rommel gave up just five hits, walked three, and struck out one. Felsch put up a rare 0-for-4 and would have to wait until the next day to connect.

On August 21, the Cleveland Indians were swept in a doubleheader by the Boston Red Sox, 12–0 and 4–0. A day before, the White Sox had swiped two from Philadelphia, 7–4 and 5–2. This gave the Sox sole possession of first place in the American League for the first time since May. Felsch went 5-for-8, raising his batting average to .329 on the year. "Eddie Collins, [Amos] Strunk, Weaver, Felsch, and J. Collins carried all the heavy artillery," reported the *Chicago Tribune*.[22] The next day, Cleveland split a twin bill with the Red Sox while Gleason's men defeated the Washington Senators.

As August shut its doors in 1920, one could not fit a slivered almond between the White Sox and the Indians. However, Chicago picked the wrong time to register its longest losing streak of the season: seven games. This not only eradicated their advantage, but also allowed the previously cold New York Yankees to rejoin the intense race. The White Sox now teetered in third place, though just one game out of first. Felsch kept up his end of the bargain, going 9-for-29 during the skid, a .310 clip. The opposing culprits were the aforementioned Yankees, Boston Red Sox, and the lowly St. Louis Browns. Even before the Yanks took care of the Sox this time around, they had already clinched the season series between the two clubs.[23]

Closing out August was not just about hits, runs, walks, and strikeouts. After a 7–3 loss to the Boston Red Sox on August 31, *Boston Globe* sportswriter Jim O'Leary wrote that the White Sox had played just like they had in the 1919 World Series. The writer was perplexed over Cicotte's unusual penchant for giving up hits when he got two strikes on a batter. When the team returned to Chicago, Eddie Collins approached Charles Comiskey to assert that the game had been thrown, fixed, sacrificed for additional greed. Eliot Asinof wrote in *Eight Men Out* that Comiskey barely reacted and, worse yet, took zero action.[24]

The day before the unfortunate slide, the White Sox scored a season's best 16 runs in a thumping of the surging Yankees. Felsch logged a 3-for-5 day with three runs scored, four RBI, and his 32nd two-bagger of the season. Babe Ruth hit is 44th home run of the season for the Yankees. He would finish 1920 with a new record of 54 home runs, which he would break the following season. The 17-hit barrage off three New York hurlers could have been a springboard into seizing control of the pack again. Instead, the Sox scraped up just 16 runs in the seven losses, getting blanked in back-to-back contests by the Yanks and Bosox. It would soon become too late.

The 1920 season closed with the familiar cakewalks of the past for Gleason, and the effort to repeat as league champs proved daunting. As his team remained in a dogfight for American League supremacy, Oscar Felsch did not ease up on his unforgiving assault on the poor mound saps that could not seem to find a way to solve his mighty stick. Beginning on September 7, Felsch hit safely in the next 12 games. The Sox followed up the losing streak by grabbing wins in seven of the next eight games. After defeating Cleveland on September 11, the Yankees held a half-game lead over the Indians and White Sox.

Despite their persistence in staying in the pennant race, with several players, including Felsch, having wonderful seasons, the taint of scorn that festered off and on during the 1920 campaign was just as relentless and unforgiving as the White Sox's play on the field. Historian Victor Luhrs wrote: "Had every major leaguer who bet on a game or offered or received a 'gift' in 1920 been banned on a given day, sixteen major league baseball parks might as well have closed down the next day."[25]

Bill Veeck, Sr., owner of the Chicago Cubs, received a telegram stating that a recent game between his club and the Philadelphia Phillies had been rigged. The story had broken on September 4 and three days later, a special Cook County grand jury convened. Before Judge Charles McDonald, the legal throng would investigate this allegation and baseball gambling in general. Leading the investigation was District Attorney Maclay Hoyne, who insisted that he would "bring to justice the ring of gamblers whose operations threaten to besmirch baseball."[26]

After soliciting the aid of a detective agency, Veeck asked for help from the Chicago chapter of the Baseball Writers' Association of America, naming Sam Hall of the *Chicago Herald and Examiner* the chairman of the effort. "Were the reflection on the Cubs the only matter entering the affair, I would not call for such assistance," said Veeck. "But it is more serious than that. Baseball is much greater than the mere standing of the Cubs, and there must be no question as to its honesty. If your investigation develops that there is one man on the team who has done a single dishonest act, you will have rendered a service so great that its value cannot be estimated."[27]

The beat writer for the *Chicago Tribune*, Jim Crusinberry, was sick up to his eyeballs of the total lack of action on what had become a rampant sea of gambling escapades on ball games, with blood-sucking bookies swarming like mosquitoes around ballparks, hotels, and dens of iniquity. Crusinberry called Fred M. Loomis, a prominent Chicago businessman, hoping that word from such a well-known local figure would stir up the necessary outrage that had been lacking. Loomis insisted that the statement carry an angry tone, to be written by Crusinberry over Loomis' signature.[28]

In the last month of the season, Felsch's reign of terror on American League pitchers did not cease. The White Sox began a crucial three-game set against the Yankees on September 16. They sat 2½ games short of first-place New York in third place, 1½ game behind second-place Cleveland. In the opener, behind Dickey Kerr, the Sox squashed the easterners, 8–3. Felsch went just 1-for-5 in the game, but scored two runs and drove in another. The Sox jumped on Yankees starter Jack Quinn for four runs in the second and never looked back. Every player in the lineup except Ray Schalk got a hit.

The White Sox won again the next day, 6–4, then completed a three-game sweep with a 15–9 slugfest triumph. Felsch went 4-for-4 in the final game, scored four times, and knocked in three runs with two singles, his 38th double, his 15th triple and a bases on balls. Gleason's lumber company tallied a season-high 22 hits with Weaver and Shano Collins joining Felsch in the four-hit club. In the meantime, the Indians were beating up on the Senators, and when the sun came up on September 20, the Sox had vaulted into second place ahead of the Yanks, 1½ games behind the league-leading Indians.

On September 24, the Sox were blanked by the Indians 2–0, Babe Ruth smacked his 55th home run of the season for the Yankees, eclipsing his own record from the year before, and an unexpected shoe dropped in the developing saga of corruption. In the Chicago Criminal Courts Building, New York Giants pitcher John "Rube" Benton told the legal eagles that Hal Chase and Buck Herzog had offered him $800 the previous September to throw a game. Although nothing came of this particular story, Benton later returned and testified that he knew of the 1919 World Series fix and that he, from a tip received from Hal Chase, won $3,800. Meanwhile, former Cubs owner Charles Weeghman testified that he had spent the 1919 World Series in Saratoga, NY, where an old friend, Monte Tennes, had told him that Abe Attell recommended that he bet heavily on Cincinnati. Asked why he had not told anybody about this previously, Weeghman simply said that it must have slipped his mind.[29]

The startling news slowly and subtly leaked out of the grand jury. On September 25, a story carried in the Chicago Tribune meticulously detailed the principals of the alleged fix, naming Oscar Felsch and the reputed Chicago eight: Weaver, Jackson, Risberg, Gandil, Williams, Cicotte and McMullin. On September 27, James Isaminger wrote a story for the Philadelphia North American entitled: "Gambler Promised White Sox $100,000 to Lose." Isaminger's source for the story was none other than small-time gambler Bill Maharg, who willingly outlined the entire deal. The day after the story broke, Eddie Cicotte and Shoeless Joe Jackson were the first to sing their confessionary tunes to a Chicago grand jury, on September 28, 1920.[30]

On the same day, a story ran in the Chicago Tribune stating that Charles

Comiskey admitted to being convinced that someone had "fixed" some of his players. He conveniently joined forces with National League President John Heydler. Why not with American League chief Ban Johnson? It had been public knowledge that the two were not on speaking terms and had been involved in several verbal scuffles long before this. Heydler said that Comiskey was "all broken up" after the first game of the 1919 World Series. This curious sympathy notwithstanding, the proverbial shit hit the fan, and the Chicago White Sox would finish two games behind the new American League champion Cleveland Indians.[31]

Happy Felsch finished his season on September 26 with a flurry, going 2-for-2 with a run scored and an RBI in an 8–1 victory over the Detroit Tigers. But the entire season, his crowning achievement, took a back seat to the lingering realities of scandal. His final numbers, .338/.384/.540 with 15 homers and 115 RBI, were all career highs.

12

Say It Ain't So, Oscar

The gamblers had drawn a lemon when they hooked Happy.

—Victor Luhrs in *The Great Baseball Mystery:*
The 1919 World Series

Novelist James T. Farrell, 16 years old at the time, later recounted one of the most infamous (and disputed) events, which he remembered happening after the September 27, 1920, game transpired:

I had a box seat for the game on Sunday, September 27. It was a muggy, sunless day. I went to the park early and watched the players take their hitting and fielding practice. It looked the same as always. They took their turns at the plate. They had their turns on the field. They seemed calm, no different, no different than they had been on other days before the scandal had broken. The crowd was friendly to them and some cheered. But a subtle gloom hung over the fans. The atmosphere of the park was like the muggy weather. The game began. Cicotte pitched. The suspected players got a hand when they came to bat. The White Sox won easily. Cicotte was master of the Detroit Tigers that day. One could only wish that he had pitched as well in the 1919 Series.

After the game, I went under the stands and stood near the steps leading down from the White Sox clubhouse. A small crowd always collected there to watch the players leave. But on this particular Sunday, there were about 200 to 250 boys waiting. Some of the players left. Lefty Williams, wearing a blue suit and gray cap, was one, and some of the fans called to him. A few others came down the steps. And then Joe Jackson and Happy Felsch appeared. They were both big men. Jackson was the taller of the two and Felsch the broader. They were sportively dressed in gray silk shirts, white duck trousers and white shoes. They came down the clubhouse steps slowly, their faces masked by impassivity.

A few fans called to them, but they gave no acknowledgment to these greetings. They turned and started to walk away. Spontaneously, the crowd followed in a slow, disorderly manner. I went with the crowd and trailed about five feet behind Jackson and Felsch. They walked somewhat slowly. A fan called out:

"It ain't true, Joe."

The two suspected players did not turn back. They walked on, slowly. The crowd took up this cry and more than once, men and boys called out and repeated:

"It ain't true, Joe."

This call followed Jackson and Felsch as they walked all the way under the stands to the Thirty-Fifth Street side of the ball park. They left the park and went for their parked cars in a soccer field behind the right field bleachers. I waited by the exit of the soccer field. Many others also waited. Soon Felsch and Jackson drove out in their sportive roadsters, through a double file of silent fans.

I went back to the clubhouse. But most of the players had gone. It was getting dark. A ball park seems very lonely after the crowd has cleared away. Never was a ball park lonelier or more deserted for me than on that September Sunday afternoon, It was almost dark. I went home. I sensed it was true. But I hoped that the players would get out of this and be allowed to go on playing.[1]

The mythological phrase often romantically uttered from the story above is that the little kid uttered "Say it ain't so, Joe." Although the accuracy of the quote was debunked soon after, the historical association of those five words has endured for almost 100 years. The precious link of a little boy to his unconditional hero worship gives this story legs and, despite its factual emptiness, there is little doubt that one or more youngsters spoke to Jackson that day, a backdrop for the scandal itself and the fight to clear Jackson from guilt even today.

Manager Kid Gleason told Comiskey that Eddie Cicotte was extremely upset and ready to spill the beans, or at least his version of them. The two went downtown to the law offices of Alfred Austrian. Cicotte was asked to sit in the waiting room, which he did for nearly 20 minutes, his hands sweating profusely over shaky nerves. Heading into Austrian's office, tired and beaten, Cicotte broke down in front of him, Comiskey, and Gleason.

"I know what you want to know—I know," he sobbed. "Yeah, we were crooked, we were crooked." Comiskey, apparently without looking at Cicotte, blurted out: "Don't tell me. Tell it to the grand jury."[2] Cicotte continued as if he had not heard Comiskey at all. "I don't know what you'd think of me, but I got to tell you how I double crossed you. Mr. Comiskey. I did double cross you. I'm a crook. I got $10,000 for being a crook."[3]

A grand jury's chief purpose is to consider evidence brought against the accused; they do not determine guilt or innocence but only whether further prosecution is warranted. One of the main differences between this and a jury trial is secrecy; the only participants are the accused, the grand jury members, a stenographer, clerical personnel, and the prosecutor. The secrecy does not extend to the purpose of the hearing, meaning people on the outside know that it is occurring, nor are the witnesses a secret. The other principle difference, and this is huge, is that the only side presenting its case is the government.[4]

As William Lamb pointed out in *Black Sox in the Courtroom*, in this particular grand jury hearing, with the public exposure afforded by professional baseball players, the oath of secrecy encouraged multiple leaks. As Lamb writes: "In hindsight, perhaps the most remarkable aspect of the grand jury proceedings in the Black Sox case was the reaction to its unorthodox modus operandi. There was none."[5]

Cook County Circuit Judge Charles A. McDonald, first elected to the court in 1920, was a huge baseball fan and sternly alerted the Cook County grand jury of the gravity of the scandal. Following the game, he read the newspaper accounts of the scandal and was understandably zealous in wiping out the corruption in the game, stating that this was "a matter of public importance which is the duty of the grand jury to investigate thoroughly . . . so that everyone implicated in the infamous conspiracy to bring the national game of baseball into disrepute and to injure the business of the respective club owners and their individual players should be brought to speedy justice and exposed to public scorn."[6]

In light of the revelation, or rather, the publicity behind it, Charles Comiskey sent telegrams to all eight suspected players, complete with suspensions. The telegrams read:

> You and each of you, are hereby notified of your indefinite suspension as a member of the Chicago American League Baseball Club. Your suspension is brought about by information which has just come to me, directly involving you and each of you in the baseball scandal now being investigated by the Grand Jury of Cook County, resulting from the World Series of 1919.
> "If you are innocent of any wrongdoing, you and each of you will be reinstated; if you are guilty, you will be retired from organized baseball for the rest of your lives if I can accomplish it.
> Until there is finality to this investigation, it is due to the public I take this action even though it costs Chicago the pennant.
> Chicago American League BB Club
> by Charles A. Comiskey[7]

Major league fans would never again see these players on major league diamonds. On September 29, Happy Felsch's hometown newspaper, the *Milwaukee Sentinel*, ran this biting headline on page 1: "*Prison Terms Now Looming for Indicted Sox Players.*"[8]

Felsch completed his best season by far, hitting .338/.384/.540. All three metrics bested all previous seasons; his composite previous highs were .308 (1917)/.352 (1917)/.428 (1919). If he was preoccupied with what happened in 1919 or even heavily involved in any fixing during the 1920 season, his performance did not show it. This doesn't imply that the wheels of guilt were not spinning inside his head. There is ample evidence in today's game, particularly the so-called "steroid era," that lying, concealment, and denial are common attributes of some professional athletes, as well as those of us in the normal world.

The boulder of guilt slid down the mountain at a steady pace, striking the eight men one by one, leaving trails of doubt, conflicting details, and shameful confessions. Each accusation of wrong-doing piled on top of the previous one, and the media had a field day. Reporters inquired about the backbone of the fix, not limiting their curiosity to the players. They wanted the entire gambling ring to endure the rampant publicity heaped upon the White Sox players, to drag everyone involved slowly through the mud.[9]

Former star and future Hall of Famer Honus Wagner, who participated in two World Series with the Pittsburgh Pirates, was stunned by the news. The Flying Dutchman hoped that this stain on the game would force further action to cleanse it. "I am for the thing that will bring about conditions that mean the rescue of baseball from the fate that has befallen wrestling, boxing, and horse racing," said Wagner. "There should be quick retribution for every player who has allowed himself to be reached, while the tempters of the players should be railroaded along with Cicotte and others of the White Sox who have betrayed their employers and fellow players." Chick Gandil, laid up in the hospital with appendicitis, issued this statement through his doctor: "There is absolutely nothing I care to say regarding the charges."[10]

A Federal grand jury might convene after the disclosures made in Chicago, according to Assistant District Attorney Thomas Morrow. On Monday, October 4, the new Hamilton County grand jury was summoned to look into the circumstances surrounding the fix.[11] The defiant vow of silence exhibited by Gandil and others would not last long (Gandil would lie through his teeth throughout). Felsch did not delay singing his own confessionary document. The world of Oscar Emil "Happy" Felsch would take a tragic spin.

At the *Chicago American* newspaper offices, young reporter Harry Reutlinger was curious as to why the information surrounding the scandal was a jumbled mess, lacking real clarity and definition. His reporter's instincts knew to snag a source to obtain the real scoop. Not a sports guy, he waltzed over to the sports desk and asked the guys who was the dumbest player on the White Sox team. The answer was Oscar Felsch. "The one they call 'Happy'?" asked Reutlinger. "That's right," replied one of the guys."[12]

Baseball writers thought that Felsch possessed an even lower IQ than Shoeless Joe Jackson. Writer Victor Luhrs: "Happy absorbed some education and could read and write. But like a sage in possession of a split atom, he didn't know what to do with his awesome knowledge. None of these boys were exactly threats to King Solomon's throne on the basis of wisdom." According to Luhrs, Felsch, while admitting guilt, had not intentionally flubbed plays, and "the gamblers had drawn a lemon when they hooked Happy."[13]

Reutlinger was told he could find Felsch at the Warner Hotel. On September 29, 1920, the inquisitive reporter accompanied his pen and pad with one of Felsch's favorite libations, a bottle of Scotch whiskey that Reutlinger concealed inside a newspaper. Felsch answered the door wearing a bathrobe. Seeing that Felsch was nursing a bad toe, the opportunistic reporter said, "Hap, I can cure that bad toe. All we need is a couple of glasses." Noticing no objection from Felsch, Reutlinger released the bottle from the makeshift package and the interview commenced.[14]

With drink in hand, Felsch poured out his heart as fast as the hard stuff slid down his gullet, his confession ripe with contradiction, dismissal, admission, and self-pity. Felsch was the fourth player to confess but the first player to talk outside the bounds of the legal system. He opened the interview with this statement: "Well, the beans are all spilled and I think I am through with baseball. I got my five thousand and I suppose the others got theirs too. If you say anything about me, don't make it appear that I am trying to put up an alibi. I'm not. I'm as guilty as any of them. We were all in it alike."

Throughout the interview, while consuming volumes of whiskey, he openly admitted to taking money and attending meetings, but conveyed no specifics about so-called flubbed plays on the field. In addition, very few specifics were offered (certainly much fewer than offered by Cicotte), mostly because he was largely in the dark about anything that might have transpired along the way. What appeared universal in the minds of all the accused players was that they felt double-crossed by the gamblers from Game One on. For some, this was corroborated by their suddenly stellar play in Game Three and decent effort in subsequent games.

"It looked easy to me, too," Felsch told Reutlinger. "It's just as easy for a good ballplayer to miss a ball as it is to catch it—just a slow start or a stumble at the right time or a slow throw and the job is done. But you can't get away with that stuff indefinitely. You may be able to fool the public, but you can't fool yourself."[15]

These passages certainly point to Felsch's mindset during the Series. Taking anything these eight players said as gospel truth is naïve at best, although it appears that Cicotte's confession was contrite. For Felsch, one wonders whether, if he had done his best to help blow the Series for the White Sox, he would have nothing else to lose had he sung like a canary. He talked in generalities, but whether or not these ideas were put into motion by him during the Series is still a mystery.

Wrapping up the interview, Reutlinger asked Felsch about how Cicotte got $10,000, more than the other players. Felsch's answer not only solidified how gullible and naïve these men were, but also how they were involved to disparate degrees—some actively sought out their piece of the pie, while others sat back passively, hoping that more money would fall into their laps.

"Because he was wise enough to stand pat for it, that's all," said Felsch. "Cicotte had brains. The rest of us roundheads just took their word for the proposition that we were to get an even split on the hundred thousand. Cicotte was going to make sure of his share from the jump off. He made them come across with it."

Felsch closed with a comment on the futility of the entire scandal and an open admission of how vulnerable these players were to the shrewdness of the gamblers, the people working on behalf of the gamblers, and to one of their own, Arnold "Chick" Gandil. Lost in trying to analyze every single word of these confessions, or pseudo-confessions, is the reality that eloquence was not common for these guys.

"I got my five thousand dollars," said a defeated Felsch. "I could have got just about as much by being on the level if the Sox had won the Series. And now, I'm out of baseball—the only profession I knew anything about, and a lot of gamblers have gotten rich. The joke seems to be on us."[16]

If one did not know that Felsch had reached only the sixth grade—probably reaching that academic level by the skin of his teeth—one could make the case that the interview with Reutlinger was a pack of genius rolled up in a sea of confusion. Conversely, this was a simple, regretful fellow who became painfully aware of his fate as a baseball player. Felsch's claim that Comiskey had treated him fairly was odd since he once quit the team over a contract dispute. Perhaps he thought the reporter, not being a sports guy, was simply unaware of the dirty details of money squabbles between players and owners. More likely, Felsch's babble was simply a desire to blurt out general bromides about the fix, without citing specific events or plays.

Baseball historian Harold Seymour wondered if Felsch and Jackson were so open with their confessions because they were trying to convince the gamblers that they had made an effort to fix the Series. Stories of the players being threatened by gamblers percolated and gained legs over the years. However, whether threats existed or not, they are far past being provable with any certainty. Throughout the interview, Felsch denied putting his intentions into action on the field, all while pointing out that it was otherwise easy to do so. The idea of players fearing retribution should they win the Series is not implausible. Jackson later claimed that Swede Risberg, a noted roughneck, himself threatened Jackson with bodily harm.[17]

The final accused player to testify to the grand jury was pitcher Lefty Williams, who sang his version. Williams stated, as had others, that it was Chick Gandil who first approached him before they all met outside the Ansonia Hotel in Cincinnati. After the meeting, Williams said he told Gandil, "anything that they did would be agreeable to me, if it was going to happen anyway. That I had no money, I may as well get all I could." He later said that he was supposed to get $10,000 after the second game, but did not receive it until after the fourth game. "I figured there was a double-cross someplace," added Williams.[18]

The confessions of Felsch and Lefty Williams were made public on September 29, 1920. After this story exploded, Felsch escaped north to Waupaca, Wisconsin, site of Fox Lake Camp. He owned a place on the lake, a quiet, somber respite from all the scandal talk. He chatted with old friend Teddy Tetzlaff, manager of the local club in the Central State League. "It's all over, and I'm glad of it," Felsch told Tetzlaff. "I want to forget, so let's not talk about it." Felsch most likely remained up north until duck hunting season ended.[19]

On September 29, the *Chicago Tribune* reported that Felsch's "Ma-in-law" said that Felsch told them to bet on the White Sox, which seemed rather strange given the fact that they were supposedly playing to lose. "Just before the World Series, Happy told us to place our money on the White Sox to win," said Mrs. Casper Wagner. "My husband placed $100 and my son Herbert about $25 on the series."[20]

One of Felsch's friends, Milwaukee bowling alley operator, John C. Rehberg, echoed Felsch's family's statement on his gambling tips. "If it is true that Happy was in on the alleged deal in the 1919 World Series, it will be a sad blow to his friends," said Rehberg. "Why, at the close of last season, we bought him a $95 gun as a token of our esteem. Three days before the World Series opened last year, he was here and he advised his friends to bet their money on the White Sox. And later, even after they had lost three games, he told his father-in-law to bet on his team."[21]

After the interview, Reutlinger returned to his office and combed over the Cicotte and Jackson confessions to the Cook County grand jury, comparing them to Felsch's comments. He was stricken by how utterly disorganized the fix was. No ballplayer knew what the others were doing at nearly every point in the Series. Nobody checked on the whereabouts of the money. Eliot Asinof later referred to the players, including Felsch, as "passive participants in their own destruction." All Chick Gandil needed from the others was a simple "yes" and whatever happened after that was, well, whatever happens, happens.[22]

Four days after Felsch told Harry Reutlinger that he had not yet hired legal counsel, he did just that, joining Weaver, McMullin, and Risberg to retain attorney Thomas D. Nash. Their goal? To fight their way back into major league baseball. To that end, Felsch was the first to retract his confession, on October 3.[23] Risberg had been the defiant one thus far, snubbing his nose at even the suggestion of a confession. Felsch, still on his fishing trip, left the details to the others. The *Milwaukee Sentinel* referred to Felsch as the "easy-going, happy-go-lucky chap," a characteristic that mostly likely contributed to his tragic baseball demise.

Like Felsch, Lefty Williams was seen as an "easily led" type, a tag that appeared to have out-numbered the witty, conniving members of the eight. James L. Killgallen wrote that Williams, despite his propensity to follow and not lead, was not the type of person to get mixed up in trouble. For some reason, Killgallen mentioned Williams' well-combed brown hair and dark brown eyes as indicators of his surprise participation, saying that he looked like a college ballplayer. Cicotte and Jackson shuffled off to their home bases of Detroit and Atlanta, respectively. Cicotte was apparently deeply depressed, and Shoeless Joe hung out in a pool room that he owned.[24]

On October 29, 1920, the grand jury formally indicted Felsch, Weaver, Gandil, Jackson, Cicotte, McMullin, Risberg, and Williams, along with five gamblers, Attell, Sullivan, Rachael Brown (associate of Arnold Rothstein), Nat Evans, and former White Sox pitcher Bill Burns on five counts to obtain money by false pretenses and/or a confidence game.[25] Extradition papers were prepared by the state's attorney, Harley Replogle, to corral the 13 indicted parties to return to Chicago to face the music.[26]

On November 8, after a slew of meetings and disagreements over the direction of the game, Judge Kenesaw Mountain Landis was easily elected as the first-ever Commissioner of professional baseball, voting 9 to 3 to give predominant power to one man. Ban Johnson and his "loyal five" did not have enough influence to prevent this from happening. The *New York Times* reported that Johnson was "reluctant to relinquish power that was passing from his hands." In the midst of this transition, Johnson had been working on the permanent ouster of Charles Comiskey over his team's 1919 World Series transgressions.[27]

Landis, born on November 20, 1866, in Millville, Ohio, was the son of Dr. Abraham Hoch Landis, who joined the Union in the Civil War after the family moved to Georgia, and became a brief prisoner of the North—this all before the famed Battle of Kenesaw Mountain. This conflict was one of the worst endured by the Union in the entire war, but it did not deter Dr. Landis and the Mrs. from naming their son after the battle, a decision that took quite a bit of time. "For months after I was born," said the future judge, "my folks couldn't agree on a name for me." His father's fascination with the bloody battle eventually won out.[28] As baseball historian Donald Honig pointed out: "Well, considering there were also battles at Spotsylvania and Yellow Tavern, it could have been worse."[29]

Landis played baseball as a child but wasn't much of an athlete. He spent his days as a newsboy, later working as a clerk in the general store for $3 a week, not a paltry sum for a boy in the 1800s. He decided later to study law in Cincinnati, and in 1905 was appointed as a Federal Judge in Illinois by President Theodore Roosevelt.[30] Sportswriter Leonard Koppett wrote of Landis: "Judge Landis was everything a judge should never be. His prejudices, strong ones, dictated his decisions. He ignored the law. If Landis were alive today, he wouldn't be a judge, but instead a right-wing talk show host."[31]

His experience on the bench aside, his immediate, confident decisions after being elected to rule baseball are perceived by most to have been necessary, prudent, and ultimately effective in eradicating the filthy stain that invaded the game. He was not a shy man, his decisions always accompanied by verbal lectures and emotional tirades. This often muddied the reasoning behind his rulings. Landis obviously felt comfortable delivering these pronouncements.

Two weeks after being elected, Landis sternly declared:"There is absolutely no chance for any of them [the eight accused players] to creep back into baseball." The Judge wasted little time in digging into the circumstances surrounding the scandal, and his single-minded determination would later define the future of the game as it was heading into the Live Ball Era.[32] The league, media, and fans would get to know this no-nonsense, grumpy-looking, small-statured man. Landis certainly knew how to read the tea leaves of public opinion, too.[33]

His strict, assured comments notwithstanding, Landis was not stepping into a cakewalk position. He worked to pacify the owners whose opinions, demeanors, and modes of self-preservation varied as much as Babe Ruth and Fred Merkle did at the plate."If the judge is a big man," noted *The Sporting News*, "sure enough, he will stand no nonsense and the pin-headed magnates who are looking out for their own pockets soon will find this out. In bringing about peace the magnates have wriggled out of a ridiculous predicament, the necessity for organizing that 12-club nightmare."[34]

Months passed before further legal wrangling transpired for the 13 who were indicted. In a joint meeting of the baseball minds on January 21, 1921, the new commissioner ratified a new National Agreement, which gave Landis broad, far-reaching powers. Predictably, Ban Johnson attempted to limit Landis' autonomy by playing with the language of the agreement; the last-minute sabotage failed quickly. His new job did not deter Landis from keeping his day job on the federal bench. His motives for institutional cleanliness now applied to baseball."If I catch any crook in baseball," Landis said,"the rest of his life is going to be a hot one."[35]

In the midst of the scandal-laden events and chatter, the 1920 World Series proceeded without a hitch, pitting the American League champion Cleveland Indians against the National League's triumphant Brooklyn Robins. After losing two of the first three games in the Series, Cleveland charged back to take the final four, capturing the championship, five games to two.

Happy Felsch had relinquished the sanctity of the baseball field and entered the unfamiliar, unpredictable morass of legal entanglement. The regular, tobacco-chewing rubes he felt comfortable around had surrendered to high-priced, educated, manipulative legal eagles, sprinkled in with questions from fans and the press that had nothing to do with singles, doubles, or shoestring catches.

13

Legal Dodge, Here Comes the Judge

Good bye, good luck, and to hell with you.

—Chick Gandil to Ban Johnson
after the 1921 Black Sox Trial

On November 13, 1920, the *Los Angeles Times* reported that Happy Felsch had retracted his confession to the *Chicago American* newspaper reporter, Harry Reutlinger. According to Felsch, because the interview "claimed" to have been conducted on the phone, the confession was rendered phony. How a person consumes Scotch whiskey through a phone line is a mystery, but the lying train picked up steam in a flash. Joe Jackson similarly denied throwing games, but unlike Felsch, Shoeless Joe's testimony was official, having occurred in front of the grand jury. Fred McMullin confidently declared that he, Felsch, Weaver, and Risberg would be cleared of any charges.[1]

That same week, Judge Landis was formally elected as the new chief baseball executive. The man named after a Civil War battle did not hesitate to establish his extreme powers, stating that the baseball fate of the accused eight was not necessarily predicated on their guilt or innocence in a court of law.[2] This was, in effect, the first warning shot fired by the new dictator of baseball; it is easy to imagine the players quivering at the prospect of never wearing a major league uniform again. Blind confidence was another passenger on that train.[3]

In early 1921, the legal wrangling peppered the landscape after Judge William Dever declared the grand jury indictments of Cicotte, Williams, and Jackson to be faulty. This pleased the battery of brilliant defense attorneys,[4] but sent state attorney Robert Crowe and his assistant, George Gorman, scrambling into a legal panic after several players submitted affidavits retracting their confessions.[5] This prompted the prosecution to request additional time to prepare, claiming an urgent need to dig up new evidence to re-indict the players.

Some predicted that a trial would never materialize. In February 1921, defense requested that the confessions of Eddie Cicotte, Lefty Williams, and

Joe Jackson be excluded from the evidence pool. On March 17, charges against Cicotte, Williams, Jackson, Felsch, Risberg, McMullin, and Weaver were dismissed, with charges presented in their stead one day later. Charges against others, including Chick Gandil, were declared inactive for six months. Robert E. Crowe was diligent in his solitary goal. "We are going after the evidence that will convict these men, and we know where to get it," exclaimed Crowe.[6]

Judge Landis placed the accused on an "ineligible list," which Charles Comiskey declared unnecessary since he had created his own list. "Those players are on my ineligible list," proclaimed Comiskey. "There is absolutely no chance for them to play on my team again unless they can clear themselves to my satisfaction of the charges made against them by three of their teammates."[7] Not averse to avoiding egg on his face, the Old Roman soon after released the eight players from his club, terminating their contracts.[8]

In the spring of 1921, Felsch, Jackson, Risberg, Williams, McMullin, and Gandil formed their own squad called The Major Stars. Looking to compete against independent and industrial teams around Chicago, the financial backer was a local investment broker. Buck Weaver rejected an offer to join them, steering clear of the fellow accused while relentlessly proclaiming his innocence.[9] The eager-to-play fallen stars were shunned at every turn. Not wanting to draw the ire of organized baseball, teams respectfully declined their repeated offers, while foregoing the lure of lucrative gate receipts that these flawed men would have garnered.

On April 14, the retooled Chicago White Sox opened the 1921 season against the Detroit Tigers at Navin Field, losing 6–5. Only Ray Schalk and Eddie Collins appeared in the box score as returning positions players; Dickie Kerr started on the hill for Kid Gleason. Johnny Mostil, playing in his first full regular season, supplanted Felsch in center and would parlay his opportunity into a nice season, hitting .301/.379/.406. The team would drop five spots in the standings from the previous season, finishing seventh. Felsch and the other Black Soxers who were absent from the box scores would soon be engaged in another battle—a fight for their professional baseball lives.

Preliminary motions and jury selection commenced on June 27, 1921, a day that brought an unexpected heat wave to Chicago, reaching the 90-degree mark. Just 11 of the 18 people who were called to appear bothered to show up. All eight accused players appeared, along with some of the gamblers who were indicted. Missing were two of them, Ben Franklin and Carl Zork, both key witnesses for the prosecution. Their attorneys filed affidavits stating that their clients were under the weather.[10] Judge Hugo Friend granted a continuance. Assistant State's Attorney George E. Gorman proclaimed the need to corral them all. "It is absolutely imperative that these two defendants are present," said

Gorman. "If they are not here, it will virtually be impossible to place the responsibility of the plot to throw the 1919 world's series games. If the gamblers are not present, they will be blamed by the ball players, and if only a few of the gamblers are present, those here will accuse the absent ones."[11]

The Honorable Hugo Friend served for 46 years on the bench, but at the time of the Black Sox trial was considered a courtroom novice, having practiced mostly civil law. As William Lamb, former New Jersey prosecutor, wrote in *Black Sox in the Court Room*, the decision to hand Friend this extremely public case was puzzling. Ironically, both sides agreed to the appointment, one of the few aspects on which they concurred. In addition, Friend was an avid Chicago baseball fan, a trait that disqualified several prospective jurors but allowed the judge to keep his robe and gavel.[12]

The accused players sat in separate groups in the Chicago courtroom. Felsch sat with Risberg; Cicotte, Williams, and Jackson—the only three who had testified to the grand jury—assembled together. Chick Gandil and Buck Weaver both sat alone, with Weaver staying a fair distance from all the others. Walking past his teammates, Weaver made no eye contact and kept silent.[13] This physical gap was a metaphor for how disjointed this entire plot was, a constant detachment that seemed to mirror the trial itself.

Several days passed before the jury was finalized. Prospective jurors (numbering nearly 100)[14] were asked by the state whether they ever played baseball at any level, leading the *Milwaukee Journal* on July 6 to surmise that there was 'little prospect of securing a jury immediately.'[15] One Chicagoan was excused after stating that he attended a Cubs game, but had never set foot in Comiskey Park.[16] To speed up the selection process, Judge Friend instructed attorneys from both sides to deliver a prepared list of general questions. In addition, each attorney would query all prospective jurors at once, instead of each juror individually.[17] As hoards of candidates were ushered in to complete the pool, many admitted harboring opinions about the case, leading to rampant disqualification.[18]

While subpoenas were served on Saturday, July 16, to the alleged conspirators on the White Sox team, some of the players formed a semi-pro team in Milwaukee. Advanced ticket sales pointed to many fans showing interest in seeing their flawed stars play on the local grounds. This unconditional support by local rooters provided welcome solace to the indicted, who had not seen each other in nearly a year.[19]

The counts outlined against Felsch and his pals included the following:

+ conspiracy to defraud Ray Schalk [White Sox catcher]
+ conspiracy to commit a confidence game [informally known as a con or scam]
+ conspiracy to defraud the public
+ conspiracy to injure the business of the American League
+ conspiracy to injure the business of Charles Comiskey[20]

The defense opened with a motion to have the entire case tossed out, claiming that the grand jury indictments were illegal under Illinois law. A week later, on July 5, Judge Friend denied their gallant attempt to pretend the entire matter was fiction. This appeared to be a consolation prize for the prosecution; however, they were also hampered by two factors: (1) to prove conspiracy, the agreement between the parties must include an overt act or conduct by one or more conspirators that takes the plot beyond just the meetings; (2) Illinois law did not contain statutes that criminalized the corruption of sporting events. Regarding the first, conspiracy is legally separate from the act (throwing games) to which the conspiracy pertains. Illinois later adopted such a law but it did not apply to the alleged 1919 World Series corruption.[21]

This legal distinction would prove challenging to the prosecution, akin to separating the white from a grain of rice. From Judge Friend: "The state was to prove that it was the intent of the ball players that have been charged with the conspiracy through the throwing of the World Series to defraud the public and others, not merely to throw ball games."[22] The reasoning that one of the consequences of throwing games was defrauding several stake-holders apparently carried no legal weight.

Following the preliminary proceedings, attorneys from both sides couldn't resist the temptation to inject baseball metaphor into their legal arguments. "We used our weakest lineup and shut them out," said prosecutor George Gorman. "Wait until our real hitters get in." Defense attorney Thomas Nash shot back with: "We took everything they sent over and didn't even burn our hands. We'll fan their heavy hitters."[23]

On July 28, tragedy struck the Felsch family. Oscar's 68-year-old father passed away at home from a cerebral hemorrhage. Judge Friend allowed him to return to Milwaukee for his father's funeral but wanted him back in court in Chicago on Monday, August 1. Milwaukee defense attorney Ray Cannon objected, and Felsch was allowed to attend the funeral on that Monday.[24]

The culpability, quasi-denial, and claims of innocence during Felsch's 1920 newspaper interview were fretted out in legal drama and sloppy jurisprudence. One of his legal eagles was Michael Ahern, who would later represent the venerable Chicago mobster himself, Alphonse Gabriel "Al" Capone. Though Felsch was relegated to spectator status during the two weeks of proceedings, his unique confession to the reporter provided an eerie metaphor to the trial events, legal clumsiness of the time, and the verdict itself.[25]

> **Felsch:** I got five thousand dollars. I could have got just about that much by being on the level if the Sox had won the Series. And now I'm out of baseball—the only profession I knew anything about, and a lot of gamblers have gotten rich. The joke seems to be on us.[26]

Whether collective regret existed is anybody's guess. Even before the trial got on the main track, Felsch smelled personal doom. How the players had mustered up any semblance of focus in 1920 was astounding, if not indicative of a pathological unawareness of the gravity of their misdeeds. Never in doubt was the support of their cleaner White Sox comrades. On July 11, about a week prior to presentation of evidence, several of the other White Sox players, along with manager Kid Gleason, graced the courtroom with their presence, a scene that favored star-struck fans who came to support their heroes and snatch an autograph or two.

Smiles and handshakes abounded in a curious web of team solidarity, akin to being in full uniform on the ball field, before, during, and after a hard-fought battle. Felsch called out to his mates: "Hope you win the pennant, boys." The good-ole boys responded with: "Thanks, Happy. Good luck to you and your trial."[27] Swede Risberg called out to Kid Gleason, "Hello, Kid. How's the boy?" Gleason countered with: "Pretty good, Swede. How's yourself?" The love fest continued with Gleason bestowing Buck Weaver with some encouraging words.[28]

Some viewed this unity as a stain on baseball, a validation of dirty baseball by those who had not participated. Some went so far as to suggest that Gleason and the clean players should be kicked out of the game themselves.[29] Team loyalty can be an impenetrable force, not easily shut off like a faucet. Far from unified was the amount of money that each player in this ring had received. The modest amount that Felsch received was downplayed during the trial, as the prosecution focused on the "major" players/earners, including Cicotte.

> **Felsch:** I didn't want to get in on the deal at first. I had always received square treatment from Commy [Comiskey] and it didn't look quite right to throw him down. But when they let me in on the idea, too many men were involved.[30]

The veracity of Felsch's statement about "Commy" was predicated on the customary player-owner dynamic, not on some whimsical admiration by Felsch.[31] On July 18, 1921, the jury trial commenced with a tempestuous exchange between defense attorney Benjamin Short and Charles Comiskey. Short's strategy was to portray the Old Roman as a systemic hypocrite. "It is a fact," asked Short, "is it not, that you jumped from the Brotherhood to the National League in the early '90s [1890s]?" Comiskey, shaking his finger in defiance, shouted back: "It is not. I have never broken a contract. I haven't broken any or jumped any. You can't get away with that with me."[32]

This verbal swap followed a tedious recitation of basic facts by Comiskey, including the value of his franchise, the ballpark's seating capacity, and other mundane particulars that, because of the defense's unwillingness to offer opening statements, compelled the prosecution to prove every minute—even inconsequential—aspect of the case.[33] This slight-of-hand strategy may have created the effect of lulling the jury into focusing on tiresome tidbits, instead of prima facie evidence pertinent to a conviction. Burden of proof proved a useful tool.

Judge Friend sustained several objections by the prosecution during the defense's attempts to divulge the meticulous details of Comiskey's financial acumen. Despite this whiff, Comiskey's claims that his business had been damaged by the fix were debunked later on by the defense, who showed that the club's gate receipts had nearly doubled from $521,175.75 in 1919 to a whopping $910,206.59 in 1920.[34]

> **Felsch:** Who was responsible for the double-cross, I couldn't say. I suspect Gandil because he was the wisest of the lot and had sense enough to get out of baseball before the crash came. But I have heard since that it was Abe Attell. Maybe it was Attell. I don't know him but I heard that he was mixed up with the gamblers who were backing us to lose. I'm not saying that I double-crossed the gamblers, but I had nothing to do with the loss of the World Series. The breaks just came so that I was not given a chance to throw the game.[35]

The gamblers that Felsch denied ever double-crossing, notably Sleepy Bill Burns and Billy Maharg, became the prosecution's star witnesses. Burns, in particular, maintained a calm, stoic demeanor and confident poise during his testimony. Burns spent parts of three days on the stand, attesting to meeting Felsch, Cicotte, Gandil, Risberg, Weaver and McMullin at the Sinton Hotel in Cincinnati, and testifying to his offer to the players of $100,000 to tank the Series. Repeated denial of a double-cross later in this melodrama took a back seat to Felsch's claims of playing the game squarely.

Burns was asked to recount his recollection of the pre-Series events. He identified Arnold Rothstein, Abe Attell, and David Zelcer (supposedly aliased as Curly Bennett) as the fix financiers. He testified that Eddie Cicotte and Chick Gandil promised the first two games would be "thrown" and that the errant hit-by-pitch by Cicotte in Game One would indeed signal that the fix was live and real. He quoted Cicotte as saying that he would throw the first game if he had to throw the ball clear out of the Cincinnati ballpark. Burns blurted out a litany of details across three days, drawing the sinister glare of several defendants, including Cicotte and Gandil.[36]

The smugness of Burns exposed itself after cross-examination by defense attorney Benjamin Short, who asked him: "You don't like me much, do you Bill?" "Sure I do," answered a cocky Burns. "You're a smart fellow and I wish we had someone like you as the head of this deal. We'd all be rich right now." After chuckles from the gallery, Burns stepped down and the prosecution wore the face of extreme confidence.[37] Their "home run" opening witness might have given them the early edge.

> **Felsch:** Whether I could actually have gotten up enough nerve to carry out my part in throwing the game, I can't say. The gold looked good to all of us, and I suppose we could

have gone ahead with the double cross. But as I said, I was given no chance to decide. When we went into that conference in Cicotte's room, he said that it would be easy for us to pull the wool over the eyes of the public, that we were expert ballplayers and that we could throw the game scientifically.[38]

That Felsch and other "follower" members of the conspiring eight were largely left out of most discussions, especially those that contained meticulous planning, served to benefit them in the eyes of the law. Although Felsch was not privy to much of what transpired behind closed doors, he received an early Christmas present from the prosecution, which failed to mention his interview with Harry Reutlinger. This unfathomable blunder by the state helped Judge Friend declare the following: "There is so little evidence against these men [Felsch and Weaver] that I doubt I would allow a guilty verdict to stand if it were brought in. But as some evidence has been brought against them, I will not dismiss unless the state is willing to 'nolle prosse.'" [dismiss charges unilaterally][39] The trial proceeded with Felsch and Weaver as defendants, and their legal representatives introducing a flurry of motions to dismiss charges, strike testimony, and set the table for their turn in front of Judge Friend's court.[40]

Felsch: They warned me after the game to be more careful about the way I muffed flies.[41]

That statement represented an infrequently mentioned theme that contributed to the pervasiveness of the scandal's mystery. Several of the accused eight men claimed they were intimidated throughout the Series. Who were the heavies? Did, according to Eliot Asinof, Arnold Rothstein send one of his henchmen, known only as Harry F., to converse with Game Eight starter Lefty Williams?[42] Curiously, Harry F. was merely a fictional character invented by Asinof. This exercise in editorial creativity enhanced Asinof's narrative, but added little to concrete truth.

Certainly, when the defense got their crack at cross-examination, they hoped that a majority of Burns' testimony would be interpreted as mysterious, maybe even fictitious. Michael Ahern, Max Luster, and Benjamin Short all took quizzical shots at Burns, questioning his audacious memory of events. "You have a good memory, have you?" Lusker asked Burns. "I can remember faces," retorted Burns. "Backs too, I suppose," quipped Lusker. The courtroom filled with laughter, including Burns. Short closed by getting Burns to admit that there was double-crossing, which came into question his motives for coming forward.[43]

Felsch: The records show that I played a pretty good game. I know I missed one terrible fly ball, but you can believe me or not, I was trying to catch the ball. I lost it in the sun and made a long run for it, and looked foolish when it fell quite a bit away from where it ought to be. The other men in the know thought that I lost the ball deliberately and that I was putting on a clown exhibition.[44]

The assertions that plays were muffed intentionally in the World Series were perhaps the most difficult aspect of the case to prove. This wasn't 2014; painstaking analysis of game footage was not an option in 1921. What wasn't arduous to prove was that the grand jury confessions of Cicotte, Williams, and Jackson were nowhere to be found. "Ask Arnold Rothstein," said State Attorney George Gorman. "Maybe he knows." Ban Johnson turned Gorman's innuendo into a full-blown accusation, releasing this statement:

> I charge that Arnold Rothstein paid $10,000 for the grand jury confessions of Cicotte, Jackson, and Williams. I charge that this money, brought to Chicago by a representative of Rothstein, went to an attache of the State's Attorney's office under the Hoyne administration [Hoyne preceded Gorman in this role]. I charge that after Rothstein had examined these confessions in New York City, and had found that the ballplayers had not involved him to the extent of criminal liability, he gave the documents to his friend, the managing editor of a New York newspaper. I charge that the editor offered these documents for sale, broadcast throughout the country.

This new development gave temporary relief and confidence to the defense, thinking that the absence of the testimonies would spell a better chance of acquittal. Judge Friend soon doused this self-assurance by declaring that the confessions would be admissible.[45] Along with the Judge's pronouncement that Felsch and Weaver were immune from prosecution, these developments for the defense were perfect segues to their portion of the proceedings.

The defense summoned several gambling figures to the stand to make some look like upstanding citizens and others, including East St. Louis theatre owner/gambler Harry Redmon, look like lying sacks of potatoes.[46] David Zelcer admitted to betting huge sums of loot on the Cincinnati Reds, but denied ever knowing or meeting Burns, Maharg, or Rothstein. This was allayed by his admittance that he had shared a hotel room with Abe Attell, even making the reservation for them both.[47]

The recurring theme of the Reutlinger interview was that Felsch admitted being complicit with the fix, not hiding what he knew and what he didn't know. However, he remained boastfully vehement about not carrying out the plot on the field. The latter was the main focus of the defense during its half of the proceedings, a tactic which the prosecution continuously objected to and Judge Friend overruled.

Despite being eliminated as official evidence, the defense was aided by four of Felsch's teammates—Eddie Collins, Ray Schalk, Roy Wilkinson, and Dickie Kerr—during defense counsels' turn to present their side of this circus. They, along with manager Kid Gleason, refuted Sleepy Bill Burns' evidence that the players had met him at the Sinton Hotel immediately prior to the World Series. The "clean" Sox testified that Felsch, Cicotte, Gandil, et al. were perched at Redland Field at the time they supposedly met with the gamblers.

After defense rested, the prosecution scrambled to dig up additional evidence. They had previously failed to call reporter Harry Reutlinger to the stand to testify about the Felsch interview; attempts to do so now were quashed by Judge Friend because this did not constitute "rebuttal" evidence.[48]

> **Felsch:** Cicotte's story is true in every detail. I don't blame him for telling. He knew the grand jury had a case against him and there wouldn't have been any object in holding out. He did the best thing to do under the circumstances. Because he [Cicotte] was wise enough to stand pat for it, that's all. Cicotte had brains. The rest of us roundheads just took their word for the proposition that we were to get an even split on the hundred thousand. Cicotte was going to make sure of his share from the jump off. He made them come all across with it.[49]

Closing arguments commenced, with the prosecution leading off. Felsch's lauding of Eddie Cicotte as the speaker of truth and the landlord of intelligence echoed the state's focus on the players' grand jury testimonies. Lead prosecutor Edward Prindiville identified Chick Gandil as the "ringleader of the corrupted players" and castigated Eddie Cicotte, referring to the right-hander as "Judas-like." Although Cicotte and Williams had confessed, Prindiville believed that the jury should still "go the limit in punishing them." The prosecution walked the jury through the events one more time. The strategy of hammering on key morsels of evidence while focusing on the dominant players was prompted, in part, by the realization that the defense would do the same with Burns.[50]

St. Louis gambler Carl Zork's attorney, Henry Berger, handed the baton to senior counsel A. Morgan Frumberg, who lambasted AL President Ban Johnson for being the so-called protector of Arnold Rothstein.[51] Frumberg addressed the jury with this curious query: "Why were these defendants in the courtroom? Why were these under-paid ballplayers, these penny-ante gamblers from Des Moines and St. Louis who bet a few nickels perhaps on the World Series, brought here to be the goats in the case?" Frumberg continued: "Ask the powers of baseball. Ask Ban Johnson."[52] Prindiville wrapped up his summation with this verbal lashing of the defendants[53]:

> These men are killers. The conspired to kill baseball, to murder our greatest sport, to defraud the public and their comrades—even to defraud the children of this country— your children and my children who pay their bleacher admission fee to watch their heroes play a game they believe to be honest. A murderer deserves the utmost in punishment. Eddie Cicotte, Joe Jackson, Happy Felsch, Buck Weaver, Claude Williams, Chick Gandil, and these gamblers conspired to murder baseball and I demand that you twelve gentlemen inflict the maximum punishment of a $2,000 fine and five years in the penitentiary on each of them.[54]

> (**Felsch:** I didn't like to be a squealer and I knew that if I had stayed out of the deal and said nothing about it, they would go ahead without me and I'd be that much money out without accomplishing anything. I'm not saying this to pass the buck to others. I suppose that if I had refused to enter the plot and stood my ground, I might have stopped the whole deal. We all share the blame equally.[55])

Felsch's regret of not "stopping the deal" was an admirable, perhaps even humbling admission. Gandil's attorney, James C. O'Brien, climbed further up the baseball food chain, slamming American League President Ban Johnson for turning a blind eye towards the gambling epidemic that pervaded the game. Thomas Nash grabbed the defense baton from O'Brien, accusing the American League president of devising the plan to prosecute the players for the sole purpose of ruining Charles Comiskey.[56]

Michael Ahern—attorney for Felsch, Weaver, and Risberg—focused his closing venom on the state's attorneys, saying they had "no more control over the prosecution than a bat boy has over the direction of play at a World Series game." Ahern then switched to Billy Maharg. "He lied," shouted Ahern. "He makes me think of a drink of moonshine. It looks good but when you drink it, it gives you a stomach ache."[57]

After the defense rested, the prosecution saw no purpose in delivering lengthy rebuttal remarks. They firmly believed their case to be rock solid, briefly citing the grand jury confessions of Cicotte, Williams, and Jackson. In closing, they focused on the allegiance of the fans of the game. "They came to see a ball game. But all they saw was a con game."[58] Felsch, self-proclaimed "roundhead," had certainly felt suckered as well, his feelings not rising to the audacity of a paying customer. Was this simplified crux enough to render a fair verdict?

The time arrived for the jury to deliberate on a verdict. Judge Hugo Friend's earlier edict that the state had to do more than just prove that the players planned to throw games came back to the surface. The state also needed to prove that the players intended to defraud the public. This became the sticking point of what was to follow. Felsch had escaped individual prosecution, compliments of Judge Friend's previous exoneration. Was this enough to return him to his status as an emerging ballplayer that one day could be considered an all-time great?

After approximately two hours and 40 minutes, the jury re-entered the court room with their rendered verdict, beginning with Claude "Lefty" Williams: "We, the jury, find the defendant Claude Williams NOT GUILTY." The courtroom erupted with cheers as one by one, the names of the remaining accused players, including Felsch, were accompanied by "not guilty" verdicts.[59]

Elation filled the courtroom. Tossed hats flew upward in the tense air. Papers were flying everywhere, as the sea of celebration became more turbulent. Eddie Cicotte jumped up and down, patted Joe Jackson on the back in a show of unconditional solidarity, then scampered off to the jury box, grabbed the foreman's hand, and shouted: "Thanks. I knew you'd do it." Judge Friend congratulated the jury for delivering a just verdict, and foregoing judicial objectivity for a brief stint, wore a great big smile on his face. Even the bailiffs joined the excitement with cheers of their own.[60]

Buck Weaver and Swede Risberg were the most animated of the group, grabbing each other by the arms and shouting vociferously in exultation. "I knew I'd be cleared," said Weaver. "I'm glad the public stood by me until the trial was over." A grinning Happy Felsch was "tickled to death," while adding: "I never had anything to do with any conspiracy." A relieved Joe Jackson said: "I'm through with organized baseball. I've got a store here in Chicago. This will be my home. I'm going to play ball with Williams in Oklahoma for a while this summer. At present, I'm contemplating taking a position as coach for a university team in Japan."[61]

In a fit of jubilation and relief, Felsch proclaimed he had nothing to do with the so-called conspiracy. We have seen the multitude of contradictions in Felsch's interview, his subsequent denial of said interview, and his utter cluelessness about the sheer gravity of the malfeasance to which he had been unavoidably linked. This dichotomy would play itself out during future events in Felsch's life. For now, he was deeply sucked into the merriment of having defeated the system and was primed to cap off the acquittal with several ounces of his favorite liquid relief.

A denial-filled Chick Gandil opined: "Never was in doubt about the verdict. I knew where I stood and knew I had done no wrong. I'm going to try to get hold of a good ball club and manage it." Claude "Lefty" Williams stated: "How could the verdict have been anything else? I'm going to stick in semi-professional baseball."[62] During the flurry of celebration, the jurors filed out of the courtroom and were greeted with congratulatory utterances from nearby spectators.[63]

After convening at a local restaurant for a celebration with the acquitted players, one un-identified juror summed up their decision in this way: "We felt from the time that when the State finished that we could not return any verdict other than not guilty. We thought the State presented a weak case. It was dependent on Bill Burns and Burns did not make a favorable impression on us." William Lamb wrote that the intention to defraud the public was inherent in the grand jury statements of Cicotte, Williams, and Jackson. The legal hairsplitting occurred even after, as Lamb stated, the confessing players had basically confessed to the exact charges levied against them.[64]

The acquittal spared the accused of heavy fines and jail time. This generosity by the so-called jury of their peers fell on deaf ears with the baseball brass, purveyors of the players' livelihood. Ban Johnson declared that despite the verdict, the players had sufficiently stained the game to the point of irrefutable certainty. "The fact that the outfit was freed by a Cook County jury does not alter the conditions one iota or minimize the magnitude of the offense," said Johnson. Not surprisingly, Charles Comiskey said that he would have nothing to do with the accused players until they could satisfactorily explain their confessions.[65]

The day after the monumental decision, the concerns of baseball men and some of the media that justice was not served the right dish were laid to rest. Although the eight men were not legally guilty of the precise charges against them, their bad judgment, innate naiveté, and marginal morality burned them in the end. The white-haired, oligarchic savior, Judge Kenesaw Mountain Landis, pleased the palates of those who had hired him, making this forceful declaration:

> Regardless of the verdicts of juries, no player that throws a ball game; no player that undertakes or promises to throw a ball game; no player that sits in a conference with a bunch of crooked ballplayers and gamblers where the ways and means of throwing games are planned and discussed and does not promptly tell his club about it, will ever play professional baseball. Of course, I do not know that any of these men will apply for reinstatement, but if they do, these are at least a few of the rules that will be enforced. Just keep in mind that regardless of the verdict of juries, baseball is entirely competent to protect itself against crooks, both inside and outside the game.[66]

The gavel had fallen. The infamous eight were left without careers, paychecks, and reputations. Many had sensed their imminent demise but now it became cruel reality. From 1921 until today, speculation as to why this jury came down on the wrong side of integrity is virtually unlimited. Some point to hero worship of the players as the main culprit. Despite their flaws, could they possibly have looked as shady as the gamblers? After all, who played the game professionally and who merely sought to profit tangentially? The scattered events of the scandal were most certainly parsed legally. How else could the striking, doubtless confessions by Cicotte, Jackson, and Williams fall short of single-handedly sealing their fate?

The gauntlet that fell on Felsch's professional baseball career conjured up this quote from his most famous post-scandal interview:

> I don't know what I'm going to do now. I have been a ballplayer during the best years of my life, and I never got into any other kind of business. I'm going to hell, I guess. I intend to hang around Chicago awhile until I see how this thing is going to go. Then, maybe, I'll go back to Milwaukee.[67]
>
> I wish I hadn't gone into it. I guess we all do. We have more than earned the few dollars they gave us for turning crooked. All this season the memory of the World Series has been hanging over us. The talk that we threw games this year [1920] is bunk. We knew we were suspected and we tried to be square. But a guy can't be crooked part of the time and square the rest of the time. We knew that sooner or later, somebody was going to turn up the whole deal.[68]

The tragedy that had unfolded over several months culminated with more losers than winners. Felsch and his compatriots fell on the former side. Judge Landis' punishment is, to this day, picked apart—especially by the tenacious supporters of Joe Jackson and Buck Weaver. One was deemed too dimwitted, the other unaware that a single mistake—attending that initial meeting—could spell career doom.

In the end, the dearth of meticulous planning led to erratic execution. The sloppy logistics mixed with rampant underestimation made it easier to expose and more difficult to escape. The gamblers, who most believe were the lucky winners during and after the trial, never considered the inherent strength of the eight players' loyalty. The blind trust of the gamblers by the players was a grave mistake, one from which the law could not liberate them to return to the field.

Left with picking up the pieces, Happy Felsch's professional baseball career ground to a halt, just as his legal machinations would persist, mostly by his own misguided volition.

14

Not My Signature

The only thing in anybody's mind now is to make baseball what the millions of fans throughout the United States want it to be.

—Judge Kenesaw Mountain Landis

The winds of scandal tempered their wrath for a stint, but stockpiled enough small breezes to resurrect more greed, perpetual lies, and courtroom skirmishes. In late April 1922, Felsch sued the Chicago White Sox, seeking $1,120 in back pay from 1920 and a $1,500 sweetener for an alleged promised bonus in 1917. Two additional claims were: (1) Injury to Felsch's professional reputation rising from the assertion that he participated in the fixing of the 1919 World Series, and (2) restraint upon Felsch's livelihood caused by a conspiracy to blacklist him and thereby prevent Felsch from playing organized baseball anywhere in the United States.[1]

Felsch hired bulldog Milwaukee attorney Ray Cannon as his counsel. Cannon had pitched in the Wisconsin-Illinois league during his high school and college years before he opted for the law, and also played ball with Felsch briefly. Cannon was vehemently against baseball as a big business, with their contractual noose hampering the freedom of players to switch teams. In 1922, he began to form a players' union to counteract what he believed to be a violation of the Sherman Anti-Trust Act. "I found a spirit of discontent about many conditions … and every player I talked with regretted the fact that there was no real appeal," said Cannon. "The only chance, they felt, was to unionize."[2]

On behalf of Felsch, Cannon served a summons for Charles Comiskey to appear in Milwaukee under the state's discovery status. Felsch, as the saying goes, should have left well enough alone.[3] Probably not expecting a generous, signed check from his former employer, Felsch met a predictable resistance to his claims from those who probably wished this nightmare in their—and baseball's—history would fade without a trace. Comiskey wasted little time in balking at the summons, his attorneys proclaiming their intention to challenge the request.

"There is no necessity for bringing the Comiskeys to Milwaukee, and I will oppose the move," said George Hudnall, one of Comiskey's legal eagles. "Efforts were made several months ago to settle their dispute. The management of the White Sox team sent a check to Mr. Felsch. Six months later, they received a letter that the check had not arrived. The check had apparently been lost, so they mailed a second check. Mr. Felsch returned it."[4]

Cannon, unfazed by Hudnall's presumptive claims, issued a dramatic, if not threatening response: "We have not revealed all we know. We have evidence which will stun the baseball world and shake organized league baseball to its very foundation." The sharp Milwaukee attorney also criticized Commissioner Landis, who delivered a snarky snap of his own: "No one would pay much attention to what Felsch had to say."

Not intimidated by the passionate, controversial Landis, Cannon snapped back: "His statement indicates he is a mouthpiece for the magnates. I rather think Mr. Landis made a bold remark in regard to Felsch's suit. I should think it would have been more in keeping with his duties as high commissioner of baseball to have withheld a statement until he had time to give careful consideration to what Mr. Felsch has said. Several months ago, Mr. Felsch and I made an effort to settle this controversy without court action. I was referred by Comiskey to their attorney who, in turn, referred me back to Comiskey. After that, we were referred to Mr. Landis, then back to Comiskey, then back to the attorney again."[5]

The verbal "hot potato" between the Felsch camp and the evasive Comiskey contingent demonstrated that most of the parties involved, particularly on Comiskey's side of the legal ledger, would stay mum until absolutely required to speak. But this wasn't like today, where the accused swiftly muzzle themselves, then defer to legal counsel. There was nothing concealing the eager lips of Harry Grabiner, faithful team secretary.

"There is no truth to the charges made by Felsch," retorted Grabiner. "Felsch is just a discredited player who was kicked out of the game because he betrayed his employer, and all charges are nonsense. He and other black-listed players had an opportunity to take the stand and tell these things during their trials. Why didn't they do so? Why do they make them now?"

The repartee persisted, this time from American League President Ban Johnson. Although a noted adversary of Comiskey, the never reticent Ohioan landed on the side of the Old Roman in this case. He also revealed that he knew that White Sox players had raised a fund in 1917 to reward the Detroit Tigers to entice them to defeat the White Sox's rivals, so that Felsch and the boys could secure the pennant. Predictably, Johnson also described his own sleuthlike exploration, this time presenting a quasi-defense of the Sox players.

Felsch's story is nothing new, for we had all this evidence ready in the trial of the corrupt Sox players last summer, but it was never presented. I will not take any action in the matter and can't speak for Judge Landis, who knew of the matter last summer. I unearthed the evidence in my own investigation and told Judge Landis about it. It must be borne in mind that the money was not used to make any players throw games. It was simply a reward for a player to use extra effort against a pennant rival of the White Sox. Of course, it was wrong-doing and not permissible, yet it was not a criminal act like the Sox committed in the World Series of 1919, when they deliberately threw games to Cincinnati.

Despite his curious rationale for bribery, Johnson held steadfast in his belief about whether any of the Sox players had a leg to stand on after their 1919 bungle. "I can't say where the matter will end, for the case is in the hands of Commissioner Landis," continued Johnson. "Of course, as far as Felsch and the other banished Sox are concerned, they are merely seizing this straw to get money out of organized baseball, but they won't get a cent."[6]

Yet another rumor of scandal in the sport most certainly was not going to help Felsch's case, or other Black Soxers who initiated frantic pleas for retribution. These post-Black Sox trial lawsuits primarily added clarity to what people already knew, but added to the embarrassment of faulty deeds past. White Sox Manager Clarence "Pants" Rowland, the manager in 1917, claimed ignorance of the alleged monetary encouragement by his players to their peers in the Motor city. "So far as I know," said Rowland, "no one connected with the White Sox organization conspired to make a pool of $50 each from the Sox players, and we never 'fixed' Detroit pitchers or any other pitchers we played against with my knowledge."[7]

Never averse to blurting out sordid details about this, or any other, act of defiance to which he was proudly linked, Swede Risberg claimed that they had contributed $45 each to reward the Detroit Tigers for their cooperation and Pants Rowland knew all about it. He mentioned another game in 1919 when the White Sox had clinched the pennant but Detroit was battling for third place. "We paid Detroit by sloughing off two games to the Tigers," said Risberg. "I know I played out of position and Jackson, Gandil, and Felsch also played out of position." (Other White Sox players quickly denied Risberg's claims of impropriety.)[8]

Regarding Felsch's lawsuit, Hudnall claimed that Felsch and his legal team could get Comiskey's statements from Chicago, asserted via a section of the law which said that Comiskey did not have to appear in Milwaukee. Hudnall claimed that Felsch was suing the Chicago club as an organization, not Comiskey directly.[9] This splitting of hairs defied the obvious notion that Comiskey "was" the Chicago White Sox and that attempting to differentiate one from the other was futile.

Hudnall claimed that Cannon's affidavit contained no material related to the premise of the lawsuit, saying that the causes of action were for back pay for 1920 and a bonus for 1917, in addition to the conspiracy to force Felsch out of baseball. Cannon asserted that Felsch was not allowed to testify in the Black Sox trial because Comiskey was afraid that Felsch would incriminate him. This dubious claim made no legal sense, but once again called Comiskey's character into question.[10] Was Charles Comiskey a squeaky-clean owner who remained unaware throughout, or was he truly complicit in masking the fix? The Old Roman would get another chance to clear his name.

Around May 12, 1922, Cannon brought two more lawsuits against the club, filing civil actions in Milwaukee on behalf of Felsch's former teammates Joe Jackson and Swede Risberg. Risberg's suit was more similar to Felsch's, while Jackson's centered on a breach of contract.[11] On June 22, 1922, meanwhile, Cannon pitched eight no-hit innings against Merrill on the team that also featured Felsch, Risberg, Cicotte, and Weaver.

Amidst the storm of legal pursuits and occasional ball playing, Felsch welcomed a son to the family, Oscar Ray, born in July of 1922. Soon after, he left to tour with ex-major leaguers including Risberg, Weaver, Williams, and Cicotte. The team also featured Cannon. Over 20 games were scheduled and drew many eager fans from Merrill and Marion in northern Wisconsin.[12]

In mid–June 1923, parts of Felsch's and Risberg's complaints were tossed out by Milwaukee Circuit Court Judge Gregory. Felsch sued for another $100,000 and claimed that his "name and reputation has been permanently impaired and destroyed" because he had been excommunicated from any organized baseball league in the United States." Most of 1923 was marked by legal maneuvers, new motions, and complaints.[13]

The legal scuffling of 1923 dragged into 1924. On January 28, 1924, the two sides appeared in Milwaukee for the trial; the plaintiff was Joe Jackson, the defendant the Chicago White Sox. Jackson and Felsch sat in the back of the courtroom. Comiskey parked his backside at his counsel's table. The gender makeup of the jury was decidedly one-sided: ten men and two women. This was not only typical, it did not muster the criticism it might have garnered today. The two women said they had never heard of Jackson or Felsch.[14]

The plaintiff opened with the questioning of Jackson. Although the January 31, 1924, *Milwaukee Sentinel* headlined that "Jackson Matched Wits" with defense attorneys, parts of his testimony reminded some of why certain people should never set foot on a witness stand. Jackson denied making several statements attributed to him in his grand jury testimony prior to the 1921 Black Sox trial, answering, "I didn't make any answer that you are reading from there" and denied knowledge of any money offered to him to fix games.[15]

Regarding the supposed confusion of Jackson signing his 1920 contract, his wife, according to Jackson, was unhappy that it had occurred without her in the room, and that she was demanding $10,000 per season for three seasons, not the $10,000 for one year or $8,000 per year for three years offered by Harry Grabiner on behalf of Comiskey.[16] It's doubtful that Jackson could match wits with anybody, and his wife obviously knew this while rushing to his defense back in 1920.

Cannon, Jackson's attorney, tried to salvage his disastrous testimony by calling Midwest Associated Press sports editor Charles W. Dunkley and AP sportswriter James C. Hamilton, the latter stating that the only suspicious play he could ascertain during the series was when Eddie Cicotte cut off Jackson's throw from the outfield. Both gentlemen focused on the stellar play of Jackson.[17] Their lauding of his play fell short of saving him from Judge Gregory's wrath later on; several rebuttal witnesses also contradicted Jackson's sudden amnesia. Sox attorney Alfred Austrian reiterated that Jackson had confessed to him.[18]

The parade of witnesses continued throughout the three weeks of the trial, with much of the testimony echoing what was previously stated during the Black Sox trial. The plaintiffs and defense regurgitated information and testimony to satisfy their cases. Similar to the 1921 trial, the battle focused on confessions, previous testimony, and meetings vs. play on the field. But Jackson had denied making many of his previous statements, which put Cannon and their case in a legal pickle and watered down the obvious statistical proof that Jackson had an excellent 1919 World Series.

The plaintiff received unintentional help from Charles Comiskey's detective, J. R. Hunter, who claimed that his investigative trek to San Francisco and back prior to the 1921 trial yielded a modest amount of evidence. The devious detective had posed as a reporter when approaching the players for juicy tidbits, one being Felsch. A reporter can never have too many sources. Hunter also interviewed the owner of a manicure shop players supposedly frequented, but came up empty. Hunter's main sources were newspaper and magazine articles, which, as we know, merely hinted at wrongful acts.[19]

Eventually, it was Felsch's turn on the stand, and like Jackson, he only sabotaged the case as a rebuttal witness and made Jackson's attorney sweat bullets. He testified that Harry Grabiner signed him to a 1920 contract at his Teutonia Ave. home in Milwaukee, with Harry "pulling a fountain pen out of his pocket." During cross examination, the courtroom was greeted with a stunning turn of events. Hudnall showed Felsch a copy of the contract, as well as several other documents he had signed. To everyone's chagrin, Felsch denied that any contained his signature. Cannon interceded with: "If it's your signature, Happy, say so." Once again, Felsch uttered his denial.[20]

Felsch became nervous, shifting his torso from side to side and alternating placing both arms on and off the back of the witness chair. Hudnall requested that Felsch sign his name to a blank piece of paper. Cannon vehemently objected to this tactic, luckily sustained by Judge Gregory. Then Felsch, not realizing he wasn't in a Milwaukee bar shooting the breeze with his friends, perpetuated his festival of lies by blurting that he had nothing to do with the throwing of the 1919 World Series. He also claimed that he did not receive a cent from anybody.

At this point, Cannon probably wanted to muzzle his flustered witness before any more damage was done. After further testimony, Judge Gregory summoned both attorneys to the bench for a five-minute conversation, announced, "This case is adjourned until 10 o'clock tomorrow morning," then left the bench.[21]

This shocking testimony by Felsch injected sudden glee into Comiskey's legal team. "Where is Felsch at now with his own suit?" said one of them. When the trial resumed the next day, Judge Gregory summoned Felsch back to the witness stand, before the jury entered. At Gregory's request, Milwaukee County District Attorney Roland Steinle attended the proceedings. The judge announced that Felsch had "defiantly" committed perjury, and instructed the bailiffs to take him into custody. His bail was set at $2,000.[22]

Having heard of Felsch's plight, two Milwaukee attorneys, Joseph A. Padway and George Damman, paid the $2,000 to spring Felsch out of the County Jail. A perjury charge could earn Felsch a two-year vacation in the state penitentiary. "I'm sorry, very sorry for Happy Felsch," said Charles Comiskey. "He was a great baseball player."[23]

The trial resumed after Felsch's unceremonious exit, beginning with handwriting experts to shed some clarity on the signature matter. Cannon presented Professor W. W. Way, who testified that the same pen was used to ink both contracts (Felsch and Jackson) and that: (A) it was a fountain pen, and (B) the signature on Jackson's contract was written "awkwardly and clumsily."[24] Both Way and John F. Tyrell, the defense team's widely known expert, used microscopes to stamp their points.[25] As if two experts were not sufficient, the court requested that Marquette University chemistry professor J. Vernon Steinle add more scientific verification to the mix. Apparently, his testimony added little to the clear up the signature blur.[26]

The legal mess that Felsch heaped on himself drew an eerie similarity to Joe Jackson's. When the court disposed of the confused Felsch, it was Jackson's turn to take punishment for idiocy. At 6:00 p.m. on February 14, soon after he was summoned to the witness stand, and before his seat was warm, he too was hauled out of court on a perjury charge. Curiously, his bail was set at $5,000; the same two Milwaukee attorneys who had sprung Felsch bailed out Jackson.[27]

The *Milwaukee Sentinel:* "The arrest of Jackson, once an idol of baseball, came with astounding suddenness. The court's summary action fairly stupefied the packed court room."[28]

A motion to order judgment on the jury's verdict was made by Jackson's lawyers. Jackson was awarded $16,711, the full amount of the suit. The jury determined that White Sox team secretary Harry Grabiner had misled Jackson about his 1920 contract, and that Charles Comiskey had promised his players a bonus in 1917.[29]

Undoubtedly with two perjury charges on his mind, Judge Gregory set aside the verdict, thereby dismissing the case because perjury had been committed during the trial. Instead, the verdict would come from answers from the jury for a set of pre-defined questions.[30] "You have failed to discharge your duty," Gregory scolded the jurors. "How you could answer some of those questions in the manner you have, the court cannot understand. Jackson stands before this court a convicted perjurer and has been committed to jail. It did not need a court or a jury to determine that. Jackson determined that for himself."[31]

On May 19, 1924, Felsch entered a not guilty plea on the perjury charge. Author William Lamb wrote that another preliminary hearing and trial would not bode well for Felsch's own lawsuit filed a couple years earlier, and the ongoing battle would soon turn ugly.[32] But before that, Felsch decided it was time to get away and play some baseball. In the summer of 1924, he hooked up with the Twin City Red Sox, those cities being Sauk City and Prairie Du Sac in central Wisconsin. The baseball diamond was clearly Felsch's sanctuary, which a stale court room or jail cell could not equal.[33] Felsch's triumphant arrival with the Twin City Red Sox drew this affirmative publicity from the local newspaper:

> Felsch reported to the manager Nigbar of the Twin City Red Sox at Sauk City Monday and roamed over the ball park in the afternoon in his "civies" to look the bunch over before getting down to business. The Sox were at batting practice and invited "Happy" to try his batting eye. The old boy didn't need any coaxing and to prove that his lamps were still working, swatted the second ball thrown on the nose with such force that it landed over the center field fence. Felsch promises us many more just like that one during the season and if you want to see a real big leaguer in action, just follow the Twin City Red Sox around this summer and you will have thrills aplenty. Every man on the team is a star in his place and a slugger for fair.[34]

Stephen J. Rundio, III, in his wonderful piece "From Black Sox to Sauk Sox," states that Felsch's status as a "big leaguer" was undisputed. Felsch was the first White Sox player to drive in over 100 runs in a season (102 in 1917) and the first to register double figures in home runs (14 in 1920). The local fans of Sauk County might not have been privy to the statistical measures of Felsch's professional accomplishments. But as soon as they saw him play in person, any doubt washed away.[35]

Felsch's debut with his new club was scheduled for May 10, but Judge Kenesaw Mountain Landis' iron-fisted tendencies had extended his post–Black Sox threats to non–major league baseball. Any team that allowed one of the accused eight to play on their club would disqualify any player on that team from ever playing professionally. All but one of the Blues players wanted him to play, but Felsch's debut was delayed. After the Blues lost their first few games sans Felsch, they received a welcoming letter from the Manitowoc team, which declared that they "would" play with Felsch on the field.[36] Was this loyalty from his former team? Regardless, this eliminated the trepidation of the Red Sox and Felsch's debut came on May 24.

Writing off the distant commands of the white-haired curmudgeon Landis, a crowd of 1,000 (half the population of the area) waited anxiously to see the former White Sox star. Fans came from neighboring towns of Lodi, Black Earth, and Cross Plains. Felsch did not disappoint, going 4-for-5 while drawing well-deserved accolades from the local press. After his exhaustive battles in the courts, scorn from the major league press and jilted fans, Felsch probably sensed relief and joy, a mental rewinding of glorious times past.[37]

Their next series of games were against the Gilkerson Colored Giants, led by Robert Gilkerson, who competed all over the country in the 1920s and 1930s. Felsch's self-imposed professional exile was juxtaposed against players who were marginalized as second-class citizens simply because of their race. This was 1924, not 2004, but the Giants had no qualms about playing on the same diamond as the tainted Felsch. They hoped that their treatment in Sauk County would be better than they had received in Madison, where persistent taunting led to unfortunate physical altercations.[38]

The Sauk County club played several contests against the talented traveling team of Gilkerson's, with the local squad triumphant in a majority of the contests. In early August, the entertaining series came to a halt after the teams split a twin bill, the opener going to the Sox, 10–7; the nightcap went to the Giants, 10–0.

In early 1925, Felsch's and Risberg's own suits were settled, just before the cases were slated for trail before the Honorable Judge Byron B. Park.[39] Comiskey's attorney, George B. Hudnall, told the court that his client's health was in a "precarious condition" and would prevent him from enduring a lengthy trial. Hudnall pleaded that a long trial would not render a different outcome than the 1924 trial and could cost Milwaukee County too much trouble for the effort.[40]

On May 18, 1925, Felsch appeared in court, represented by Cannon and Winfred C. Zabel. Their state counterparts were George B. Skogmo, special assistant district attorney, and C. Stanley Perry, assistant district attorney.[41]

Felsch was given one year's probation for his "false swearing" charge. Both former players received far less than requested. Felsch received his final two paychecks for the 1920 season ($1,166.66) plus interest and incurred costs for a grand total of $1,575.35. The charges against him and Joe Jackson had lingered in obscurity for quite some time.[42]

15

Big Skies, Cow Pastures
and Moonshine

*In Scobey, no one asked where you came from or what you did;
they were interested in your performance, here and now.*

—from "Scobey's Touring Pros" by Gary Lucht, 1970

With tiresome legal battles now behind him—at least for the moment—
Felsch focused on getting into the tavern business, entertaining eager patrons,
and playing more baseball. Now nearly 34 years old, the seasoned Deutsche
slugger still considered himself a productive player, albeit against lesser competition. This mattered little as throngs of supportive fans came out to see the
former Milwaukee sandlot legend. His next stop on the "tour of the castaway"
was Scobey, Montana, to play for the Scobey Giants; one of his teammates was
fellow Black Soxer Swede Risberg.

Scobey, Montana, was a booming, vivacious town in 1925. The Great
Northwest Railroad established a line there in 1913, and the bustling area soon
became the transportation hub of western Montana. During this period, Scobey
also boasted the extraordinary privilege of being the primary wheat shipper in
the United States, an honor that lasted until 1926 when the railhead was
expanded to Opheim.[1]

A group of local Scobey businessmen chipped in $3,015 to assemble a base-
ball team in Plentywood, located 37 miles east. They aspired to propel Plentywood into respectability and cultivate a healthy baseball relationship between
the two locales. The plentiful cash and eager competiveness created a heated
rivalry. In Felsch's favor, the area hoisted baseball players onto a pedestal; those
who could not hack it quickly fled town.[2]

The hunt for willing players extended from Canada down through the Dakotas, Minnesota, Wisconsin, and Ohio. This sudden interest in accumulating
top-notch talent wasn't exactly the level of the Yankees'"Murderers Row.""Good

money bought quality talent," said *Montana Magazine* in its May/June 2001 issue. Preceding Felsch and Risberg were lesser-known stars such as George "The Indian" Eastman, Porky Dallas (a Winnipeg find), and John Chief" Meyers (former New York Giants star).[3]

The ancient Scobey ballpark had no outfield fence. Rows of Model Ts served as a temporary border between the playing field and fans. Both entities chipped in towards maintaining the place, especially vital after frequent, heavy downpours. Mud holes were soaked up by heavy blankets, greasy spots draped with gasoline and set ablaze. Legend had it that gophers packed their bags every fall after spending summers avoiding flying baseballs.[4]

Felsch and Risberg signed contracts for $600 per month each, plus expenses. This was a magnificent sum for a small-town club, but both spent generous amounts on "broads and booze." Despite their morally questionable tastes, their spending habits meant their money stayed home. Their alcohol preferences were not limited to beer and garden-variety liquor. They often sampled the local moonshine, coupled with escapades that stretched into dawn's early glow. As Gary Lucht wrote: "It has been said that most of the team members had permanent rings over their noses from drinking moonshine from quart fruit jars."[5]

After introducing the local fans to his hitting proficiency, Felsch was quickly "adopted as a native son." He played several positions but his stick carried them to victory after victory. Matches included tussles with nearby teams, including Plentywood. They also barnstormed in Minnesota and across the border in Regina, Saskatchewan. At home, they sold out all of their games, with gate receipts approximating $1,200 per contest. Curiously, several clubs shrouded the day's lineup in secrecy until the very last moment. Sometimes, these tactics delayed the starts of games. They might not have wanted to reveal their most recent player acquisition; petty bickering often ensued when this occurred.[6]

The announcement of lineups sometimes came with gaudy flamboyance. Prior to one game, a small airplane landed in the outfield, from which the Scobey starting pitcher emerged. Fans let out a huge roar. The hurler, Chief Seeley, had been flown from South Dakota as the team's new recruit. Nobody knew who he was other than the team, which hardly mattered as that was the only game in which Seeley appeared for Scobey.[7]

Keith Wipple, a former teammate of Felsch's there, said years later that Felsch and Risberg, as adored as they were in Scobey, were booed mercilessly elsewhere. "I remember one game in Moose Jaw, Saskatchewan," said Wipple. "When things got a little rough for the team. Everywhere we played, the opposition fans would ride Hap Felsch and Swede Risberg. If the two didn't play their best game each game, the fans would ride them about their former big league standing and remind them of their present cow pasture status."[8]

In one game, a particularly obnoxious fan stood out, firing vulgar language at Felsch. Happy warned the loud gent that if he didn't shut up, he would get a tonsillectomy with his baseball bat. Luckily for all parties, local Mounties interceded and escorted the gutsy man out of the ball park. Later that night, Felsch and teammate Meyers encountered the ousted fan at their hotel and did not hesitate to teach him a cruel lesson. Felsch clobbered him first and Meyers' fists followed.[9]

One of the recent acquisitions by Plentywood was an African American pitcher named James Donaldson, formerly of the Negro Leagues' Kansas City Monarchs. Despite being disallowed from playing in the major leagues for another 20+ years, Negro players (as they were called back then) were not always shunned by local teams. Donaldson did not escape scorn from the paying crowd, but the jeering did not deter him from his duties on the mound. Classless insults were not exclusive to the fans; Felsch also slipped in some verbal jibes. During one contest, Felsch yelled: "You black so and so, you couldn't hit the side of a barn with a handful of rice." Donaldson shot back: "Why Mr. Felsch, why is you so irate? I could pitch from second base and strike you out."[10]

The drinking and debauchery displayed by the child-like former big leaguers extended into the night streets after a game. Apparently practicing their pitching, the two rubes used rocks as baseballs and fired them at street lamps on Scobey's main street. Their liquor-induced raucousness was never stopped by passing locals. The unfettered behavior was protected by their status as ballplayers. Armchair psychology might reveal that neither was especially thankful for his chance at playing baseball again.[11]

Betting was prevalent in these games, a sick irony given the crux of their big league ousting. Bill Stephens was the "bag man" for Scobey, ostensibly the gent who secured the loot. Even during games, Stephens scurried around the park taking bets. Plentywood had their own bag man, nicknamed "Jew Backer." Allowing the ex-Black Soxers to play was one thing; freely and openly permitting wagering was a distant slap in the face to the Landis people.[12]

In July, the *Plentywood Herald* published this comparison between the eschewed Donaldson and the spoiled ex-White Soxers: "One made by nature and can't help it; the other one [Risberg] naturally became so after getting his sox dirty and being awarded a spanking by Judge Landis. Scobey will be flanked by Happy Felsch, also of a muddy complex."[13]

Scobey went 20–7 on their 1925 barnstorming tour and played Plentywood seven times, but disbanded in September of that year.[14] After the season, Felsch returned home to Milwaukee and was lured back to Montana in 1926. The flair of the Scobey team dissipated quickly and local coverage of games and Felsch was scarce. The town eventually dropped semi-pro ball and opted to use local amateur players.[15] Felsch, not giving up on baseball just yet, continued his sojourn through outlaw ball.

Between steady stints of his rejuvenated baseball career, Felsch probably wished there was no off-season. Judge Landis had requested that several former White Sox players appear before a hearing to determine whether Swede Risberg lied about the team helping the Detroit Tigers in 1917. Pants Rowland, Ray Schalk, Eddie Collins, and a slew of former Tigers were summoned. "Propelled unwillingly in the spotlight," Felsch was deluged by a host of callers wanting his opinion on the issue. Instead, he shuffled north with a few friends to ice fish.[16]

Incorporated as a city in 1903, Regina became the capital of the Saskatchewan province three years later. On May 14, 1927, the headline in the sports section of the *Regina Morning Leader* read: "Hap Felsch to Have Charge of the Semi-Pros." The man who could barely police himself was now a player/manager for a team in Canada called the Regina Balmorals.[17] (A balmoral is a Scottish hat.) He might have been given the manager's hat, but it was his playing that was most revered. "Hap is well known in these parts as a stellar performer," said the paper.

The semi-professional team opened their season on May 25. Felsch played first base, batted third, and went 1-for-2 in a 2–1 squeaker over Wildrose.[18] Hap would play multiple positions during the 1927 season and rarely had a hitless game. His notoriety was not wasted as the team frequently used his name in newspaper advertisements to lure fans to their next game. The team did not have a regular schedule, so marketing game-by-game was vital. Instead of the expected title of "Regina Balmorals," public notices and game accounts routinely referred to the club as "Hap's Balmoral," "Felsch's Balmorals" or simply "The Felschmen."[19]

The spring weather in Saskatchewan was frequently brutal, with stiff breezes often scaring away all but the most ardent patrons. On June 4, the "Felschmen" battled a team from Lignite, North Dakota, which included a reunion with Swede Risberg, who now played for the Lignites. Felsch greeted his former teammate by going 2-for-2 with a run scored in a 5–0 victory. Apparently, the Lignites left the field in disgust after several disputes with the umpire.[20] One could picture the feisty Risberg jostling his way into the middle of any quarrel without hesitation.

Two days later, the Balmorals swept a doubleheader from Risberg's club, with Felsch doing more damage. In the nightcap, he smacked a long home run and went 3-for-5. He also played his traditional center field position in both games, with no traces of rust. "The crowd gave Hap a great ovation when he pulled down a sure three-base hit in the seventh, making a running catch of Colliton's long fly to deep centre," reported the *Leader*.[21]

The irregular schedule of the team mixed in home stands with lengthy road trips, some as far away as St. Paul, Minnesota. Canadian stops filled the card, including delightfully named towns like Moose Jaw and Saskatoon and the more recognizable Edmonton and Calgary. In a 4–3 win over the latter, Felsch once again cornered the market on publicity, not undeserved. "Connecting for a home run and two singles, his former one being one of the longest drives ever made in Calgary, Happy Felsch featured the Regina Balmorals 4–3 over the Calgary Athletics here tonight."[22]

Even the most humble and grounded athlete would have enjoyed repeated ego boosts had he been in Felsch's shoes. After a 4–2 dispatching of Edmonton, the headline made clear who the star of the club was:

"Hap Felsch Figures In Sensational Fielding and Heavy Clouting Episode"

Felsch made a one-handed shoestring catch "in the centre pasture that threw eight hundred odd onlookers into a tumult of excitement." Felsch received a "tremendous hand" for his eighth inning fielding gem. His 2-for-3 showing at the plate included a double.[23] The competition was obviously weaker than the American League but at age 36, his consistent wrecking of local pitching sufficed. Add to that the positive attention that had eluded him in recent years, and Felsch probably didn't mind being hundreds of miles away from home, where constant reminders of his previous misdeeds would have busted his eardrums and psyche.

In early August, with the season winding down, Regina agreed to play Bosetown for bragging rights in a Saskatchewan Province championship series, the first ever semi-pro title event there. The teams played two games in Regina, two in Bosetown, and two in a neutral venue, Saskatoon. In the opener, Felsch let his bat do the talking, cranking two home runs in 4–0 blanking. The clouts came in successive at-bats for the first baseman.[24]

Game two featured another pasting of Bosetown, 7–1. Felsch didn't hit any bombs, but still led them to victory. "Felsch failed to duplicate his sensational home run hitting of Monday night when the Bals won 4–0 but the same 'Hap' connected for two doubles, again the big hitter of the night," said the *Leader*.[25] The Balmorals won three of the final four games to earn the inaugural title of Saskatchewan Champions!

In the lone defeat, Felsch went 3-for-3 with another home run. In game five, he even toed the pitcher's mound for a few batters. His hurling occurred in a 12–9 slugfest, and Felsch played sacrificial lamb to save his regular pitchers.[26] Regina outscored Bosetown, 33–17 in the series. Time to repeat the cycle: return to Milwaukee and anticipate another invite to display his dissipating baseball skills.

Later that year, the law found him again. Felsch was charged with a pro-hibition law violation after federal authorities found "a quantity of beer" at the soft drink parlor that he had gained control of just three days earlier. He was arraigned in front of a federal commissioner and bound over to a grand jury under $500 bail.[27] The Eighteenth Amendment to the United States had been ratified eight years earlier. Given Felsch's proclivity towards the wet stuff, per-haps it was only a matter of time before he breached Section 1 of that amend-ment.[28]

In April of 1928, Felsch signed to play with the Kosciuszko Reds in the new Wisconsin State League. The following statement was issued on Felsch's behalf:

> Every club in the league was willing that Hap should have the chance and when Judge A. J. Hedding, president of the league, gave his consent. Manager Al Moran quickly got Felsch's name on the dotted line. Judge Hedding explained that Felsch's case is not unlike that of a juvenile first offender. He has paid for his mistake with the Black Sox and will be given another chance here. That he will be a big drawing card for the Poles, if able to show any considerable part of his marvelous ability of old, goes without saying.[29]

The rousing endorsement was momentary. Nine days later, the league rep-resentatives decided to ban "outlaw" players, which included Felsch. Curiously, Moran stated that even if the ruling had not been issued, he would not permit Felsch to play. Did the league have cold feet? Did some members believe Felsch was too much of a risk?[30]

The ghosts of deeds past presented a slight hiccup. But with his celebrity status well-established in several Canadian environs, Felsch returned to the States and the familiarity of Plentywood, Montana, in 1928. The team manager, Backer, announced that the "nationally known" Felsch was joining the club called the Plentywood All-Stars. This season on the semi-professional circuit mirrored his previous campaigns. His thirst to stay active in the game he loved was matched only by his exceptional performances.

The All-Stars played the Cuban Giants and a House of David team, in addition to clubs from Canada, Montana, Iowa, and the Dakotas. In a 20–4 whupping of his former team, Scobey, Felsch smacked two triples, two doubles and a home run, going 5-for-5.[31] On June 8, Plentywood played the Cuban Giants for the fourth time, having won the first three matchups. Apparently, the umpiring was less than stellar, with the local newspaper reporting that "poor umpiring can spoil a good game and neither Plentywood nor Scobey can afford to have games become continual arguments between players, umpires, and man-agers."[32]

As Felsch maintained his on-field gems, Scobey was apparently ticked about the constant thumpings by his new team. Constant bickering over gate receipts also fueled the tension. Monetary squabbles notwithstanding, the local paper offered that "Hap Felsch might get one of those long hits like he did off Donaldson, and he might strike out; either event is a treat for the fans."[33]

In one of the last games of the summer, Felsch singled, tripled, scored, and gunned down a runner at home in a 5–3 victory over the Hanford Eskimos. The *Sioux City Journal* called Felsch "one of the greatest throwers who ever played baseball" as he "unleashed a peg about ten feet above the ground from center field to the catcher's mitt."[34] Another scandal-free season was in the books for Felsch. He was not ready to hang up the cleats just yet, despite knocking on the 40-year-old door.

The trend, albeit maybe not entirely conscious by Felsch, was to stay away from the middle-lower 48 states as much as possible. Towns such as Scobey, Plentywood, and Grand Forks were remote enough to keep him safe from the lively scorn of Judge Landis. The next stop on his twilight baseball journey— his last away from his hometown Milwaukee—was Virden, Manitoba, in 1929 and parts of 1930. The aging ballplayer, as he had done throughout his post-banishment years, made a pleasant impression on the star-starved Virden club.

"Hap Felsch and his merry men are just about the smoothest all-around combination that has invaded Wesley diamonds for a long, long time," said the *Virden Empire-Advance*. "Hap has slowed up some, but his gardening last night left nothing to be desired." In an 11–4 thrashing of the Toronto Oslers, Felsch proved that his fielding wasn't the only aspect of his game still packed with juice. "Spring had Hap Felsch's number in three out of five trips the clever performer made to the plate with a slow ball offering which made the centre fielder hit weakly. However, his long triple to the south bleachers in the fourth atoned for his unnecessary attempts, while his sharp single in the first was a hit in any league."[35]

In the last series of 1929, Virden battled Felsch's former team, the Regina Balmorals. The local paper lauded team manager Harry Allan for his dedicated, selfless efforts towards promoting the ball club. The extensive on-field coverage afforded Felsch consistent publicity of his own, earned legitimately by his clutch play and consistent production in leading "Hap Felsch's Virden All-Stars."[36]

In 1930, Felsch began play with a barnstorming team, the American-Canadian Clowns. He eventually returned to the Virden club to finish the season. In an early-season matchup against Virden, Felsch did not fare so well, going 0-for-5 while batting third in the order. The Clowns triumphed in the back-and-forth affair, 5-3. When Felsch returned to his former club, he reprised his prolific hitting, collecting a triple and a homer in an 8–4 doubling up of the Brandon Greys.[37] Despite not fading ultra-fast on the field, Felsch decided to hang up his glove and cleats after the 1930 season and return to Milwaukee. In 1931, Felsch was identified in the local directories as a ballplayer, but his presence was largely outside the bounds of the diamond spotlight.[38]

During the 1930s, Felsch opened a tavern and mixed in some appearances on local Milwaukee diamonds, even finding himself back in the headlines. Playing for the A.A.A. Triangle Billiards team, Felsch soaked up the admiration of local fans, especially children who were obviously clueless about his checkered past. The caption below a picture in the *Milwaukee Journal* was entitled: "Felsch Has His Kid Admirers." The adjoining article waxed nostalgic over the bigger hype years as a member of the Chicago White Sox. "Fifteen years ago, if Happy was like the rest of us, he was lustily singing in the evening over the beers 'It's a Long Way to Tipperary.'"[39]

Whenever Felsch hit a baseball, fans marveled at seeing their hometown hero in person. Older fans claimed he was as good as ever, while young ladies were "squealing" when he hit one. His gestures were immediately familiar, from pulling on his nose and cap to squinting at the pitcher, as if to warn the hurler of impending doom. Pitchers who tried to make him fish for stinkers soon discovered that fooling the old bird was a waste of effort. The *Milwaukee Journal* noted that Felsch was "hitting them on a line, with the same easy, natural swing."

In a game against the Bucher Malts, Felsch even stole home and wreaked havoc on the base paths to the bitter end. One writer surmised that "most men in the soft drink business don't slide for home, except on Saturday nights."[40] With Felsch living above the tavern on Teutonia Avenue, the local city directory listed his profession as "soft drinks," not a misprint given the era of Prohibition, although his previous run-in with the law would naturally draw suspicion.[41]

With the years catching up on Felsch, his playing days dissipated as well. Joining the Bucher Malts team in 1933, Felsch began in his familiar outfield position but as his "fighting" weight of 165 pounds ballooned to 200, he became relegated exclusively to first base. In late May, the newspaper headline read "15,000 Fans Watch Happy Felsch Play Star Role" as he led the Malts to an opening day, 4–1 victory over the Ziemer Sausages.

The "Big Man" of the Auer Avenue diamond was idolized by swarming fans as they peered in awe when his clouts sailed over their heads in the outfield, ruled doubles to make the game fair for others. His second double was equally colossal, this time landing on a Burleigh Street front porch, an easy souvenir for its residents. "There goes a window," shouted manager Steinke. Three of Felsch's hits contributed to the four tallies.[42] His baseball survival now hinged on his bat. Luckily, as of June 13, Felsch was atop the league leaders with a .526 average.

With Felsch now living above his tavern on 17th and Center, his establishment became the prime gathering place of sandlot players and managers. The lifting of Prohibition in 1933 turned the "soft drink" parlor into a full-fledged watering hole. Felsch served free peanuts, and in true pub style, the shells were ceremoniously tossed to the ground. Drinking and baseball chatter lasted late into the night; some patrons drew comparisons between Felsch and the new stars of the 1930s. Discussions about the 1919 scandal were infrequent, and never broached by Felsch.[43]

Scandal talk did not draw Felsch's ire too much, but other annoyances did. In May of 1934, he got into an altercation at his tavern. Apparently, a female customer brought in a big glass pitcher and asked to "fill 'er up." Felsch didn't take kindly to the woman's brash request, an argument ensued, a male patron stood up for the woman, and Felsch allegedly belted the man in the eye. Deputy Clerk of Criminal Courts August C. Schmidt slapped an "assault and battery" charge on him.[44] It was unclear whether Felsch was upset over the gall of an aggressive woman or the risk of unsanitary beer pitchers, but surely, his German temper percolated with little warning.

After playing with the Triangle Billiards, Felsch spent time playing in Oconomowoc and back home for his first amateur club, Sissons and Sewells. He also appeared in several exhibition games in the immediate vicinity of Milwaukee County. Well into his 40s, Felsch settled down with his business and family, who left the Center Street tavern and moved to the 2500 block of Teutonia Avenue. In mid–May of 1937, the 45-yar old Felsch took another crack at baseball, this time joining his old friend Elly Luderus' Verifine team.

Many AAA managers sought to recapture the glory of years past, signing older, experienced players. Luderus was credited with luring Felsch back to the Milwaukee sandlots in 1932. Felsch's presence immediately drew more fans than would have attended otherwise. Being requested to increase attendance was overshadowed by his unrelenting thirst to play the game he still loved. The former sandlot heroes' teams recruited players that might have been Felsch's equal on the field, but not in legendary splendor.

The 1940s brought another tavern for Felsch, this time the Barn Grove on the northwest side of town. Oscar and Marie lived above the tavern as well. Their nomadic existence lasted until the mid–'40s, where more moves and additional vocations carried Felsch into retirement and, eventually, growing illness. After serving as assembler and night watchman for various companies, Felsch became a crane operator at George Meyer Company from 1949 to 1962.[45]

Now reaching age 70, Felsch battled varicose veins and leg abscesses, which left him semi-ambulatory. His three children, Oscar Jr., Shirley, and Marilyn, had produced 11 grandchildren. His frequent travels, both as a professional with the Chicago White Sox and later in several Midwestern and near-western towns, probably took a toll on his family back home. They finally settled in their final residence on North 49th Street in an upper flat. His final days were drawing closer.

16

If You Pour, He Will Talk

When wine, women, and song get to be too much for you, give up singing.

—Felsch to a patron in his Milwaukee tavern

In the fall of 1956, reporter Westbrook Pegler wrote a series of five articles based on interviews with Eddie Cicotte, Swede Risberg, and Felsch. A friend of Pegler's in Detroit said it would be futile to reach the now-reclusive Felsch at his home. But as long as he had other business to tend to in Milwaukee, Pegler saw no harm in trying. He first stopped to talk with Milwaukee Circuit Court Judge Robert C. Cannon, son of Ray Cannon, Felsch's attorney. The Judge gathered a hoard of documents from his vault for Pegler's perusal. During his two days in Cannon's chambers, Pegler pondered a visit with Felsch and remembered an old reporter saying "Always do what you can."[1]

Pegler looked up Felsch in the phone book and hopped a cab to the "wooden shoe" district of Milwaukee. "The address was a two-story frame building," wrote Pegler. "There was no name at either bell so I stabbed one and the buzzer [Felsch's] snarled, unlocking the door at the foot of the stairs. It was almost dark. A gruff voice behind a glass door called 'Who is it?' I told him. 'Well what do you know,' said Hap Felsch. 'Are you back on sports? Come on in.'"[2]

Felsch led Pegler to the kitchen, where he had something propped up for his leg, "ugly with disease down near the ankle." "I got an abscess on a varicose vein," said Felsch. "I don't sleep more than four hours any night." Pegler's friend had wired him ahead of time to inform him that Felsch had been isolated for years, refused to talk any baseball, and had not seen any baseball in quite a while. This friend also said that argumentative drinkers ran him out of the tavern business. Felsch had claimed that one night as he left a dinner at which the 1919 World Series was rehashed, he discovered that his tires had been slashed.[3]

When asked if it was true that he was now a crane operator, Felsch replied: "That's right. I am running a crane for George Meyer Company, bottling equipment. I am 65 but the only thing wrong is this ankle and I don't use that to run the crane. I had this tavern 14 years and when I sold it, I spent a couple of thousand bucks in two weeks. So I said 'I gotta cut this out' so I got this job."[4]

Felsch switched the subject to baseball. "Say what is the matter with those crazy broadcasters," continued Felsch. "What do they mean by a slider? It sounds to me like an in-shoot although they think it is old-style to call it an in-shoot. I know. I looked at it. Sure it dropped a little but all in-shoots fall off." Pegler agreed and said: "Swede Risberg thinks it's an old-fashioned forget-me-not out-curve, with a little downer. But I agree with you. Slider sounds like new publicity for an old throw."[5]

Contrary to Pegler's friend's account, Felsch was happiest talking baseball, never averse to conveying his expertise. His next offering about a future Hall of Famer seems silly now, but his assessment of a particular play had credence. "Did you hear about that switch [Lou] Boudreau pulled on Mickey Mantle?" said Felsch. "Pulled the whole club [fielders] to the right. And he [Mantle] popped one right in the middle of that mob. If you did that on our club, you went to Cedar Rapids. Mantle could have had a sure single to left. He doesn't know how to use a bat."[6]

Pegler asked Felsch if he had seen Chick Gandil. He had not, but had kept in contact with Buck Weaver for a while after the scandal dust settled. He said that Weaver got a raw deal in the whole mess, his performance being solid proof that he did not throw games. A discussion on the botched cut-off relay by Cicotte in Game Four of the 1919 World Series followed. Felsch claimed that he heard catcher Ray Schalk yell towards Cicotte to cut off Jackson's throw. Pegler told Felsch that Schalk wondered how the outfielder could have heard anything from a hundred yards away. The differing opinions and viewpoints continue today, so why not in the late 1950s?[7]

"We all get old and I don't mind except the reputation they gave us," said a tiring Felsch. "I played my best all the time. And they never paid me my money for the time we finished second in 1920, the year they broke up the club. That was my money. I earned it and somebody else got it. I could use it today. So could the others—those who aren't dead. Well, I am glad you come. It is fun to talk old times to old timers once in a while."[8]

As Pegler walked down the stairs, he repeated his friend's advice in his head: "Always do what you can." Felsch is still the blond Bavarian Heine who whipped off a bartender's apron as a kid in Milwaukee nearly 50 years ago to be a cog in the most beautiful baseball machine ever put together." The reporter's next step was to arrange an interview with Risberg, which eventually took place in a California tavern.[9]

Eliot Asinof, famed author of *Eight Men Out*, published in 1963, has been since scrutinized for the journalistic liberties that he took in describing some of the events of the scandal. Despite the embellishments, the work was the first of its kind—at least on a large scale—on the 1919 debacle. Shortly before the book hit the streets, Asinof became the last person to interview Felsch. In the weeks prior, Asinof called and wrote the old ballplayer, starting a dialogue that perhaps would earn him a face-to-face meeting.

Prior to his arrival, Asinof stopped at a local Milwaukee tavern for a couple of brews. The bartender was too young to remember the Black Sox scandal, but an older gentleman at the bar told the writer that he used to frequent Felsch's drinking establishments and said that Felsch was a real good guy. "Everybody liked him," said the man. "Always used to tell crazy riddles. 'How do porcupines screw?' Then he'd answer, 'Very, very carefully.'" Asinof listened as the man told more stories, hanging on to every word, imagining what it was like back then at those local watering holes. He sensed a remote intimacy with Felsch, picturing him standing behind the bar with such respect and command.[10]

Asinof hailed a cab and arrived at the Felsch home. He remembered how Harry Reutlinger had snagged an interview with Felsch in 1920, by bringing a fifth of Chivas Regal with him. If it worked once, it might work again; Asinof too had a bottle with him as he rang the doorbell. Felsch's wife, Marie, answered and welcomed him upstairs. She had remembered the calls, so this wasn't a stranger at the door. "Be kind to him," she said. Felsch was asleep, with his heavily bandaged foot propped up. Marie turned off the TV, which awakened Happy. "Oscar, you have a visitor," she said.[11]

Asinof extended his hand in greeting and said "How do porcupines screw?" "Very, very carefully," replied Felsch. "I need your help," said Asinof. "I can't drink all this scotch myself." "Don't seem like much to me," replied Felsch, a seasoned veteran of the hard stuff. Marie retrieved a couple of tumblers and left the men alone to talk. "You must have put the whammy on her," quipped Felsch. The ice was broken and Felsch opened up.[12]

Felsch began by describing his childhood. Asinof found him to be a delightful, humble storyteller who did not appear to take life too seriously. Felsch condemned Charles Comiskey for being cheap, then took a shot at the sportswriters. "He made us feel like dogs," he said. He called the sportswriters "company men." "You could bet they'd write what the old man wanted. The player didn't have a chance. No matter what was happening, if he felt Comiskey wouldn't like the story, he wouldn't write a word. I might be dumb, but most of those writers don't know half of what I know. Writers can't hit a baseball. If they could, they wouldn't be writers."[13]

After Felsch described his love for the game, Asinof got brave and asked: "How then, did you come to sell out the game you loved?" The writer sat in fear, thinking Felsch would kick him out for even broaching the subject, which had been taboo for many years. But Happy acquiesced and explained[14]:

> It was a crazy time. I don't know what happened, but it did, all right. I've thought about it plenty over the years and I don't know. Maybe it was one of those God awful things that just happens to you. You don't know what you're doing, then one day you wake up and it's there, real as life. I guess that comes from being dumb. God damn, I was dumb, all right. Old Gandil was smart and the rest of us was dumb. We started out gabbing about all the big money we would take, like a bunch of kids pretending to be big shots, you know? It just seemed like a bunch of talk. I never really believed it would happen. I don't think any of us even wanted it to happen, 'cept Gandil. But it happened all right. Gandil gave Cicotte ten grand the night before the opener, and the next thing we knew, we were all tied up in it.[15]

The conversation continued and arrived at an aspect of the scandal that was most vague, or as some would believe, a fable. Were threats levied against the players at any point, or at least paranoia on the part of the players? Felsch answered: "There was so much crookedness around, you sort of fell into it. Once when I was playing factory ball [in Milwaukee], some guy calls me in the outfield—they stood around the fence out there, you know. He shows me this gun he's packing and he said, 'Oscar. I want you to drop the next fly ball comes your way!' I couldn't believe it, but the next inning, some guy hits a long one to center and I got to thinking. That crazy coot is gonna shoot me." Asinof asked Felsch if he made the catch. Felsch replied: "Are you kidding? The thing stopped rolling halfway to the fence and I kicked it the rest of the way."[16]

Felsch talked more despairingly about Comiskey, not mincing words, which Asinof concluded was bottled up for many years. The reasons Felsch got mixed up in the fix seemed, to the writer, not his own. Going along with the crowd meant equal guilt, as Felsch admitted to playing to lose. But were these ideas his own? Felsch led Asinof through the Series, play by play. The specific details were not published, but some of Felsch's words almost seemed like they came from a script. "Playing rotten, it ain't that hard to do when you get the hang of it," said Felsch. "It ain't that hard to hit a pop-up when you take what looks like a good cut at the ball. It ain't that much fun either."[17]

A week after the interview, Asinof called the Felsch home. Happy was sleeping, but Marie chatted for a bit. She told the writer that her husband was afraid of the gamblers and that they had even threatened to hurt their children. The shame was clear, as was the stupidity. He had returned to the baseball fields for years after he was kicked out of professional ball. Happiness came with playing, chatting with old friends, and of course, drinking. His varicose veins and messed-up body came from his two main loves: baseball and booze.[18]

On Monday, August 17, 1964, the man they said was born laughing died from a coronary blood clot due to arteriosclerosis, at St. Francis Hospital in Milwaukee. He had taken a turn for the worse six months before his passing.

His host of maladies included a liver ailment, diabetes, and a pancreatic tumor. He was survived by his wife, Marie, son Oscar Jr., daughters Shirley and Marilyn, and 11 grand-children. Also surviving him were two sisters.[19]

In his later years, many of Felsch's teammates and friends faded into the sunset. Long after some die, perspective on one's life, although perhaps not entirely clear, can bring kinder words and indelible loyalty. One of Felsch's ex-teammates from his Triangle Billiards team was a gentleman named Howard Neustedler, Twenty-five years after Felsch's death, in 1989, the 78-year-old was living out his years in a Milwaukee area nursing facility. *Milwaukee Journal* baseball writer Tom Flaherty interviewed him that year. The headline said it all[20]: "Those Happy Days: Former teammate recalls Hap Felsch as a good man, not as a Black Sox"

Neustedler joked about his nickname, "Noisy." "I'm not mistaken, said Howard, "Happy Felsch was responsible for that. Baseball in those days featured talking it up. Talk it up! Talk it up! I guess I did fairly well at that. So the name 'Noisy.' It went with the pronunciation of my name." The frail ex-sandlot player who never came near Felsch's lifetime success, delighted in revealing that Felsch took him under his wing at a time when there was no true benefit to the old White Soxer other than being helpful.[21]

> When we played on the team, he kind of took me over. He worked with me and corrected all my mistakes. It made me a better ball player. And he let me use his bat, which was something. He still had one of those old hickory black bats. As a player, he was tops. As a person, he left nothing to be desired. He was an excellent person. Harry Kresbach lived where Hap Felsch grew up, around 19th and Center. This man knew Happy quite well. When I was old enough to understand, he took me aside and gave me the full pitch about Happy Felsch. He told me all the stories on Happy Felsch were not true. I placed a lot of confidence on his word because I knew he and Happy were real close.[22]

As a player, Neustedler made quite an impression on the ex-big leaguer. "That kid has got that way about him that makes a great ballplayer," explained Felsch. "He's what they call nonchalant. Nothing fazes him and he has the whole world licked."[23]

The irony of that last statement summed up the wasted baseball career of Oscar "Happy" Felsch. Perhaps if his career had mirrored Neustedler's, someone who played his tail off to make it big, but fell short, Felsch would have lived a much happier life. The man born laughing died with solemn remorse.

"You know the biggest regret? I got kicked out of baseball the year they souped up the ball," said Felsch. "Why, I would've hit forty homers with that lively ball! Like Ruth!"[24]

Postlude: Was Felsch a Future Hall of Famer?

Baseball from the 1910s to the 1920s presented the most dramatic change in baseball history. Opinions differ about whether the baseballs were harder. More tangible reasons for the offensive renaissance were the outlawing of spitballs, shine balls, and emery balls, and the more frequent use of newer balls during the course of a game. Prior to this change, balls would be replaced only if they could not be retrieved from the stands.[1]

Happy Felsch had his best season in 1920, when the average runs per game in the American League rose to 4.75, up from 4.10 in 1919. The league batting average climbed to .283 from .268, a sizable jump in one season. Dave Shiner, a Society for American Baseball Research member, projected that Felsch lost 50 percent of his career with his premature departure. Below are Felsch's actual and Shiner's projected career statistics.[2]

	G	AB	Runs	Hits	D'bles	Triples	HR	RBI	.AVG
Actual	749	2812	385	825	135	64	38	446	.293
Projected	1603	5939	715	1815	374	125	128	861	.306

These are not automatically Hall of Fame numbers, even for that time period. The projected 1,815 hits falls well short of today's standard, but below are some current inductees who had fewer than 2,000 hits in their careers:

+ Home Run Baker (1,838)
+ Lou Boudreau (1,779)
+ Mickey Cochrane (1,652)
+ Ray Schalk (1,345)
+ Frank Chance (1,274)

Felsch's projected power numbers and his superior defense could have put him over the voting hump. Boudreau is the most modern member of this group; he played mainly in the Live Ball Era. Schalk, Felsch's teammate in Chicago, lasted into the Live Ball Era, playing through 1929. Chance and Baker preceded 1920, with the former starting his career in 1898.

Another Milwaukee-born player, who actually idolized Felsch while he was sowing his youthful baseball oats, was Al Simmons, who debuted with Connie Mack's Philadelphia A's in 1924. Born Aloisius Szymanski, "Bucketfoot Al" referred to Felsch as his "lodestar" and put up tremendous numbers in a long career. He also benefited from the immense spike in offensive advantages in the 1920s and 1930s. Raised on Milwaukee's south side by Polish immigrants, Simmons is widely regarded as the city's all-time greatest player.

Adjusted for era and considering Felsch the superior defensive player, some might consider them very close. Felsch debuted with the White Sox at age 24, Simmons with the A's at age 22. Felsch's happy disposition was counter to Simmons's fierce, unbending, competitive spirit, the latter gaining the reputation of not being well-liked. They did, however, share an unabated passion for the game, and Milwaukee has not produced players quite as good since.

In the end, we will never really know how good Oscar "Happy" Felsch would have been. In White Sox and major league history, he stands proudly in a few all-time categories.

Major League History
+ 15 double plays in 1915 is still a major league record for outfielders today

White Sox History
+ 14 home runs in 1920 were the highest to date for the White Sox and was not surpassed until 1930 by Carl Reynolds, who hit 22
+ 13th in doubles (40) for a single season in 1920 (tied with several, including Shoeless Joe Jackson)
+ 13th all time with 64 career triples
+ 19th all-time in career slugging percentage (.427). Most who are ahead of him played in the modern era
+ 18th in single-season batting average, .338 in 1920

Chapter Notes

Introduction

1. Sean Deveney, *The Original Curse: Did the Cubs Throw the 1918 World Series to Babe Ruth's Red Sox and Incite the Black Sox Scandal* (New York: McGraw-Hill, 2010), 1.
2. Daniel A. Nathan, *Saying It's So: A Cultural History of the Black Sox Scandal* (Champaign: University of Illinois Press, 2003).

Chapter 1

1. John Gurda, *The Making of Milwaukee* (Milwaukee: Milwaukee County Historical Society, 1999), 59–63.
2. *Ibid.*, 68–69.
3. *Ibid.*, 61.
4. Kathleen Neils Conzen, *Immigrant Milwaukee 1836–1860: Accommodation and Community in a Frontier City* (Cambridge, MA: Harvard University Press, 1976), 85–90.
5. Eliot Asinof, *Bleeding Between the Lines* (New York: Holt, Rinehart & Winston, 1979), 113.
6. *Ibid.*, 114.
7. *Ibid.*, 115.

Chapter 2

1. Dennis Pajot, *The Rise of Milwaukee Baseball: The Cream City from Midwestern Outpost to the Major Leagues, 1859–1901* (Jefferson, NC: McFarland, 2009), 8.
2. *Milwaukee Sentinel*, April 3, 1911.
3. *Ibid.*
4. *Milwaukee Sentinel*, April 8, 1911.
5. *Milwaukee Sentinel*, April 10, 1911.
6. *Milwaukee Sentinel*, July 18, 1911.
7. *Milwaukee Sentinel*, July 17, 1911.
8. *Milwaukee Sentinel*, July 31, 1911.
9. *Milwaukee Sentinel*, August 7, 1911.

10. John Gurda, *The Making of Milwaukee* (Milwaukee: Milwaukee County Historical Society, 1999), 215.
11. *Milwaukee Sentinel*, April 21, 1912.
12. *Ibid.*
13. Peter Morris, *A Game of Inches: The Story Behind the Innovations That Shaped Baseball* (Chicago: Ivan R. Dee, 2006, 2010), 219.
14. *Milwaukee Sentinel*, May 27, 1912.
15. *Milwaukee Sentinel*, June 3, 1912.
16. *Milwaukee Sentinel*, June 10, 1912.
17. *Milwaukee Sentinel*, May 12, 1912.
18. *Ibid.*
19. *Milwaukee Sentinel*, May 27, 1912.
20. Chris Jaffe, *Evaluating Baseball Managers: A History and Analysis of Performance in the Major Leagues, 1896–2008* (Jefferson, NC: McFarland, 2010), 80–81.
21. *Manitowoc Herald*, June 24, 1912.
22. *Ibid.*
23. *Manitowoc Herald*, July 8, 1912.
24. *Ibid.*
25. *Milwaukee Sentinel*, March 24, 1933.
26. *Stevens Point Daily Journal*, July 25, 1912.
27. *Stevens Point Daily Journal*, August 1, 1912.
28. *Stevens Point Daily Journal*, August 5, 1912.
29. *Stevens Point Daily Journal*, August 31, 1912.
30. *Stevens Point Daily Journal*, September 7, 1912.
31. *Milwaukee Sentinel*, April 30, 1913.
32. *Ibid.*
33. Neil J. Sullivan, *The Minors: The Struggles and the Triumph of Baseball's Poor Relation From 1876 to the Present* (New York: St. Martin's Press, 1990), 33.
34. *Milwaukee Sentinel*, May 5, 1913.

35. *Milwaukee Sentinel*, May 8, 1913.
36. *Milwaukee Journal*, May 28, 1913.
37. *Milwaukee Sentinel*, June 1, 1913.
38. *Ibid.*
39. *Milwaukee Sentinel*, June 21, 1913.
40. *Milwaukee Sentinel*, June 22, 1913.
41. *Milwaukee Sentinel*, June 23, 1913.
42. *Milwaukee Sentinel*, June 24–25, 1913.
43. *Milwaukee Sentinel*, July 29, 1913.
44. *Milwaukee Sentinel*, August 7, 1913.

Chapter 3

1. *Milwaukee Journal*, November 27, 1932.
2. Bill O'Neal, *The American Association: A Baseball History 1902–1991* (Texas: Eakin Press, 1991), 1–10.
3. *Ibid.*, 44.
4. Marshall D. Wright, *The American Association: Year-by-Year Statistics for the Baseball Minor League, 1902–1952* (Jefferson, NC: McFarland, 1997), 68–80.
5. *Ibid.*
6. Brian A. Podoll, *The Minor League Milwaukee Brewers: 1859–1952* (Jefferson, NC: McFarland, 2003), 96.
7. *Milwaukee Sentinel*, August 8, 1913.
8. *Milwaukee Sentinel*, August 11, 1913.
9. *Ibid.*
10. *Milwaukee Sentinel*, August 18, 1913.
11. *Milwaukee Sentinel*, August 19, 1913.
12. *Milwaukee Sentinel*, August 23, 1913.
13. *Milwaukee Sentinel*, March 11–17, 1914.
14. *Milwaukee Sentinel*, March 16, 1914.
15. *Milwaukee Sentinel*, March 22, 1914.
16. *Milwaukee Sentinel*, March 30, 1914.
17. *Milwaukee Sentinel*, April 7, 1914.
18. *Milwaukee Sentinel*, April 12, 1914.
19. *Milwaukee Journal*, April 15, 1914.
20. *Milwaukee Sentinel*, May 4, 1914.
21. *Milwaukee Journal*, August 8, 1914.
22. *Milwaukee Journal*, August 9, 1914.
23. *Ibid.*
24. *Ibid.*
25. *Milwaukee Journal*, August 11, 1914.

Chapter 4

1. Bill James, *The New Bill James Historical Baseball Abstract: The Classic–Completely Revised* (New York: Free Press, 2001), 94.
2. *The Sporting News*, July 1, 1915.
3. *The Day* newspaper, June 9, 1915.
4. Harvey Frommer, *Shoeless Joe and Ragtime Baseball* (Lincoln: University of Nebraska Press, 1992), 59–64.

5. *Chicago Tribune*, February 27, 1915.
6. *Chicago Tribune*, March 5, 1915.
7. *Chicago Tribune*, March 7, 1915.
8. *Chicago Tribune*, March 4, 1915.
9. *Chicago Tribune*, April 3, 1915.
10. *Chicago Tribune*, April 2, 1915.
11. *Chicago Tribune*, April 16, 1915.
12. *The Sporting News*, April 29, 1915.
13. *The Sporting News*, May 6, 1915.
14. *Chicago Tribune*, May 19, 1915.
15. *Chicago Tribune*, May 31, 1915.
16. *Chicago Tribune*, June 9, 1915.
17. *Chicago Tribune*, June 10, 1915.
18. *Chicago Tribune*, June 19, 1915.
19. John Thorn, and Pete Palmer, and Michael Gershman, *Total Baseball: The Official Encyclopedia of Major League Baseball–Seventh Edition* (New York: Total Sports, 2001).
20. *Chicago Tribune*, August 2, 1915.
21. *Chicago Tribune*, August 22, 1915.
22. Jim Nitz, SABR Bio Project, *Happy Felsch.*
23. Harvey Frommer, *Shoeless Joe and Ragtime Baseball* (Lincoln: University of Nebraska Press, 1992), 66.
24. Geoffrey C. Ward, and Ken Burns, *Baseball: An Illustrated History* (New York: Alfred A. Knopf, 1994).
25. Connie Mack, *My 66 Years in the Big Leagues* (Philadelphia: Universal House, 1950).
26. *The Sporting News*, September 16, 1915.
27. *Milwaukee Journal* and *Milwaukee Sentinel*, October 29, 1915.

Chapter 5

1. Bill James, *The New Bill James Historical Baseball Abstract: The Classic–Completely Revised* (New York: Free Press, 2001), 220.
2. *Chicago Tribune*, April 19, 1916.
3. *Chicago Tribune*, April 27, 1916.
4. *Washington Post*, May 23, 1916.
5. Richard C. Lindberg, *Total White Sox: The Definitive Encyclopedia of the World Champion Franchise* (Chicago: Triumph Books, 2006), 17–18.
6. *Chicago Tribune*, May 27, 1916.
7. *Chicago Tribune*, June 5, 1916.
8. *The Sporting News*, July 6, 1916.
9. Bill James, *The New Bill James Historical Baseball Abstract.*
10. *The Sporting News*, July 6, 1916.
11. *Chicago Tribune*, August 17, 1916.
12. David S. Neft, and Richard M. Cohen, and Michael L. Neft, *The Sports Encyclopedia:*

Baseball (New York: St. Martin's Griffin, 2007).

13. *Pittsburgh Press*, November 28, 1916.

Chapter 6

1. Harold Seymour, and Dorothy Seymour Mills, *Baseball: The Golden Age* (New York: Oxford University Press, 1971), 294–303.

2. *The Sporting News*, March 31, 1917.

3. *The Sporting News*, March 29, 1917.

4. *Hall of Fame Library file on Oscar Felsch*, August 17, 1964.

5. *The Sporting News*, April 26, 1917.

6. *Chicago Tribune*, April 12, 1917.

7. *Chicago Tribune*, April 16, 1917.

8. Bill James, and Rob Neyer, *The Neyer/ James Guide to Pitchers: An Historical Compendium of Pitching, Pitchers, and Pitches* (New York: Fireside Books, 2004), 40–41.

9. *Chicago Tribune*, May 25, 1917.

10. Gerald E. Shenk, *Work or Fight: Race, Gender, and the Draft in World War One* (New York: Palgrave, 2005).

11. *Chicago Tribune*, June 17, 1917.

12. Daniel E. Ginsburg, *The Fix Is In: A History of Baseball Gambling and Game Fixing Scandals* (Jefferson, NC: McFarland, 2003), 100–134.

13. Harvey Frommer, *Shoeless Joe and Ragtime Baseball* (Lincoln: University of Nebraska Press, 1992), 70–84.

14. *Chicago Tribune*, July 2, 1917.

15. *Chicago Tribune*, July 11, 1917.

16. John Thorn, and Pete Palmer, and Michael Gershman, *Total Baseball, 7th Edition* (Tampa, FL: Total Sports Publishing, 2001).

17. *Chicago Tribune*, July 26, 1917.

18. *The Sporting News*, July 12, 1917.

19. *Chicago Tribune*, August 3, 1917.

20. *Chicago Tribune*, July 24, 1917.

21. *The Sporting News*, September 6, 1917.

22. *Ibid.*

23. *Ibid.*

24. *Chicago Tribune*, September 22, 1917.

25. *Milwaukee Journal*, September 22, 1917.

26. *Chicago Tribune*, October 2, 1917.

Chapter 7

1. Bill James, *The Bill James Guide to Baseball Managers: from 1870 to Today* (New York: Scribner, 1997), 48.

2. *Chicago Tribune*, October 3, 1917.

3. Bill James, and Rob Neyer, *The Neyer/ James Guide to Pitchers: An Historical Compendium of Pitching, Pitchers, and Pitches* (New York: Fireside Books, 2004), 377.

4. *Milwaukee Journal*, October 7, 1918.

5. *New York Times*, October 5, 1917.

6. *Chicago Tribune*, October 6, 1917.

7. *Ibid.*

8. *Chicago Tribune*, October 2, 1917.

9. *Chicago Tribune*, October 7, 1917.

10. *New York Times*, October 7, 1917.

11. *Chicago Tribune*, October 7, 1917.

12. *Milwaukee Journal*, October 7, 1917.

13. *New York Times*, October 7, 1917.

14. *Ibid.*

15. *Milwaukee Journal*, October 7, 1917.

16. *Milwaukee Journal*, October 10, 1917.

17. *New York Times*, October 8, 1917.

18. *Chicago Tribune*, October 8, 1917.

19. *Ibid.*

20. *Ibid.*

21. *Ibid.*

22. *New York Times*, October 8, 1917.

23. *New York Times*, October 10, 1917.

24. *The Sporting News*, October 11, 1917.

25. *Chicago Tribune*, October 12, 1917.

26. *Chicago Tribune*, October 13, 1917.

27. *Chicago Tribune*, October 14, 1917.

28. *Ibid.*

29. *New York Times*, October 10, 1917.

30. *New York Times*, October 14, 1917.

31. *Chicago Tribune*, October 14, 1917.

32. *Ibid.*

33. *New York Times*, October 14, 1917.

34. *Chicago Tribune*, October 15, 1917.

35. *New York Times*, October 16, 1917.

36. *Chicago Tribune*, October 16, 1917.

37. *Milwaukee Journal*, October 18, 1917.

38. *Chicago Tribune*, October 16, 1917.

39. John Thorn, and Pete Palmer, and Michael Gershman, *Total Baseball: The Official Encyclopedia of Major League Baseball—Seventh Edition* (New York: Total Sports, 2001), 293.

40. Harvey Frommer, *Shoeless Joe and Ragtime Baseball* (Lincoln: University of Nebraska Press, 1992), 77–87.

41. *Milwaukee Journal*, October 10, 1917.

42. *Milwaukee Journal*, October 18, 1917.

43. *Pittsburgh Press*, October 24, 1917.

Chapter 8

1. Harvey Frommer, *Shoeless Joe and Ragtime Baseball* (Lincoln: University of Nebraska Press, 1992), 84–94.

2. David S. Neft, Richard M. Cohen, and Michael L. Neft, *The Sports Encyclopedia:*

Baseball (New York: St. Martin's Griffin, 2004), 84–85.

3. *Chicago Tribune*, March 19, 1918.

4. *Chicago Tribune*, March 20, 1918.

5. *Chicago Tribune*, March 25, 1918.

6. *The Sporting News*, March 28, 1918.

7. *Chicago Tribune*, May 10, 1918.

8. *Ibid.*

9. Frommer, *Shoeless Joe and Ragtime Baseball*, 77–83.

10. Harold Seymour and Dorothy Seymour Mills, *Baseball: The Golden Age* (New York: Oxford University Press, 1971), 274–278.

11. *Chicago Tribune*, June 3, 1918.

12. *Chicago Tribune*, June 4, 1918.

13. *Milwaukee Sentinel*, July 2, 1918.

14. *Chicago Tribune*, July 2, 1918.

15. *The Sporting News*, January 9, 1919.

16. *Milwaukee Sentinel*, July 3, 1918.

17. *Ibid.*

18. *Milwaukee Sentinel*, July 15, 1918.

19. *Milwaukee Journal*, July 29, 1918.

20. *Milwaukee Sentinel*, August 19, 1918.

21. *Milwaukee Sentinel* and *Milwaukee Journal*, October 15, 1918.

22. *Chicago Tribune*, January 1, 1918.

23. *The Sporting News*, January 9, 1919.

24. *Chicago Tribune*, January 23, 1919.

25. *Chicago Tribune*, February 21, 1919.

Chapter 9

1. *The Sporting News*, January 2, 1919.

2. Donald Gropman, *Say It Ain't So, Joe: The True Story of Shoeless Joe Jackson and the 1919 World Series* (New York: Lynx Books, 1979), 170–178.

3. *The Sporting News*, January 23, 1919.

4. *Chicago Tribune*, March 21, 1919.

5. *Ibid.*

6. *Chicago Tribune*, April 24, 1919.

7. *Chicago Tribune*, May 3, 1919.

8. *Chicago Tribune*, May 8, 1919.

9. Bill James, and Rob Neyer, *The Neyer/James Guide to Pitchers: An Historical Compendium of Pitching, Pitchers, and Pitches* (New York: Fireside Books, 2004), 164.

10. *Chicago Tribune*, May 23, 1919.

11. *Chicago Tribune*, May 26, 1919.

12. *Chicago Tribune*, May 28, 1919.

13. *Chicago Tribune*, May 31, 1919.

14. *The Sporting News*, June 19, 1919.

15. *Chicago Tribune*, July 2, 1919.

16. *Chicago Tribune*, June 25, 1919.

17. *Milwaukee Sentinel*, October 9, 1919.

18. *The Sporting News*, July 3, 1919.

19. *Chicago Tribune*, July 3, 1919.

20. *The Sporting News*, August 21, 1919.

21. *Chicago Tribune*, September 12, 1919.

22. *The Sporting News*, September 18, 1919.

23. William A. Cook, *The 1919 World Series: What Really Happened* (Jefferson, NC: McFarland, 2001), 83–95.

24. Eliot Asinof, *Eight Men Out: The Black Sox and the 1919 World Series* (New York: Holt, Rinehart & Winston, 1963), 34–37.

25. Wayne Anderson, *The Chicago Black Sox Trial: A Primary Source Account* (New York: Rosen Publishing Group, 2004), 8–12.

26. *Ibid.*, 11–16.

27. Asinof, *Eight Men Out*, 35–39.

28. Gene Carney, *Burying the Black Sox: How Baseball's Cover-Up of the 1919 World Series Fix Almost Succeeded* (Washington, D.C.: Potomac, 2007), 112–116.

29. Asinof, *Eight Men Out*, 37–40.

30. Anderson, *The Chicago Black Sox Trial*, 8–12.

31. *Ibid.*, 13–14.

32. *Sports Illustrated*, September 17, 1956.

Chapter 10

1. *Chicago Tribune*, October 1, 1919.

2. *Ibid.*

3. *Washington Post*, October 1, 1919.

4. Eliot Asinof, *Eight Men Out: The Black Sox and the 1919 World Series* (New York: Holt, Rinehart, and Winston, 1963), 53.

5. *Ibid.*, 47.

6. *Ibid.*, 59.

7. Victor Luhrs, *The Great Baseball Mystery: The 1919 World Series* (South Brunswick, NJ: A. S. Barnes, 1966), 167.

8. *New York Times*, October 2, 1919.

9. Asinof, *Eight Men Out*, 66.

10. Fred Lieb, *Baseball As I Have Known It* (Lincoln: University of Nebraska Press, 1977), 106.

11. *Washington Post*, October 2, 1919.

12. *Milwaukee Sentinel*, October 2, 1919.

13. John Lardner, "Remembering the Black Sox" *Saturday Evening Post*, April 30, 1938.

14. Asinof, *Eight Men Out*, 93–97.

15. Wayne Anderson, *The Chicago Black Sox Trial: A Primary Source Account* (New York: Rosen Publishing Group, 2004), 17–19.

16. *Washington Post*, October 3, 1919.

17. *Chicago Tribune*, October 3, 1919.

18. *New York Times*, October 3, 1919.

19. *Ibid.*

20. *Chicago Tribune*, October 3, 1919.

21. *Milwaukee Sentinel*, October 3, 1919.

22. Asinof, *Eight Men Out*, 94.

23. *Washington Post*, October 4, 1919.

24. *New York Times*, October 4, 1919.

25. *Chicago Tribune*, October 4, 1919.

26. *The Spalding Baseball Guide*, 1920.

27. *Washington Post*, October 4, 1919.

28. Daniel E. Ginsburg, *The Fix Is In: A History of Baseball Gambling and Game Fixing Scandals* (Jefferson, NC: McFarland, 2003), 117–124.

29. Gary Gillette, and Pete Palmer, *The ESPN Baseball Encyclopedia*, fifth edition (New York: Sterling, 2008), 184–185.

30. Eliot Asinof, *Eight Men Out: The Black Sox and the 1919 World Series* (New York: Holt, Rinehart, and Winston, 1963), 104–105.

31. *Chicago Tribune*, October 5, 1919.

32. *Ibid.*

33. *Ibid.*

34. *Ibid.*

35. *Cincinnati Post*, October 5, 1919.

36. *Washington Post*, October 5, 1919.

37. *Chicago Tribune*, October 7, 1919.

38. *Ibid.*

39. *Ibid.*

40. *Washington Post*, October 7, 1919.

41. *Ibid.*

42. Asinof, *Eight Men Out*, 108.

43. *Ibid.*, 109–110.

44. *Los Angeles Times*, October 8, 1919.

45. Victor Luhrs, *The Great Baseball Mystery: The 1919 World Series* (South Brunswick, NJ: A.S. Barnes, 1966), 72–75.

46. *Los Angeles Times*, October 8, 1919.

47. Asinof, *Eight Men Out*, 115–116.

48. *Chicago Tribune*, October 8, 1919.

49. Michael T. Lynch, Jr., *It Ain't So: A Might-have-been History of the White Sox in 1919 and Beyond* (Jefferson, NC: McFarland, 2009).

50. *New York Times*, October 8, 1919.

51. *Chicago Tribune*, October 9, 1919.

52. *Ibid.*

53. William A. Cook, *The 1919 World Series: What Really Happened* (Jefferson, NC: McFarland, 2001), 87–93.

54. *Chicago Tribune*, October 9, 1919.

55. Asinof, *Eight Men Out*, 111.

56. *Washington Post*, October 9, 1919.

57. William A. Cook, *The 1919 World Series*, 91–94.

58. Victor Luhrs, *The Great Baseball Mystery: The 1919 World Series* (South Brunswick, NJ: A.S. Barnes, 1966), 72–77.

59. *New York Times*, October 9, 1919.

60. *Washington Post*, October 9, 1919.

Chapter 11

1. Irv Goldfarb, SABR Bio Project, *Charles Comiskey.*

2. Daniel E. Ginsberg, *The Fix Is In* (Jefferson, NC: McFarland, 1995).

3. Jim Nitz, SABR Bio Project, *Happy Felsch.*

4. Daniel E. Ginsburg, *The Fix Is In*, 131–133.

5. Harold Seymour, and Dorothy Seymour Mills, *Baseball: The Golden Age* (New York: Oxford University Press, 1971), 296–297.

6. Robert C. Cottrell, *Blackball, the Black Sox, and the Babe* (Jefferson, NC: McFarland, 2002), 201.

7. Leonard Koppett, *Koppett's Concise History of Major League Baseball* (New York: Carroll & Graf, 1998), 151–154.

8. *Chicago Tribune*, March 26, 1920.

9. *Milwaukee Journal*, April 11, 1920.

10. *Ibid.*

11. Robert C. Cottrell, *Blackball, the Black Sox, and the Babe* (Jefferson, NC: McFarland, 2002), 143–146.

12. *Chicago Tribune*, May 25, 1920.

13. *Chicago Tribune*, May 30, 1920.

14. *Chicago Tribune*, July 18, 1920.

15. Eliot Asinof, *Eight Men Out: The Black Sox and the 1919 World Series* (New York: Holt, Rinehart, and Winston, 1963), 145–146.

16. *Ibid.*, 146.

17. *Ibid.*, 143.

18. *Chicago Tribune*, August 16, 1920.

19. Seymour and Mills, *Baseball: The Golden Age*, 88.

20. *Ibid.*

21. Bill James, and Rob Neyer, *The Neyer/James Guide to Pitchers: An Historical Compendium of Pitching, Pitchers, and Pitches* (New York: Fireside Books, 2004), 364.

22. *Chicago Tribune*, August 22, 1920.

23. *Chicago Tribune*, August 28, 1920.

24. Asinof, *Eight Men Out*, 148.

25. Victor Luhrs, *The Great Baseball Mystery: The 1919 World Series* (South Brunswick, NJ: A.S. Barnes, 1966), 86.

26. Seymour and Mills, *Baseball: The Golden Age*, 298.

27. Asinof, *Eight Men Out*, 151.

28. *Ibid.*

29. *Ibid.*, 156–157.

30. Seymour and Mills, *Baseball: The Golden Age*, 300–303.

31. *Chicago Tribune*, September 27, 1920.

Chapter 12

1. Eliot Asinof, *Eight Men Out: The Black Sox and the 1919 World Series* (New York: Holt, Rinehart & Winston, 1963), 163–164.

2. *Ibid.*, 170.

3. *Chicago Tribune*, September 29, 1920.

4. William F. Lamb, *Black Sox in the Courtroom: The Grand Jury, Criminal Trial and Civil Litigation* (Jefferson, NC: McFarland, 2013), 29–30.

5. *Ibid.*, 31.

6. *Ibid.*, 32.

7. Asinof, *Eight Men Out*, 179.

8. *Milwaukee Sentinel*, September 29, 1920.

9. *Ibid.*

10. *Ibid.*

11. *Ibid.*

12. Asinof, *Eight Men Out*, 188–189.

13. Luhrs, *The Great Baseball Mystery: The 1919 World Series* (New Jersey: A. S. Barnes), 185, 250.

14. Asinof, *Eight Men Out*, 188–189.

15. *Chicago American*, September 30, 1920.

16. *Ibid.*

17. Gene Carney, *Burying the Black Sox: How Baseball's Cover-Up of the 1919 World Series Fix Almost Succeeded* (Washington, D.C.: Potomac Books, 2007), 127.

18. Lamb, *Black Sox in the Courtroom*, 57.

19. *Milwaukee Sentinel*, September 30, 1920.

20. *Chicago Tribune*, September 30, 1920.

21. *Milwaukee Sentinel*, September 30, 1920.

22. Asinof, *Eight Men Out*, 193.

23. Victor Luhrs, *The Great Baseball Mystery: The 1919 World Series* (New Jersey: A. S. Barnes), 183–184.

24. *Milwaukee Sentinel*, October 4, 1920.

25. Lamb, *Black Sox in the Courtroom*, 74.

26. *Milwaukee Sentinel*, October 30, 1920.

27. Harold Seymour and Dorothy Seymour Mills, *Baseball: The Golden Age* (New York: Oxford University Press, 1971), 315–321.

28. David Pietrusza, *Judge and Jury: The Life and Times of Judge Kenesaw Mountain Landis* (Indiana: Diamond Communications, 1998), 2–6.

29. Donald Honig, *Baseball America: The Heroes of the Game and Times of Their Glory* (New York: Galahad Books, 1985), 113–114.

30. Asinof, *Eight Men Out*, 223–224.

31. Leonard Koppett, *Koppett's Concise History of Major League Baseball* (New York: Carroll & Graf, 1998, 2004), 161.

32. *Ibid.*, 173.

33. Robert C. Cottrell, *Blackball, the Black Sox, and the Babe* (Jefferson, NC: McFarland, 2002), 233–235.

34. *The Sporting News*, November 18, 1920.

35. Seymour and Mills, *Baseball: The Golden Age*, 321–323.

Chapter 13

1. *Los Angeles Times*, November 13, 1920.

2. *Chicago Tribune*, January 12, 1921.

3. *Ibid.*

4. Harvey Frommer, *Shoeless Joe and Ragtime Baseball* (Lincoln: University of Nebraska Press, 1992), 160.

5. Harold Seymour and Dorothy Seymour Mills, *Baseball: The Golden Age* (New York: Oxford University Press, 1971), 325.

6. William F. Lamb, *Black Sox in the Courtroom: The Grand Jury, Criminal Trial and Civil Litigation* (Jefferson, NC: McFarland, 2013), 90.

7. Frommer, *Shoeless Joe and Ragtime Baseball*, 161.

8. Seymour and Mills, *Baseball: The Golden Age*, 325.

9. Eliot Asinof, *Eight Men Out: The Black Sox and the 1919 World Series* (New York: Holt, Rinehart, and Winston, 1963), 237–238.

10. *Chicago Tribune*, June 29, 1921.

11. *Chicago Tribune*, June 28, 1921.

12. Lamb, *Black Sox in the Courtroom*, 103–104.

13. *New York Times*, June 28, 1921.

14. *Milwaukee Journal*, July 3, 1921.

15. *Milwaukee Journal*, July 6, 1921.

16. *Chicago Tribune*, July 7, 1921.

17. *Milwaukee Journal*, July 14, 1921.

18. *Milwaukee Journal*, July 15, 1921.

19. *Milwaukee Journal*, July 10, 1921.

20. Daniel E. Ginsburg, *The Fix Is In: A History of Baseball Gambling and Game Fixing Scandals* (Jefferson, NC: McFarland, 2003), 143.

21. Lamb, *Black Sox in the Courtroom*, 101–102.

22. Ginsburg, *The Fix Is In*, 143–144.

23. Seymour and Mills, *Baseball: The Golden Age*, 327.

24. Jim Nitz, SABR Bio Project, *Happy Felsch*.

25. Lamb, *Black Sox in the Courtroom*, 102.

26. *Chicago American*, September 30, 1920.

27. Seymour and Mills, *Baseball: The Golden Age*, 326.

28. Asinof, *Eight Men Out*, 242.

29. *The Sporting News*, August 4, 1921.

30. *Chicago American*, September 30, 1920.

31. Eliot Asinof, *1919: America's Loss of Innocence* (New York: Donald I. Fine, 1990), 320–324.

32. *Chicago Tribune*, July 19, 1921.

33. Lamb, *Black Sox in the Courtroom*, 111.

34. Seymour and Mills, *Baseball: The Golden Age*, 327.

35. *Chicago American*, September 30, 1920.

36. Asinof, *Eight Men Out*, 247–248.

37. Lamb, *Black Sox in the Courtroom*, 114.

38. *Chicago American*, September 30, 1920.

39. Lamb, *Black Sox in the Courtroom*, 128.

40. Asinof, *Eight Men Out*, 261.

41. *Chicago American*, September 30, 1920.

42. Asinof, *Eight Men Out*, 113–114.

43. *Ibid.*, 255–256.

44. *Chicago American*, September 30, 1920.

45. Asinof, *Eight Men Out*, 258–261.

46. Lamb, *Black Sox in the Courtroom*, 132.

47. Asinof, *Eight Men Out*, 261.

48. Lamb, *Black Sox in the Courtroom*, 133–134.

49. *Chicago American*, September 30, 1920.

50. Lamb, *Black Sox in the Courtroom*, 138–139.

51. *Ibid.*, 139.

52. *Washington Post*, August 2, 1921.

53. Lamb, *Black Sox in the Courtroom*, 138–139.

54. *Washington Post*, July 31, 1921.

55. *Chicago American*, September 30, 1920.

56. Lamb, *Black Sox in the Courtroom*, 139–140.

57. *Ibid.*, 140.

58. *Ibid.*

59. *Chicago Tribune*, August 3, 1921.

60. *Ibid.*

61. *Milwaukee Sentinel*, August 3, 1921.

62. *Chicago Tribune*, August 3, 1921.

63. *Milwaukee Sentinel*, August 3, 1921.

64. Lamb, *Black Sox in the Courtroom*, 142–144.

65. *Los Angeles Times*, August 4, 1921.

66. *Ibid.*

67. *Chicago American*, September 30, 1920.

68. *Ibid.*

Chapter 14

1. William F. Lamb, *Black Sox in the Courtroom: The Grand Jury, Criminal Trial and Civil Litigation* (Jefferson, NC: McFarland, 2013), 151.

2. Eliot Asinof, *Eight Men Out: The Black Sox and the 1919 World Series* (New York: Holt, Rinehart & Winston, 1963), 288.

3. *Chicago Tribune*, April 27, 1922.

4. *Chicago Tribune*, May 13, 1922.

5. *New York Times*, May 13, 1922.

6. *Ibid.*

7. *Ibid.*

8. David Pietrusza, *Judge and Jury: The Life and Times of Judge Kenesaw Mountain Landis* (Indiana: Diamond Communications, 1998), 296–299.

9. *New York Times*, May 14, 1922.

10. *Ibid.*

11. Lamb, *Black Sox in the Courtroom*, 152.

12. *Milwaukee Journal*, October 3, 1988; Jim Nitz, SABR Bio Project, *Happy Felsch*.

13. *Milwaukee Journal*, May 18, 1939; Jim Nitz, SABR Bio Project, *Happy Felsch*.

14. *Milwaukee Sentinel*, January 29, 1924.

15. *Milwaukee Sentinel*, January 31, 1924.

16. *Ibid.*

17. Lamb, *Black Sox in the Courtroom*, 172–173.

18. *Milwaukee Sentinel*, February 6, 1924.

19. *Milwaukee Sentinel*, February 11, 1924.

20. *Milwaukee Sentinel*, February 13, 1924.

21. *Ibid.*

22. Lamb, *Black Sox in the Courtroom*, 181.

23. *Milwaukee Sentinel*, February 14, 1924.

24. Lamb, *Black Sox in the Courtroom*, 181.

25. *Milwaukee Sentinel*, February 13, 1924.

26. Lamb, *Black Sox in the Courtroom*, 181.

27. *Ibid.*, 189.

28. *Milwaukee Sentinel*, February 15, 1924.

29. *Milwaukee Sentinel*, February 16, 1924.

30. *Ibid.*

31. Lamb, *Black Sox in the Courtroom*, 189–190.

32. *Ibid.*, 194.

33. Stephen Rundio III, "From Black Sox to Sauk Sox: When Oscar 'Happy' Felsch and George 'Buck' Weaver Played Baseball in Sauk County, Wisconsin," 1997 SABR Research Symposium, 1924.

34. *Ibid.*

35. *Ibid.*

36. *Ibid.*

37. *Ibid.*

38. *Ibid.*

39. *Milwaukee Journal*, February 9, 1925.
40. *Milwaukee Sentinel*, February 10, 1925.
41. *Milwaukee Sentinel*, May 25, 1925.
42. Lamb, *Black Sox in the Courtroom*, 196–197.

Chapter 15

1. Gary Lucht, "Scobey's Touring Pros: Wheat, Baseball, and Illicit Booze" *Montana: The Magazine of Western History* (Summer 1970): 88–92.
2. *Ibid.*
3. *Ibid.*
4. *Ibid.*
5. *Ibid.*
6. *Ibid.*
7. *Ibid.*
8. *Ibid.*
9. Dorothy Rustebakke, "Prairie Baseball in 1920's Featured Pro Players," *Daniels County Leader*, November 3, 2005.
10. Keith Whipple interview, as told to Dorothy Rustebakke.
11. Rustebakke, "Prairie Baseball in 1920's Featured Pro Players."
12. Gary Lucht, "Scobey's Touring Pros: Wheat, Baseball, and Illicit Booze," *Montana: The Magazine of Western History* (Summer 1970): 88–92.
13. *Plentywood Herald*, July 10, 1925.
14. Gary Lucht, "Scobey's Touring Pros."
15. Jim Nitz, SABR Bio Project, *Happy Felsch*.
16. *Milwaukee Sentinel*, January 3, 1927.
17. *Regina Morning Leader*, May 14, 1927.
18. *Regina Morning Leader*, May 26, 1927.
19. *Regina Morning Leader*, June 14, 1927.
20. *Regina Morning Leader*, June 4, 1927.
21. *Regina Morning Leader*, June 14, 1927.
22. *Regina Morning Leader*, June 22, 1927.
23. *Regina Morning Leader*, June 7, 1927.
24. *Regina Morning Leader*, August 10, 1927.
25. *Regina Morning Leader*, August 11, 1927.
26. *Regina Morning Leader*, August 13, 1927.
27. *Reading (PA) Eagle*, December 1, 1927.
28. Daniel Okrent, *Last Call: The Rise and Fall of Prohibition* (New York: Scribner, 2010), 3–4.
29. *Milwaukee Sentinel*, April 19, 1928.
30. *Milwaukee Sentinel*, April 28, 1928.
31. *Plentywood Herald*, June 1, 1928.
32. *Plentywood Herald*, June 15, 1928.
33. *Plentywood Herald*, July 12, 1928.
34. *Plentywood Herald*, August 9, 1928.

35. *The Virden Empire-Advance*, July 23, 1929.
36. *The Virden Empire-Advance*, August 6, 1929.
37. *The Virden Empire-Advance*, July 1, 1930.
38. Jim Nitz, SABR Bio Project, *Happy Felsch*.
39. *Milwaukee Journal*, May 16, 1932.
40. *Ibid.*
41. *Wright's City Directories of Milwaukee*, 1932.
42. *Milwaukee Journal*, May 22, 1933.
43. *Milwaukee Journal*, August 18, 1964.
44. *Milwaukee Journal*, May 19, 1934.
45. Jim Nitz, SABR Bio Project, *Happy Felsch*.

Chapter 16

1. *The Charleston Gazette*, September 25, 1956.
2. *Ibid.*
3. *Ibid.*
4. *Ibid.*
5. *Ibid.*
6. *Ibid.*
7. *Ibid.*
8. *Ibid.*
9. *Ibid.*
10. Eliot Asinof, *Bleeding Between the Lines* (New York: Holt, Rinehart & Winston, 1979), 112–113.
11. *Ibid.*, 112–113.
12. *Ibid.*, 113–114.
13. *Ibid.*, 114–115.
14. *Ibid.*, 115.
15. *Ibid.*, 115–116.
16. *Ibid.*, 116.
17. *Ibid.*, 117.
18. *Ibid.*
19. *Milwaukee Journal*, August 18, 1964.
20. *Milwaukee Journal*, August 19, 1989.
21. *Ibid.*
22. *Ibid.*
23. *Ibid.*
24. Asinof, *Bleeding Between the Lines*, 117.

Postlude

1. Bill James, *The New Bill James Historical Baseball Abstract: The Classic—Completely Revised* (New York: Free Press, 2001), 122.
2. Jim Nitz, SABR Bio Project, *Happy Felsch*.

Bibliography

Books

Anderson, Wayne. *The Chicago Black Sox Trial: A Primary Source Account.* New York: Rosen Publishing Group, 2004.

Asinof, Eliot. *Eight Men Out: The Black Sox and the 1919 World Series.* New York: Holt, Rinehart, & Winston, 1963.

Asinof, Eliot. *1919: America's Loss of Innocence.* New York: Donald I. Fine, 1990.

Asinof, Eliot. *Bleeding Between the Lines.* New York: Holt, Rinehart & Winston, 1979.

Barthel, Thomas. *Baseball, Barnstorming, and Exhibition Games, 1901–1962: A History of Off-Season Major League Play.* Jefferson, NC: McFarland, 2007.

Carney, Gene. *Burying the Black Sox: How Baseball's Cover-Up of the 1919 World Series Fix Almost Succeeded.* Washington, D.C.: Potomac Books, 2007.

Conzen, Kathleen Neils. *Immigrant Milwaukee 1836–1860: Accommodation and Community in a Frontier City.* Cambridge, MA: Harvard University Press, 1976.

Cook, William A. *The 1919 World Series: What Really Happened?* Jefferson, NC: McFarland, 2001.

Cottrell, Robert C. *Blackball, the Black Sox, and the Babe.* Jefferson, NC: McFarland, 2002.

Deveney, Sean. *The Original Curse: Did the Cubs Throw the 1918 World Series to Babe Ruth's Red Sox and Incite the Black Sox Scandal.* New York: McGraw-Hill, 2010.

Frommer, Harvey. *Shoeless Joe and Ragtime Baseball.* Lincoln: University of Nebraska Press, 1992.

Gillette, Gary, and Pete Palmer. *The ESPN Baseball Encyclopedia,* fifth edition. New York: Sterling, 2008.

Ginsburg, Daniel E. *The Fix Is In: A History of Baseball Gambling and Game Fixing Scandals.* Jefferson, NC: McFarland, 2003.

Gropman, Donald. *Say It Ain't So, Joe: The True Story of Shoeless Joe Jackson and the 1919 World Series.* New York: Lynx Books, 1979.

Gurda, John. *The Making of Milwaukee.* Milwaukee County Historical Society, 1999.

Honig, Donald. *Baseball America: The Heroes of the Game and Times of Their Glory.* New York: Galahad Books, 1985.

Jaffe, Chris. *Evaluating Baseball Managers: A History and Analysis of Performance in the Major Leagues, 1896–2008.* Jefferson, NC: McFarland, 2010.

James, Bill. *The Bill James Guide to Baseball Managers: from 1870 to Today.* New York: Scribner, 1997.

James, Bill. *The New Bill James Historical Baseball Abstract: The Classic—Completely Revised.* New York: Free Press, a division of Simon & Schuster, 2001.

James, Bill, and Rob Neyer. *The Neyer/James Guide to Pitchers: An Historical Compendium of Pitching, Pitchers, and Pitches.* New York: Fireside Books, 2004.

Koppett, Leonard. *Koppett's Concise History of Major League Baseball.* New York: Carroll & Graf, 1998, 2004.

Lamb, William F. *Black Sox in the Courtroom: The Grand Jury, Criminal Trial and Civil Litigation.* Jefferson, NC: McFarland, 2013.

Lardner, John. *The John Lardner Reader: A Press Box Legend's Classic Sportswriting.* Lincoln: University of Nebraska Press, 2010.

Lieb, Fred. *Baseball As I Have Known It.* Lincoln: University of Nebraska Press, 1977.

Lindberg, Richard C. *Total White Sox: The Definitive Encyclopedia of the World Champion Franchise.* Chicago: Triumph Books, 2006.

Luhrs, Victor. *The Great Baseball Mystery: The 1919 World Series*. South Brunswick, NJ: A.S. Barnes, 1966.

Lynch, Michael T. Jr. *It Ain't So: A Might-Have-Been History of the White Sox in 1919 and Beyond*. Jefferson, NC: McFarland, 2009.

Mack, Connie. *My 66 Years in the Big Leagues*. New York: Amereon House, 1950.

Morris, Peter. *A Game of Inches: The Story Behind the Innovations That Shaped Baseball*. Chicago: Ivan R. Dee, 2006, 2010.

Muchlinski, Alan. *After the Black Sox: The Swede Risberg Story*. Indiana: Author House, 2005.

Neft, David S., and Richard M. Cohen, and Michael L. Neft. *The Sports Encyclopedia: Baseball*. New York: St. Martin's Griffin, 2004.

O'Neal, Bill. *The American Association: A Baseball History 1902–1991*. Austin, TX: Eakin Press, 1991.

Okrent, Daniel. *Last Call: The Rise and Fall of Prohibition*. New York: Scribner, 2010.

Pajot, Dennis. *The Rise of Milwaukee Baseball: The Cream City from Midwestern Outpost to the Major Leagues, 1859–1901*. Jefferson, NC: McFarland, 2009.

Pietrusza, David. *Judge and Jury: The Life and Times of Judge Kenesaw Mountain Landis*. South Bend, IN: Diamond Communications, Inc., 1998.

Pietrusza, David. *Rothstein: The Life, Times, and Murder of the Criminal Genius Who Fixed the World Series*. New York: Carroll & Graf, 2003.

Podoll, Brian A. *The Minor League Milwaukee Brewers: 1859–1952*. Jefferson, NC: McFarland, 2003.

Seymour, Harold, and Dorothy Seymour Mills. *Baseball: The Golden Age*. New York: Oxford University Press, 1971.

Sullivan, Neill J. *The Minors: The Struggles and Triumph of Baseball's Poor Relation from 1876 to the Present*. New York: St. Martin's Press, 1990.

Thorn, John, and Pete Palmer, and Michael Gershman. *Total Baseball: The Official Encyclopedia of Major League Baseball*, seventh edition. New York: Total Sports Publishing, 2001.

Ward, Geoffrey C., and Ken Burns. *Baseball: An Illustrated History*. New York: Alfred A. Knopf, 1994.

Wells, Robert. *This Is Milwaukee: A Colorful Portrait of the City That Made Beer Famous*. Milwaukee: Renaissance Books, 1970.

Wright, Marshall D. *The American Associa-tion: Year-by-Year Statistics for the Baseball Minor League, 1902–1952*. Jefferson, NC: McFarland, 1997.

Newspapers/Articles

The Charleston Gazette, 1956.
Chicago American, 1920.
Chicago Tribune, 1914–1935.
Cincinnati Post, 1919.
The Day, 1915.
Nitz, Jim. *SABR Bio Project*, Happy Felsch.
Lardner, John. "Remembering the Black Sox" *Saturday Evening Post*, 1938.
Los Angeles Times, 1918–1925.
Lucht, Gary "Scobey's Touring Pros: Wheat, Baseball, and Illicit Booze" *Montana: The Magazine of Western History*, Summer 1970, 88–92.
Manitowoc Herald, 1912.
Milwaukee Journal, 1911–1989.
Milwaukee Sentinel, 1911–1964.
New York Times, 1916–1925.
Pease, Neal. "The Kosciuszko Reds, 1909–1919: Kings of the Milwaukee Sandlots" 2004.
Pittsburgh Press, 1916.
Plentywood Herald, 1925–1928.
Regina Morning Leader, 1927.
Rundio III, Stephen. "From Black Sox to Sauk Sox: When Oscar 'Happy' Felsch and George 'Buck' Weaver Played Baseball in Sauk County, Wisconsin" *Montana: 1997 SABR Research Symposium*, 1924.
Rustebakke, Dorothy. "Prairie Baseball in 1920's Featured Pro Players" *Daniels County Leader*, November 3, 2005.
Shenk, Gerald E. "Work or Fight: Race, Gender, and the Draft in World War One." New York: Palgrave, 2005.
The Sporting News, 1914–1935.
Stevens Point Daily Journal, 1912.
The Virden Empire-Advance, 1929–1930.
Washington Post, 1915–1924.

Internet

www.news.google.com.
www.retrosheet.org.
www.baseball-reference.com.
www.sabr.org.

Other Materials

Wright's City Directories of Milwaukee, 1932–1936.

Index

mourir à petit feu pour ça. Puisque ta conscience est pure, il n'y a pas de raison. Ces ragots s'éteindront d'eux-mêmes.

— Non, justement. Le directeur Hardy a laissé entendre que je devrais démissionner de la présidence de ma classe.

— Jim Hardy a dit cela? s'exclama la tante Ruth, sur un ton qui traduisait un souverain mépris. Son père a été l'engagé de mon grand-père pendant des lustres. Et Jim Hardy croirait que ma nièce pourrait se mal conduire? Voyons donc!

Émilie se dit qu'elle rêvait. Sa tante prenait parti pour elle?

— Ne t'en fais pas à propos de Jim Hardy, fit celle-ci. Je vais le remettre à sa place. Ça apprendra aux gens d'ici à ne pas parler en mal des Murray.

— Il y a aussi Mme Tolliver qui m'a priée de laisser mon stand à sa cousine, au bazar, dit Émilie. C'est clair qu'elle ne veut plus de moi.

— Polly Tolliver est une parvenue et une sotte, rétorqua la tante Ruth. Depuis qu'elle a épousé son patron, Nat Tolliver, l'église St. John n'a plus jamais été la même. Il y a dix ans, Polly était une va-nu-pieds des quartiers pauvres de Charlottetown à qui nul n'eût ouvert sa porte. Et voilà qu'elle se donne des airs et veut mener la confrérie! Je m'en vais lui river son clou. Tu te rappelles comme elle était reconnaissante, l'autre jour, d'avoir une Murray dans son stand. Pour elle, ça signifiait qu'elle était acceptée dans la société.

La tante Ruth plana jusqu'à l'étage, laissant là une Émilie médusée, et en redescendit, sur un pied de guerre. Elle avait retiré ses frisettes, mis son plus beau chapeau, sa meilleure robe de soie noire et son nouveau manteau de phoque. Ainsi parée, elle fit voile vers la ville et s'arrêta à la résidence des Tolliver, sur la colline. Elle y passa une demi-heure, enfermée avec Mme Nat. Il y avait, d'un côté, la tante Ruth, petite boulotte plutôt mal fagotée, en dépit de ses vêtements neufs. Et de l'autre, Mme Nat, élégante comme une carte de modes avec sa toilette de Paris, son face-à-main et sa mise en plis *Marcelle* — mode qui venait tout juste de gagner Shrewsbury et dont elle était la première à faire étalage.

Nul ne sut jamais ce qui se dit, lors de cette entrevue. Mme Tolliver, quant à elle, n'en révéla jamais rien. Mais, quand la tante Ruth quitta la résidence cossue, Polly, nonobstant sa robe de Paris et sa permanente, pleurait toutes les larmes de son corps dans les coussins de son canapé. La tante Ruth portait, dans son manchon, un mot de Mme Tolliver à «sa chère Émilie», lui disant que sa cousine ne prendrait pas part au bazar et qu'elle serait bien bonne d'assumer la direction du stand, tel qu'elle l'avait promis.

La tante Ruth se rendit ensuite chez le docteur Hardy où elle gagna la bataille tambour battant. La domestique des Hardy rapporta, du dialogue, une phrase qu'elle avait entendue, mais qui se pouvait difficilement croire. Ruth Dutton aurait dit, à l'imposant directeur au nez chaussé de lunettes:

— Je sais que tu es un idiot, Jim Hardy, mais, pour l'amour de Dieu, essaie de prouver aux autres que tu ne l'es pas.

La domestique avait sûrement inventé ça.

— Tu n'auras plus d'ennuis, ma nièce, déclara la tante Ruth, en rentrant à la maison. Polly et Jim n'ont pas fini d'en rabattre. Quand les gens te verront au bazar, ils comprendront d'où souffle le vent et ils orienteront leurs voilures en conséquence. J'aurai un mot ou deux à dire à quelques autres personnes, quand l'occasion s'en présentera. Ce serait du joli que des garçons décents et des filles sages ne puissent échapper à la mort dans la tempête sans qu'on les calomnie. Ne t'en tracasse plus, Émilie. Ta famille t'appuie.

Quand sa tante sortit de la chambre, Émilie gagna son miroir qu'elle inclina à l'angle qui convenait le mieux. Elle sourit à Émilie-dans-la-glace d'un sourire lent, provoquant, aguichant.

«Je me demande bien où j'ai pu mettre mon calepin-Jimmy, pensa-t-elle. Il faut que je peaufine mon esquisse de la tante Ruth.»

XXII

Qui m'aime, aime mon chien

Quand les habitants de Shrewsbury découvrirent que Mme Dutton épaulait sa nièce, la flambée de commérages qui avait enflammé la ville mourut de sa belle mort. Mme Dutton, n'est-ce pas, contribuait — c'était dans la tradition des Murray —aux œuvres de l'église St. John plus que n'importe quel autre paroissien. Elle avait aussi prêté de l'argent à la moitié des hommes d'affaires de la localité et détenait un billet de reconnaissance de dettes de Nat Tolliver qui donnait à ce dernier des cauchemars. Mme Dutton connaissait les secrets honteux des familles et y faisait allusion sans la moindre délicatesse. Il allait donc de soi qu'elle ne fût pas contrariée.

Émilie vendit des chandails de bébé, des couvertures, des chaussons tricotés et des bonnets dans le stand de Mme Tolliver et sut convaincre, avec son sourire maintenant renommé, de vieux messieurs à acheter cet artisanat.

On la traita avec gentillesse et elle refleurit, mais l'épreuve avait laissé des cicatrices. Elle avait souffert si fort que la vue de quiconque avait eu un lien avec sa blessure la révulsait. Quand Mme Tolliver la pria, la semaine d'après, de servir le thé à sa réception pour sa cousine, Émilie refusa poliment, sans se donner la peine d'offrir une excuse. Et quelque chose dans l'angle de son menton et dans la nature de son regard rappela à Mme Tolliver qu'elle était toujours Polly Riordan, de la ruelle

Riordan, et qu'elle ne serait jamais autre chose, aux yeux d'une Murray de la Nouvelle Lune.

Andrew fut accueilli aimablement, lorsqu'il vint veiller, la mine penaude, le vendredi d'après, peu rassuré sur le traitement qu'on lui réserverait. Émilie se montra particulièrement charmante, s'y prenant à son gré pour rendre à Andrew la monnaie de sa pièce.

Alors qu'il répétait, naïf, les compliments reçus de son patron, elle acquiesça «qu'il était, certes, une merveille!» en relevant les paupières et en les rabaissant d'une manière telle que le cœur bien réglé d'Andrew en avait manqué un battement. Et qu'il ne saisit même pas ce qu'il y avait de sarcastique dans son acquiescement.

Ce printemps-là, tout alla bien pour Émilie. Plusieurs de ses textes furent acceptés, et rétribués, et elle commença à en tirer vanité. Sa famille prit au sérieux sa manie d'écrire, les chèques étant des documents incontestables.

— Émilie a gagné cinquante dollars avec sa plume, depuis le premier de l'An, confia la tante Ruth à Mme Drury. Je commence à croire que cette petite a trouvé un filon facile pour gagner sa vie.

Un filon facile! Qu'est-ce que la tante Ruth savait des déceptions et des échecs qui guettent les grimpeurs de cimes alpestres? Des portes qui se ferment? Des sanctuaires imprenables que sont les maisons d'édition? Des notes de refus et des tièdes compliments, plus affreux encore?

La tante Ruth ne connaissait pas ces affres, mais se mettait maintenant dans tous ses états quand les manuscrits d'Émilie lui étaient retournés.

— Quel effronté! disait-elle de l'éditeur. Ne lui envoie plus rien. Après tout, tu es une Murray.

— Il n'en sait rien, répliquait Émilie, moqueuse.

— Alors, apprends-le-lui, faisait la tante Ruth.

Shrewsbury fut en émoi, en mai, lorsque Janet Royal revint de New York au pays natal avec ses magnifiques toilettes, sa brillante réputation et son chien chow-chow. Janet n'était jamais revenue à Shrewsbury depuis son départ pour les États-Unis, vingt ans plus tôt, où cette fille brillante et déterminée avait réussi. Elle était devenue directrice littéraire d'un grand magazine féminin de la métropole et l'une des lectrices les plus appréciées d'une maison d'édition réputée. Émilie eut le souffle coupé quand elle apprit l'arrivée de Mlle Royal. Quel plaisir elle aurait à la rencontrer, à causer avec elle, à lui poser toutes les questions qui se pressaient dans sa tête! Lorsque M. Towers lui ordonna d'aller interviewer Mlle Royal pour le *Times*, Émilie ne se tint plus de joie. Et d'appréhension. Comment aurait-elle jamais l'audace d'interroger Mlle Royal sur sa carrière et de lui demander son opinion sur la politique extérieure des États-Unis et sur la réciprocité?

Elle adressa à Mlle Royal une lettre très respectueuse sollicitant la faveur d'une entrevue, lettre qu'elle retravailla une douzaine de fois. Mlle Royal lui envoya une réponse charmante.

La Cendraie, lundi

Chère mademoiselle Starr,

Bien sûr que vous pouvez venir me voir. Je vais vous confier tout ce que Jimmy Towers veut savoir de moi (le cher homme n'a-t-il pas été mon premier soupirant?) et tout ce que vous-même voulez connaître. Je vous avoue que je suis revenue dans l'île surtout pour rencontrer l'auteure de La dame qui donna la fessée au roi. *J'ai lu ce conte, l'hiver dernier, quand il a été publié dans* Roche, *et je l'ai trouvé charmant. Venez me voir et parlez-moi de vous et de vos ambitions. Vous avez des ambitions, n'est-ce pas? Je suis certaine que vous arriverez à les réaliser, et je suis prête à vous aider à le faire, si cela m'est possible. Vous possédez un don que je n'ai jamais eu: la capacité de créer, mais moi, je suis riche d'expérience. Cette expérience vous est acquise, pour peu que vous le souhaitiez. Je puis vous aider à éviter les pièges et je dispose d'une certaine influence dans certaines sphères. Venez à la Cendraie, vendredi prochain, dans l'après-midi, après la classe, et nous parlerons à cœur ouvert.*

Salutations fraternelles,
Janet Royal

Cette lettre transporta Émilie au septième ciel. «Salutations fraternelles», disait Janet Royal. Comme c'était merveilleux! Agenouillée à sa fenêtre, elle regarda avec des yeux extasiés les minces bouleaux du Bois Debout et, plus loin, les champs de trèfle couverts de rosée. Deviendrait-elle, un jour, assez brillante pour atteindre à la réussite de Mlle Royal? Cette lettre le laissait entendre. Elle laissait entendre que les rêves les plus fous pourraient se réaliser. Encore quatre jours à attendre et elle verrait sa grande prêtresse et lui parlerait.

Mme Angela Royal, qui vint rendre visite à la tante Ruth, ce soir-là, ne semblait pas considérer Janet comme une grande prêtresse, et encore moins comme une merveille. Nul n'est prophète en son pays, c'est entendu, et Mme Royal avait élevé Janet.

— Elle s'est bien débrouillée, confia-t-elle à la tante Ruth. Elle gagne beaucoup d'argent, mais c'est quand même une vieille fille. Et je la trouve plutôt bizarre, par moments.

Émilie, qui étudiait son latin dans la fenêtre en baie, s'enflamma d'indignation. Crime de *lèse-majesté**.

— Elle paraît encore très bien, dit la tante Ruth. Janet a toujours été une charmante fille.

— Oui, plutôt charmante, c'est vrai. J'ai toujours pensé qu'elle était trop intelligente pour se marier, et j'avais raison. Elle est vraiment fantasque, vous savez. Toujours en retard aux repas. Et les chichis qu'elle fait à propos de son chien: Chu-Chin, qu'elle l'appelle! C'est lui qui gouverne la maison. Mon pauvre chat ne sait plus où donner du museau. Janet n'entend pas à rire là-dessus. Quand je me suis plainte que Chu-Chin dormait sur le canapé, ça l'a tellement offusquée qu'elle m'a battu froid le reste de la journée. Elle prend la mouche facilement et là, c'est le drame. J'espère que personne ne va la contrarier avant ta visite, vendredi, Émilie, parce que c'est à toi qu'elle s'en prendra. Laissez-moi dire à sa décharge qu'elle se fâche rarement et qu'elle est la générosité même pour ses amis.

Lorsque la tante Ruth sortit pour parler au garçon livreur, Mme Royal confia rapidement à Émilie:

— Elle s'intéresse beaucoup à toi. Elle aime s'entourer de jeunesse. Ça la rajeunit, qu'elle dit. Elle trouve que tu as du

---

* En français, dans le texte.

talent. Si elle te prend en affection, tu auras tout à y gagner. Mais suis mon conseil: montre-toi aimable envers son chien. Tu serais Shakespeare lui-même, si tu offenses son chien, Janet ne voudra rien savoir de toi.

Le vendredi venu, Émilie s'éveilla, convaincue qu'elle allait vivre l'un des jours marquants de sa vie.

Il plut à torrents tout l'avant-midi, mais, à midi, le ciel se débarrassa de ses nuages, et les collines au-delà du port se pavoisèrent de bleu. Émilie rentra précipitamment de l'école, pénétrée de la solennité de l'occasion. Il lui fallait soigner sa mise. Elle porterait sa nouvelle robe de soie marine qui la faisait paraître plus vieille que son âge, mais comment coifferait-elle ses cheveux? Le chignon psyché faisait distingué et allait à son profil, sous le chapeau. Le front dégagé la faisait paraître plus intellectuelle. Mme Royal avait dit que Janet aimait les jolies filles. Alors, jolie elle serait. L'abondante chevelure noire fut coiffée bas sur le front et couronnée du nouveau chapeau de printemps qu'Émilie s'était acheté avec son dernier chèque, à l'étonnement scandalisé de ses tantes qui la trouvaient dépensière. Ce nouveau chapeau était très seyant avec sa grappe de violettes tombant en cascade sur son cou. Tout en elle était parfait: elle était tirée à quatre épingles. La tante Ruth, qui rôdait dans le couloir la vit descendre et fut subjuguée. «Elle a l'élégance des Murray», pensa-t-elle.

C'était l'accolade suprême. En fait, c'était plutôt des Starr qu'Émilie tenait son élégante minceur. Les Murray étaient imposants et dignes, mais raides.

Elle gagna à pied la Cendraie, imposante demeure nichée dans les arbres, en retrait de l'avenue et, comme un pèlerin s'approchant du temple sacré, s'avança dans l'allée bordée des ombres délicatement frangées par le printemps. Un gros chien blanc pelucheux l'attendait à mi-chemin. Émilie l'examina, curieuse: elle n'avait jamais vu de chow-chow. Le dénommé Chu-Chin était beau, sans aucun doute, mais il n'était définitivement pas propre. Il avait pataugé dans les flaques de boue. Ses pattes et son poitrail en portaient des traces. Émilie souhaita que Chu-Chin l'accepte mais qu'il garde ses distances. Pour l'accepter, il l'accepta. Faisant aussitôt volte-face, il trottina à ses côtés, agitant amicalement une queue empanachée de boue et se tint au garde-à-vous avec elle à la porte.

Il sauta d'un bond joyeux sur la dame qui vint ouvrir, la renversant presque dans son enthousiasme. C'était Janet Royal.

«Pas belle, se dit Émilie, mais tellement distinguée, de la couronne de ses cheveux d'or bronzé jusqu'au bout de ses escarpins de satin.» Elle portait une superbe robe de velours mauve et arborait un pince nez cerclé d'écaille de tortue, le premier qu'on eût jamais vu à Shrewsbury.

Le chien lui laboura les joues d'un grand coup de langue enthousiaste, puis se rua dans le salon. La belle robe mauve de Janet Royal fut maculée du col à l'ourlet de ses empreintes boueuses. Émilie se dit *in petto* que Chu-Chin méritait la mauvaise opinion qu'en avait Mme Royal et que, s'il était son chien à elle, il se conduirait autrement. Mlle Royal n'éleva aucun reproche, mais son accueil, bien que parfaitement courtois, fut plutôt froid.

— Donnez-vous la peine d'entrer, fit-elle. Veuillez vous asseoir.

Elle indiquait de la main un fauteuil confortable et s'assit elle-même sur une chaise Chippendale peu accueillante. Émilie sentit que le choix que Mlle Royal avait fait de ce siège était révélateur. Pourquoi ne s'était-elle pas laisser choir, en camarade, dans les profondeurs du canapé? Non, elle se tenait là, imposante, distante, n'ayant, à ce qu'il semblait, prêté nul intérêt aux taches qui maculaient sa belle robe. Chu-Chin avait sauté sur le canapé de peluche et y restait vautré, son regard courant de l'une à l'autre, charmé de la situation. Comme l'avait redouté Mme Royal, quelque chose, c'était évident, avait «froissé» Mlle Royal. Les espoirs d'Émilie coulèrent à pic.

— Belle journée, n'est-ce pas, balbutia-t-elle. (Il lui fallait bien dire quelque chose, puisque son interlocutrice restait muette.)

Le silence devint insupportable.

— Très belle, acquiesça Mlle Royal, les yeux fixés sur Chu-Chin, qui cinglait de sa queue mouillée un des beaux coussins de soie et de dentelle de Mme Royal.

Émilie se mit à détester Chu-Chin de tout son cœur, n'osant, encore, se permettre de détester Mlle Royal. Elle eût voulu se voir à des milliers de milles de là, mais il y avait, sur ses genoux, ce petit paquet de manuscrits qu'elle n'oserait plus, maintenant, montrer à Janet Royal. Était-ce possible que cette impératrice outragée ait été l'auteure de la lettre amicale qu'Émilie avait reçue?

Des minutes s'écoulèrent, longues comme des heures. La bouche d'Émilie était sèche, et son cerveau, paralysé. Aucun sujet de conversation ne lui venait à l'esprit. Un soupçon terrible lui vint: Mlle Royal avait eu vent des commérages sur la nuit dans la vieille maison John et son attitude fermée en découlait.

Elle se tortilla sur son fauteuil, au supplice, et son petit paquet glissa sur le parquet. Elle se pencha pour le ramasser. Au même instant, Chu-Chin fondit dessus. Ses pattes sales s'accrochèrent à la grappe de violettes qui pendait du chapeau d'Émilie et l'en arrachèrent. Émilie lâcha ses manuscrits pour retenir son chapeau. Chu-Chin lâcha les violettes et fondit sur le paquet, puis, le tenant dans sa gueule, fila par la porte menant au jardin.

Ce chow-chow du diable avait emporté sa plus récente histoire et plusieurs de ses meilleurs poèmes. Qu'est-ce qu'il allait en faire? Elle ne les reverrait sûrement plus. Au moins, elle n'aurait pas à les soumettre à Mlle Royal.

Émilie se souciait peu, maintenant, de l'humeur de sa grande-prêtresse. Elle ne souhaitait plus du tout plaire à cette femme qui laissait son chien se conduire aussi grossièrement envers une invitée, sans même le réprimander. Une femme qui paraissait même amusée par ces pitreries.

— Chien enjoué, fit-elle, sarcastique.

— Très, acquiesça Mlle Royal.

— Un peu de discipline ne lui ferait pas de tort, peut-être?

— Qui sait? fit Mlle Royal sibylline.

Chu-Chin rentra à l'instant, renversa d'un coup de queue un petit vase en verre dont il renifla, curieux, les morceaux cassés, puis sauta de nouveau sur le canapé, pantelant.

Émilie se saisit de son carnet de notes et de son crayon.

— M. Towers m'a envoyée vous interviewer, dit-elle.

— C'est ce que j'ai cru comprendre, dit Mlle Royal, qui ne lâchait pas des yeux son chow-chow adoré.

Émilie: — Puis-je me permettre de vous poser quelques questions?

Mlle Royal, (avec une amabilité forcée): — Bien entendu.

Chu-Chin, ayant repris son souffle, sauta au bas du canapé et disparut par les portes pliantes de la salle à manger.

Émilie, (consultant son carnet et posant à la diable la première question venue): — Quel sera, pensez-vous, le résultat des élections présidentielles, cet automne?

Mlle Royal: — Je ne pense jamais à cela.

(Émilie, lèvres serrées, écrivit dans son carnet: «Elle ne pense jamais à cela».)

Chu-Chin réapparut, traversa le salon comme l'éclair et courut au jardin, portant dans sa gueule un poulet rôti.

Mlle Royal: — Mon souper vient de s'envoler.

Émilie (biffant la première question): — Y a-t-il quelque possibilité que le Congrès des États-Unis se montre favorable aux ouvertures du gouvernement canadien sur la réciprocité?

Mlle Royal: — Le gouvernement canadien a-t-il fait des ouvertures sur la réciprocité?

(Émilie écrivit: «Elle n'en a pas entendu parler».)

Mlle Royal replaça son pince-nez. Émilie pensa: «Avec un nez comme celui-là et le menton à l'avenant, tu auras l'air d'une sorcière, en vieillissant.»

Émilie (à haute voix): — À votre avis, le roman historique a-t-il fait son temps?

Mlle Royal, (mollement): — Je laisse toujours mes opinions à la maison, quand je pars en vacances.

(Émilie écrivit: «Elle laisse ses opinions à la maison, quand elle part en vacances», et souhaita sauvagement écrire sa propre version de cette entrevue.) M. Thomas ne la publierait pas, bon, mais elle avait un calepin-Jimmy vierge, à la maison, et elle prit un malin plaisir à imaginer ce qu'elle y écrirait, en rentrant. Chu-Chin revint. Avait-il mangé le poulet en un si court laps de temps? En quête de dessert, il se saisit d'une des parures crochetées d'un fauteuil, rampa sous le piano en l'apportant avec lui et se mit à la mâchouiller avec bonheur.

Mlle Royal, (fervente): — Chère petite bête!

236

Émilie, (soudain inspirée): — Que pensez-vous des chiens chow-chow?

Mlle Royal: — Ce sont de délicieuses créatures.

Émilie, (in petto): «Ah ah, vous avez apporté *une* opinion avec vous. *(À Mlle Royal)*: — Nos goûts diffèrent, c'est évident, en ce qui a trait aux chiens.»

Un gros chat gris bedonnant passa à l'extérieur. Chu-Chin émergea de son repaire et fondit sur lui en courant entre les pieds d'une étagère portant une plante. L'étagère se renversa et le beau bégonia rex de Mme Royal s'écrasa au sol, au milieu d'un monceau de terre et de poterie brisée.

Mlle Royal, (la voix neutre): — Pauvre tante Angela! Elle en aura le cœur brisé.

Émilie: — Mais ça, ça n'a pas d'importance, n'est-ce pas?

Mlle Royal, (gentiment) — Oh non, aucune.

Émilie, (consultant son carnet): — Trouvez-vous que Shrewsbury ait changé?

Mlle Royal: — Oui, les gens, surtout, ont changé. Les jeunes me déçoivent.

Émilie nota cela. Chu-Chin réapparut, ayant, selon toute apparence, chassé le chat dans une autre flaque de boue, et reprit son mâchouillage là où il l'avait laissé, sous le piano.

Émilie ferma son carnet et se leva.

— Merci, ce sera tout, dit-elle, avec une morgue pareille à celle de Mlle Royal. Je regrette d'avoir pris de votre temps. Au revoir.

Elle s'inclina légèrement et sortit dans le vestibule. Mlle Royal la suivit jusqu'à la porte.

— Ne serait-ce pas préférable que vous emmeniez votre chien, mademoiselle Starr?

Émilie, qui refermait la porte extérieure, s'arrêta net et regarda Mlle Royal.

— Vous dites?

— J'ai dit: ne serait-ce pas préférable que vous emmeniez votre chien?

— *Mon* chien?

— Oui. Il n'a pas tout à fait fini la parure crochetée, mais il peut l'emporter. Elle ne sera plus d'aucune utilité à tante Angela, maintenant.

— Ce... ce n'est pas *mon* chien, s'étouffa Émilie.

— Pas *votre* chien? Alors, à qui est-il?

— Je... je croyais que c'était le vôtre, *votre* chow-chow, dit Émilie.

XXIII

La porte s'ouvre

Mlle Royal fixa Émilie, estomaquée. Lui saisissant le poignet, elle la tira vers le salon et la poussa fermement vers l'un des fauteuils Morris. Ceci fait, elle se laissa choir sur le canapé maculé de boue et se mit à rire à gorge déployée. Elle s'arrêtait, donnait des claques retentissantes aux genoux d'Émilie, puis repartait de plus belle, pâmée de rire. Émilie restait là, souriant faiblement, trop blessée, encore, pour partager une hilarité qu'elle ne s'expliquait pas.

Pendant ce temps, le chien blanc, ayant réduit la parure en miettes, se lança derechef à la poursuite du chat.

Mlle Royal se ressaisit et s'essuya les yeux.

— C'est impayable, Émilie Byrd Starr, tout simplement impayable. J'aurai quatre-vingts ans que je me souviendrai encore de ce chien et que je m'en tordrai de rire. Qui écrira cette histoire, toi ou moi? Mais à qui appartient donc ce monstre?

— Je n'en sais vraiment rien, dit Émilie, gardant ses distances. Je ne l'ai jamais vu de ma vie.

— Bon, alors, fermons vite la porte avant qu'il ne revienne. Et maintenant, chère belle, assieds-toi près de moi: il y a un coin propre ici, sous le coussin. Notre conversation, nous l'aurons. J'ai été tellement odieuse envers toi, quand tu me

239

posais tes questions, Je m'appliquais à l'être. Pourquoi est-ce que tu ne m'as pas lancé un objet à la figure? Je le méritais.

— Ce n'est pas le désir qui manquait. Pourtant, à bien y penser, vous m'avez plutôt ménagée; mon prétendu chien s'est tellement mal conduit.

Mlle Royal pouffa.

— Je ne sais pas si je peux te pardonner d'avoir cru que cette horrible bête était mon magnifique chow-chow tout de douceur et d'or roux. Tu viendras à ma chambre, tout à l'heure, lui présenter tes excuses. Il dort sur mon lit. Je l'ai enfermé à clef pour que tante Angela ne se tracasse pas au sujet de son chat. Chu-Chin ne lui ferait pas de mal. Tout ce qu'il veut, c'est jouer, mais le vieux matou est craintif et détale. Un chien ne peut s'empêcher de courir après un chat qui file devant lui. Si, au moins, cette créature s'était contentée de pourchasser le chat!

— Quel dommage pour le bégonia de Mme Royal! s'attrista Émilie.

— Oui, c'est regrettable. Tante Angela l'avait depuis longtemps. Je lui en achèterai un autre. Quand je t'ai vue t'avancer dans l'allée avec ce chien qui gambadait autour de toi, j'ai cru, bien sûr, qu'il était à toi. J'avais revêtu ma robe préférée, celle qui me fait paraître presque jolie. Je souhaitais te plaire. Quand le monstre l'a maculée et que tu ne l'as pas réprimandé et que tu ne t'es pas non plus excusée, je suis entrée en rage. Ça m'arrive, je n'y peux rien. C'est une de mes faiblesses. Mais je reprends vite mes esprits, quand de nouvelles frustrations ne viennent pas s'ajouter à l'outrage. Dans le cas qui nous occupe, les frustations n'ont cessé de s'accumuler. Je me suis juré de ne pas intervenir si tu ne tentais pas, devant moi, de discipliner ton chien. Tandis que toi, tu t'indignais avec raison que je laisse mon chien gâcher tes violettes et manger tes manuscrits.

— C'est vrai. J'étais indignée.

— Je suis désolée pour les manuscrits. Nous en retrouverons peut-être quelques-uns. Il ne peut les avoir mangés tous, mais il les a sans doute réduits en bouillie.

— Ça n'a pas d'importance. J'ai des copies à la maison.

— Et tes questions, Émilie! Elles étaient délicieuses. As-tu vraiment écrit mes réponses?

— Mot à mot. Je les aurais fait reproduire telles quelles. M. Towers m'avait donné une liste de questions pour vous, mais je n'avais pas l'intention de vous en bombarder comme je l'ai fait. Je me proposais des les intercaler avec art dans la conversation. Mais voici votre tante.

Mme Royal entrait dans la pièce, le sourire aux lèvres. Sa figure changea quand elle aperçut son bégonia. Sa nièce intervint aussitôt.

— Chère petite tante, ne pleure pas et ne perds pas connaissance, en tout cas, pas avant de m'avoir dit qui, aux alentours, possède un chien blanc frisé absolument dépourvu de manières, un vrai diable.

— Lily Bates, laissa tomber Mme Royal, au bord des larmes. Ne me dis pas qu'elle a laissé son monstre en liberté encore une fois. Il me donne bien du fil à retordre. C'est un gros chiot pas encore dressé. J'ai dit à Lily que si je le prenais encore dans mes parages, je l'empoisonnerais. Elle le garde attaché, depuis. Mais qu'est-ce qui s'est passé? Mon beau bégonia.

— Ce chien est entré avec Émilie. J'ai cru qu'il était à elle. Je me suis montrée courtoise envers lui comme envers elle, mon invitée. N'est-ce pas la coutume? Il m'a fait la bise à son arrivée: ma robe en témoigne. Il a souillé ton canapé, arraché les violettes du chapeau d'Émilie, pourchassé ton chat, jeté ton bégonia au sol, brisé ton vase et il s'est enfui avec notre poulet. C'est à n'y pas croire, tante Angela. Il a fait tout ça et je suis restée là stoïque et je n'ai pas élevé la voix pour protester. Ma conduite a été, je le jurerais, digne de la Nouvelle Lune elle-même, tu ne trouves pas, Émilie.

— Tu étais trop fâchée pour parler, c'est tout, conclut Mme Royal en relevant sa malheureuse plante.

Mlle Royal glissa un regard complice à Émilie.

— Tu vois, je ne peux rien passer à tante Angela. Elle me connaît trop bien. Je ne me suis pas montrée sous mon meilleur jour, je l'admets. Chère tantine, je te procurerai un vase neuf et un autre bégonia. Pense au plaisir que tu auras à le cajoler pour qu'il pousse. La plaisir réside bien davantage dans la prévision que dans la réalisation.

— Je m'en vais lui dire son fait, à cette Lily Bates, dit Mme Royal, quittant la pièce, en quête d'un porte-poussière.

— Et maintenant, chère petite Émilie, dit Mlle Royal, très détendue, causons.

C'était là la Janet Royal de la lettre. Émilie bavarda à cœur ouvert avec elle. Elles passèrent ensemble une heure agréable, à la fin de laquelle Janet Royal fit à Émilie une proposition qui lui coupa le souffle.

— Accompagne-moi à New York, en juillet. Il y a un poste libre dans l'équipe du *Ladies's Own*. Rien de sensationnel, toutefois. Tu servirais de bouche-trou. Toutes les besognes de routine te reviendraient d'office. Mais pense aux possibilités d'avancement. Tu serais au cœur même des choses. Tu écris bien, je m'en suis rendu compte dès que j'ai lu *La dame qui donna la fessée au roi*. Je connais l'éditeur de *Roche*; par lui, j'ai appris qui tu étais et où tu habitais. La raison pour laquelle je suis venue ici, c'est que je voulais retenir tes services. Tu perds ta vie, ici. Je sais que tu es attachée à la Nouvelle Lune. C'est un coin ravissant, plein de poésie et baigné de romanesque. L'endroit parfait pour y passer son enfance. Mais tu grandis. Tu dois devenir autonome. Il te faut, pour cela, le stimulant que donne la fréquentation des grands esprits, l'apprentissage que seule une grande ville peut offrir. Viens avec moi. Si tu le fais, dans dix ans, je te le promets, Émilie Byrd Starr sera un nom hautement prisé par les magazines d'Amérique.

Émilie en resta confondue. Mlle Royal lui offrait la clef du monde de ses rêves, de ses espoirs et de ses chimères. Derrière cette porte se trouvaient le succès et la renommée auxquels elle aspirait depuis toujours. Et pourtant, pourtant! Un étrange et timide ressentiment se faisait jour, à travers le tourbillon de sensations qui l'emportait. Mlle Royal n'affirmait-elle pas implicitement que le nom d'Émilie ne serait jamais connu, si elle ne l'accompagnait pas à New York? C'était blessant, non? Les Murray morts et enterrés ne se retourneraient-ils pas dans leurs tombes en apprenant que l'une des leurs n'atteindrait pas au succès sans l'aide d'une étrangère?

Mlle Royal ne s'était-elle pas montrée trop condescendante? Quoi qu'il en soit, cette impression empêcha Émilie de se jeter, au propre comme au figuré, aux pieds de sa bienfaitrice.

— Ce serait merveilleux, fit-elle, hésitante. J'aimerais vous suivre, mais ma tante Élisabeth n'y consentira jamais. Elle dira que je suis trop jeune.

— Quel âge as-tu?

— Dix-sept ans.

— J'avais dix-huit ans, quand je suis partie d'ici. Je ne connaissais personne à New York et j'avais juste assez d'argent pour trois mois. J'étais une provinciale sans expérience et, pourtant, tu vois, j'ai gagné la partie. *Toi*, tu partageras ma vie. Je m'occuperai de toi aussi bien que ta tante Élisabeth pourrait le faire. Dis-lui que je veillerai sur toi comme sur la prunelle de mes yeux. J'ai un joli appartement douillet où nous serons heureuses comme des reines avec mon Chu-Chin adoré et adorable. Tu aimeras vivre avec moi. Je suis très bonne et conciliante, quand je le veux bien, et je le veux presque tout le temps, et je ne perds jamais mon sang-froid. Je supporte les défauts des autres d'une âme sereine. Et je ne *dis* jamais à mes proches qu'ils ont le rhume ou qu'ils ont l'air fatigué. Oui, vraiment, je ferais une compagne d'appartement très convenable.

— J'en suis persuadée, fit Émilie, souriante.

— Je n'ai jamais, avant aujourd'hui, rencontré quelqu'un avec qui j'aimerais vivre, déclara Mlle Royal. Tu as une personnalité lumineuse, Émilie. Tu mettras de l'éclat dans les moments ternes et de la couleur dans les coins gris. Allez, décide. Tu viens, ou non, avec moi?

— C'est tante Élisabeth qu'il faudrait convaincre, dit Émilie. Si elle dit que je peux vous accompagner, je...

Émilie s'interrompit brusquement.

— ... vous accompagnerai, termina joyeusement Mlle Royal. Ta tante Élisabeth se ralliera. J'irai lui parler. Je me rendrai à la Nouvelle Lune avec toi, vendredi prochain. Il faut que tu aies ta chance.

— Je ne sais comment vous remercier, mademoiselle Royal. Je vais réfléchir à votre proposition. Elle m'éblouit. Vous ne pouvez pas savoir ce que ceci représente pour moi.

— Je crois que si, fit Mlle Royal, très douce. J'ai déjà été une jeune fille de Shrewsbury qui se rongeait les sangs parce qu'elle n'avait aucune chance de percer.

— Mais vous avez réussi à percer et vous avez gagné.

— Il m'a fallu partir de mon patelin pour y arriver. Ici, je ne serais jamais arrivée à rien. La montée a été rude. Elle m'a volé ma jeunesse. Je veux t'éviter ces difficultés. Tu iras beaucoup plus loin que moi: tu peux créer, alors que moi, je suis seulement capable de bâtir avec les matériaux des autres.Il reste que nous, les bâtisseurs, nous avons notre place: nous élevons, à défaut d'autre chose, des temples pour nos dieux et nos déesses. Viens avec moi, chère Émilie, et je mettrai tout en œuvre pour t'aider.

— Merci, merci, fut tout ce qu'Émilie put dire.

Des larmes de gratitude lui montaient aux yeux devant cette offre. Elle n'avait guère reçu de sympathie, auparavant. Profondément touchée, elle retourna chez la tante Ruth, pénétrée de l'impression qu'elle *devait* tourner la clef et ouvrir la porte magique derrière laquelle se profilait la beauté de la vie. *Si* sa tante Élisabeth la laissait libre d'en profiter.

«Je n'irai pas, si elle n'est pas d'accord», décida Émilie.

À mi-chemin du retour, elle s'arrêta soudain et se mit à rire. Mlle Royal ne lui avait pas, en fin de compte, montré son Chu-Chin.

— Peu importe, pensa-t-elle. Je le connaîtrai, si je vais à New York.

XXIV

Verts pâturages

Émilie irait-elle ou non à New York avec Mlle Royal? C'était la question à laquelle la tante Élisabeth devait répondre. La destinée d'Émilie reposait sur cette décision et elle regardait de loin ces verts pâturages que Mlle Royal avait fait miroiter à ses yeux, persuadée qu'elle ne pourrait jamais s'y reposer.

Elle ne révéla rien à sa tante de la proposition reçue jusqu'au week-end d'ensuite, alors que Mlle Royal se rendit à la Nouvelle Lune, tout miel, tout sucre et un brin condescendante, pour demander à la tante Élisabeth de laisser partir sa nièce.

La tante Élisabeth écouta en silence, et ce silence était désapprobateur.

— Les femmes de la famille des Murray n'ont jamais eu à travailler à l'extérieur pour gagner leur vie, déclara-t-elle froidement.

— Ce n'est pas exactement ce qu'on pourrait appeler «travailler à l'extérieur», chère mademoiselle Murray, fit Janet Royal, avec la patience courtoise qu'on se doit de manifester envers une dame dont les opinions reflètent celles d'une génération dépassée. Des milliers de femmes se lancent en affaires, maintenant, partout dans le monde.

— Elles n'ont sans doute rien de mieux à faire, si elles ne se marient pas, fit la tante Élisabeth.

245

Mlle Royal rougit légèrement. Elle n'ignorait pas qu'à Blair Water et à Shrewsbury, en dépit de sa position sociale et de ses revenus à New York, on la considérait comme une vieille fille et, par conséquent, comme une ratée. Elle attaqua sur un autre front.

— Émilie a des dons exceptionnels pour l'écriture, dit-elle. Des dons qu'elle pourrait mettre à profit, si l'occasion lui en était donnée. Cette occasion, elle devrait en bénéficier, mademoiselle Murray. Et il n'en existe aucune de ce genre par ici.

— Émilie a gagné quatre-vingt-dix dollars, cette année, avec sa plume, fit la tante Élisabeth.

«Le Ciel me soit en aide!» pensa Mlle Royal.

— Oui, et dans dix ans, elle gagnera quelques centaines de dollars, tandis que si elle vient avec moi, dans dix ans, son revenu sera probablement de plusieurs centaines de milliers de dollars.

— Je dois y réfléchir, conclut la tante Élisabeth.

Émilie fut étonnée que sa tante consentît à «y réfléchir». Elle s'était attendue à un refus irrévocable.

— Elle y viendra, souffla Mlle Royal, en s'en allant. Je t'aurai, chère Émilie Byrd. Je connais les Murray depuis toujours. Ils savent flairer les bonnes affaires. Ta tante te laissera libre de m'accompagner.

— Je crains bien que non, fit Émilie.

Après le départ de Mlle Royal, la tante Élisabeth interrogea Émilie.

— Aimerais-tu la suivre?

— Oui, je crois que oui, si vous n'y voyez pas d'inconvénient, fit Émilie, la voix hésitante, sans aucun espoir au cœur.

La tante Élisabeth y réfléchit pendant une semaine. Elle fit demander Ruth, Wallace et Oliver pour l'assister. Ruth déclara, à demi gagnée à cette cause:

— Nous devrions peut-être la laisser aller. C'est une occasion inespérée pour elle. Et ce n'est pas comme si elle partait seule. Janet s'occupera d'elle.

— Elle est trop jeune, trop jeune! fit l'oncle Oliver.

— Mais ça semble une bonne affaire, dit l'oncle Wallace. Janet Royal a bien réussi, à ce qu'on me dit.

La tante Élisabeth écrivit à la grand-tante Nancy, lui demandant son avis. «Et si vous laissiez Émilie décider elle-même?» répondit-elle, d'une plume mal assurée.

Repliant la lettre, la tante Élisabeth manda Émilie au salon.

— Si tu veux partir avec Mlle Royal, tu le peux, lui dit-elle. Il me semble que ce serait mal de ma part de te retenir. Tu nous manqueras. Nous aurions aimé te garder avec nous encore quelques années. Je ne sais rien de New York, sauf qu'on dit que c'est une ville de perdition. Tu as été bien élevée. À toi de décider. Laura, cesse de pleurer.

Émilie aussi avait envie de pleurer. La porte s'ouvrait devant elle et, à son grand étonnement, elle n'en ressentait ni ravissement, ni plaisir. C'était une chose que de soupirer après des pâturages défendus et une autre que de voir tomber les barrières et de s'entendre dire qu'on pouvait y entrer à loisir.

Plutôt que de se précipiter à sa chambre pour y écrire une lettre enthousiaste à Mlle Royal, en visite chez des amis à Charlottetown, Émilie sortit au jardin et y réfléchit très fort tout cet après-midi-là et le dimanche d'après. Pendant la semaine à Shrewsbury, elle fut calme et songeuse. Sa tante Ruth l'observait de près, mais n'en discuta pas avec elle. Peut-être pensait-elle à Andrew? Ou peut-être était-ce entendu, chez les Murray, que nul n'influencerait la décision d'Émilie.

Pourquoi n'écrivait-elle pas cette lettre à Mlle Royal? Certes, elle irait à New York! Ce serait ridicule que de refuser une telle occasion qui ne se représenterait sûrement pas. Tout lui deviendrait facile, alors: le sentier alpestre se muerait en chemin gentiment montant avec, au bout, le succès assuré, rapide, brillant. Pourquoi, alors, se répétait-elle tout cela, comme pour s'en persuader? Et qu'est-ce qui l'avait poussée à quémander l'avis de M. Carpenter, le week-end d'ensuite?

— Ne me dis pas que les chats ont déterré d'autres trésors, grommela celui-ci, rendu plus maussade que jamais par son rhumatisme.

— Je n'ai pas de manuscrit à vous faire lire, dit Émilie en souriant. Je viens vous demander conseil.

Elle lui conta ce qui la rendait si perplexe.

— C'est une telle chance! conclut-elle.

— Une chance? Aller se faire *Yankeefier* outre-frontière?

— Je ne me laisserai pas *Yankeefier*, protesta Émilie, froissée. Mlle Royal a vécu vingt ans à New York et elle n'est pas *Yankeefiée*.

— Je t'accorde qu'elle n'est pas comme ces petite folles qui vont travailler aux «États» et qui reviennent, six mois plus tard, avec un accent à couper au couteau. Il n'en reste pas moins que Janet Royal est *Yankeefiée*: sa conception de la vie, l'air qu'elle déplace et son style sont tous U.S. Je ne lui en fais pas reproche: à chacun sa façon, mais elle n'a plus rien de canadien, et c'est ce que je souhaite que tu restes: Canadienne pure laine, et que tu participes, dans la mesure de tes moyens, à la littérature de ton pays en véhiculant sa saveur et son piquant uniques. Ces choses-là, évidemment, ne rapportent pas beaucoup d'argent.

— Il n'y a pas d'ouvertures, ici, en littérature.

— Pas plus qu'il n'y en avait, au presbytère de Haworth.

— Je ne suis pas Charlotte Brontë, protesta Émilie. Elle avait du génie, et le génie se nourrit de lui-même. Je n'ai que du talent, et ce talent a besoin d'être soutenu et guidé.

— ... marrainé.

— Autant dire que je ne devrais pas accepter?

— Vas-y, si le cœur t'en dit. Pour devenir célèbre rapidement, il faut apprendre à se courber. Oui, vas-y. Je suis trop vieux pour en débattre. Tu serais folle de refuser. Néanmoins, il arrive que certains fous atteignent aussi la gloire par leurs chemins à eux.

Émilie quitta la petite maison du vallon avec une mine d'enterrement. Elle croisa le vieux Kelly, en remontant la colline. Il arrêta net son petit cheval dodu et sa guimbarde rouge et lui fait signe d'approcher.

— Ma poulette, v'là des pastilles de menthe pour toi. Dis donc, y est grand temps pour toir de penser à... tu sais quoi...

Il lui fit un clin d'œil.

— Je vais rester vieille fille, monsieur Kelly, déclara Émilie, le sourire en coin.

Le vieux Kelly hocha la tête en ramassant ses guides.

— Y a rien de moins certain que ça, mais je te préviens, va pas prendre un des Priest, ma poulette, jamais un des Priest.

— Monsieur Kelly, lâcha Émilie soudain, on m'offre un poste à New York dans un grand magazine. C'est une chance inespérée, mais je n'arrive pas à me décider. Qu'est-ce que vous pensez que je devrais faire?

Ce disant, il lui vint à l'idée que sa tante Élisabeth serait horrifiée qu'une Murray ait demandé conseil au vieux Jock Kelly, et elle eut un peu honte de cette dérogation aux usages.

Le vieux Kelly hocha de nouveau la tête.

— Les gars du canton sont pas dégourdis comme de mon temps. Qu'est-ce que la vieille demoiselle en pense?

— Ma tante m'a dit de faire à mon goût.

— Bon alors, c'est une affaire réglée, dit le vieux Kelly, en repartant sans plus rien ajouter.

«Pourquoi est-ce que je souhaite qu'on m'aide? pensa Émilie, qui ne se comprenait plus elle-même. Je devrais être capable de prendre mes propres décisions. Ira? Ira pas? En somme, je me rends compte que je ne souhaite pas vraiment aller à New York, mais que tout me pousse à accepter cette proposition.»

Si, au moins, Dean avait été là! Mais Dean n'était pas rentré de son hiver à Los Angeles. En parler à Teddy? Elle n'osait le faire. Rien n'était sorti de ce merveilleux moment qu'ils avaient partagé, dans la vieille maison John, rien qu'une contrainte qui gâchait leur vieille camaraderie. En apparence, ils restaient les meilleurs amis du monde, mais un impondérable s'en était détaché, et rien ne semblait être comme avant. Au fond, elle avait peur, et refusait de se l'avouer, que Teddy ne lui recommande de s'expatrier, prouvant par là qu'il se préoccupait peu qu'elle parte ou qu'elle reste.

— Bien sûr que je vais aller à New York, se répéta-t-elle à haute voix. Autrement, qu'est-ce que je deviendrai, ici, l'année prochaine? Ilse sera partie. Perry aussi. Teddy de même, vraisemblablement, puisqu'il lui faut gagner de l'argent pour ses études en art. Je n'ai pas le choix: je dois partir.

Quand elle atteignit la Nouvelle Lune, au crépuscule, personne n'était là. Elle arpenta la maison de haut en bas. Quel charme, quelle dignité elles avaient, ces grandes pièces, avec leurs bougies, leurs chaises à hauts dossiers et leurs tapis tressés! Comme elle était charmante, sa petite chambre avec son papier peint à losanges, sa jarre noire pleine de pétales de roses et son drôle de carreau déformant! L'appartement de Mlle Royal aurait-il autant de charme?

— C'est certain que je vais y aller, se répéta Émilie, non sans se dire que, n'eût été le «c'est certain», l'affaire eût été classée.

Elle sortit au jardin, qu'un printemps hâtif réveillait, et s'y promena au clair de lune le long des allées. De loin, le train de Shrewsbury l'invitait, en sifflant, à gagner l'univers auquel il menait, univers aux multiples splendeurs. Elle fit halte près du cadran solaire drapé de lichen et suivit du doigt la devise inscrite sur sa bordure: *Ainsi s'en va le temps.* Le temps s'en allait, oui, rapidement, impitoyablement, il vous filait entre les doigts, même à la Nouvelle Lune, pourtant préservée des courants du modernisme. Cette voie qui lui était proposée, ne devrait-elle pas l'emprunter?

«Connaîtrai-je encore le déclic, à New York?» se demanda-t-elle, songeuse

Qu'il était beau, le jardin que le cousin Jimmy aimait! Qu'elle était magnifique, la ferme de la Nouvelle Lune! Comment pouvait-elle penser à quitter cette chère maison qui l'avait accueillie et aimée, à quitter les tombeaux des aïeux près de l'étang de Blair Water, les champs immenses et les boisés où elle avait rêvé? Elle sut à l'instant qu'elle ne pourrait jamais les quitter, qu'elle n'avait jamais voulu partir. Et elle comprit pourquoi elle avait quêté si désespérément les avis de son entourage. Elle espérait qu'on lui dise de rester. Dean, lui, le lui aurait recommandé.

— J'appartiens à la Nouvelle Lune, se dit-elle. Je reste avec les miens.

Cette décision était irrévocable, et elle l'avait prise seule, sans l'aide de personne. Pénétrée d'une profonde satisfaction intérieure, elle remonta l'allée, entra dans la maison et alla trouver la tante Élisabeth, la tante Laura et le cousin Jimmy dans la cuisine éclairée par la magie des chandelles.

— Je n'irai pas à New York, tante Élisabeth, dit-elle. Je vais rester avec vous à la Nouvelle Lune.

La tante Laura laissa fuser un petit cri de joie. Le cousin Jimmy cria: Bravo! La tante Élisabeth finit posément un rang de son tricot.

— À mon sens, déclara-t-elle enfin, c'est là ce qu'une Murray se devait de décider.

Le lundi qui suivit, Émilie se rendit tout droit à la Cendraie. De retour de Charlottetown, Mlle Royal l'accueillit chaleureusement.

— Tu viens m'annoncer que ta tante Élisabeth a consenti à ce que tu m'accompagnes, n'est-ce pas, ma mignonne?

— Elle m'a dit que c'était à moi de décider.

Mlle Royal applaudit.

— Magnifique! Alors, tout est réglé?

Émilie était pâle, mais son visage grave reflétait l'intensité de ses sentiments.

— Oui, tout est réglé: je n'y vais pas, dit-elle. Je vous remercie du plus profond de mon cœur, mademoiselle Royal, mais je ne peux pas vous accompagner.

La regardant jusqu'au fond des yeux, Janet Royal comprit qu'il ne lui servait à rien d'insister. Elle n'en insista pas moins.

— Émilie, je ne peux pas le croire. Tu ne veux pas me suivre?

— Je ne peux pas quitter la Nouvelle Lune. Elle me tient trop à cœur.

— Je croyais que tu voulais venir avec moi, fit Mlle Royal, d'un ton de reproche.

— Je le croyais aussi. Et une partie de moi le veut encore, mais une autre partie refuse de s'en aller. Ne me croyez pas ingrate, mademoiselle Royal.

— Je ne te crois pas ingrate, mais je crois que tu fais une bêtise. Tu rejettes délibérément tes chances d'avenir. Qu'est-ce que tu pourras bien produire, ici, qui ait quelque valeur, ma chère enfant? Tu n'as pas idée des obstacles qui vont jalonner ta route. Il n'y a pas de matière littéraire, ici, pas d'atmosphère...

— Je saurai créer ma propre atmosphère, rétorqua Émilie. quant à la matière littéraire, c'est a moi d'en juger. Les gens *vivent*, ici comme ailleurs. Ils souffrent et ils jouissent. Ils pèchent et ils espèrent, tout comme les gens de New York.

— Comment le sais-tu? s'informa Mlle Royal avec humeur. Je t'assure que tu ne pourras jamais écrire quoi que ce soit de valable dans ce petit patelin. Où puiserais-tu ton inspiration? Tu n'auras jamais tes coudées franches à l'extérieur. Les éditeurs ne verront pas plus loin que l'adresse de retour: Île-du-Prince-Édouard, sur tes manuscrits. C'est un suicide littéraire que tu commets. Et c'est à trois heures du matin, par les nuits d'insomnie, que tu t'en rendras compte. Bien sûr, avec les années, tu amasseras une clientèle d'écoles du dimanche et de journaux d'agriculteurs. Mais est-ce que cela te suffira? Tu sais bien que non. C'est alors que naîtront les jalousies qui existent dans les petites agglomérations: tu auras laissé tes compagnons d'école loin derrière et plusieurs ne te le pardonneront pas. Ils croiront tous que tu es l'héroïne de tes romans, surtout si tu décris celle-ci comme jolie et charmante. Si tu écris un roman d'amour, ils seront certains que c'est le tien. Tu en auras tellement marre des gens de Blair Water, dont tu connaîtras tous les secrets, que tu auras l'impression de relire le même livre pour la vingtième fois. Je parle d'expérience. J'étais là avant que tu viennes au monde. Tu connaîtras le découragement. Le coup de trois heures, à l'horloge, en viendra à t'accabler: n'oublie pas qu'il sonne toutes les nuits. Tu finiras par tout laisser tomber et par épouser ton cousin.

— Jamais.

— Ou, alors, quelqu'un qui lui ressemble. Et tu t'encroûteras.

— Je ne m'encroûterai jamais, fit Émilie, le ton décidé. Jamais au grand jamais.

— ... et tu auras un salon comme celui de ma tante Angela. Avec un manteau de cheminée orné de photos, un chevalet portant un portrait dans un cadre de huit pouces de largeur, un album de peluche rouge recouvert d'un napperon crocheté, une courtepointe de toutes les couleurs sur le lit de la chambre des invités et, touche suprême d'élégance, un asparagus au centre de la table de la salle à manger.

— Non, dit gravement Émilie, ces choses n'ont rien de commun avec les traditions des Murray.

— Alors, disons que tu auras l'équivalent. J'imagine ta vie, dans un endroit comme celui-ci, où les gens ne voient pas plus loin que le bout de leur nez.

— Moi, je vois plus loin que ça, dit Émilie, en redressant le menton. Je vois jusqu'aux étoiles.

— Je parlais au figuré, ma chère.

— Moi aussi. Oh! mademoiselle Royal, je sais que la vie est plutôt quotidienne, dans les parages, mais le ciel m'y appartient en propre. Je ne réussirai peut-être pas, ici, mais, alors, je n'aurais pas réussi, non plus à New York.

Mlle Royal leva les bras au ciel.

— Je me rends. Tu commets une erreur, mais si, dans les années qui viennent, je m'aperçois que je me suis trompée, je t'écrirai pour te le dire. Et si *toi*, tu t'aperçois que tu t'es trompée, écris-moi. Tu me trouveras toujours prête à t'aider. Je ne te dirai même pas: Je te l'avais dit! Envoie-moi celles de tes histoires qui conviennent à mon magazine et n'hésite pas à me demander mon avis sur ce que je connais. Je retourne à New York demain. Je remettais à juillet parce que je comptais te ramener avec moi. Puisque tu ne viens pas, je pars. Je déteste vivre là où les gens pensent que j'ai mal joué mes cartes et que j'ai perdu au jeu matrimonial, et là où les vieux de la vieille passent leur temps à me dire que je ressemble à ma mère. Ma mère était *laide*. Alors, disons-nous au revoir, et qu'on en finisse.

— Mademoiselle Royal, dit Émilie, grave, j'apprécie votre bonté à mon égard, vous le savez n'est-ce pas? Votre sympathie et vos encouragements ont eu plus d'importance pour moi que vous ne pouvez l'imaginer.

Mlle Royal chassa une larme du revers de la main et posa un baiser sur la joue d'Émilie.

— Que la chance t'accompagne, dit-elle, voilà mon souhait. En ce qui me concerne, j'aimerais qu'un endroit au monde me devienne aussi cher que la Nouvelle Lune l'est pour toi. Ce serait bien.

À trois heures, cette nuit-là, une Émilie insomniaque mais heureuse se rappela qu'elle n'avait, de sa vie, vu Chu-Chin.

253

XXV

Amour de printemps

«**10 juin, 19-**

«Hier soir, Andrew Oliver Murray a demandé Émilie Byrd Starr en mariage. Émilie Byrd Starr a répondu non.

«Je suis contente que cette affaire soit réglée. Je la sentais se préciser depuis trop longtemps. À chacune de ses visites, Andrew orientait la conversation vers des sujets sérieux auxquels je ne me sentais pas prête à faire face. J'étais venue à bout, chaque fois, de le faire bifurquer sur des sujets badins, mais ça ne faisait que repousser l'échéance.

«Hier soir, je suis allée vagabonder au Bois Debout pour l'une des dernières fois. J'ai grimpé les collines couvertes de conifères et admiré d'en haut les champs de brume et d'argent du clair de lune. Au-delà du port, au couchant, s'allongeait un ciel de pourpre et d'ambre. Derrière moi, c'était l'obscurité des pins, l'antichambre des rêves, royaume du mystère, où tout peut devenir réalité.

«Je cherchais des mots neufs pour exprimer ce que je ressentais, quand est survenu Andrew, tout propret, tout compassé et distingué.

«Quel dommage que les favoris soient passés de mode, ai-je pensé. Ils lui iraient si bien!

«Andrew était venu, c'était évident, pour me dire quelque chose de spécial. Autrement, il ne m'aurait pas suivie au pays

255

du Bois Debout, mais m'aurait attendue, en tout bien, tout honneur, dans le salon de tante Ruth. Il fallait y passer: j'y passerais. L'attitude d'expectative de tante Ruth et des gens de la Nouvelle Lune devenait oppressante. Sans doute croyaient-ils tous que mon refus d'aller à New York tenait à la présence d'Andrew. Je n'allais quand même pas le laisser me demander en mariage au clair de lune, dans le pays du Bois Debout. Je risquais de répondre oui, ensorcelée par le décor. Alors, quand il a laissé tomber: C'est joli, ici; restons-y un moment, j'ai dit, gentiment mais fermement, qu'il faisait trop humide pour une personne menacée de tuberculose et que je préférais rentrer.

«Nous rentrâmes. Je m'assis face à lui et m'absorbai dans la contemplation d'un bout de laine tombé sur le tapis. Ce bout de laine, je me souviendrai de sa couleur et de sa forme jusqu'à ma mort. Andrew se mit à parler d'abondance de choses et d'autres, semant, çà et là, des indices: il obtiendrait la gérance de son entreprise dans deux ans, au plus tard... c'était bien, selon lui, de se marier jeune... et ainsi de suite. Il s'enferrait dans son discours. J'aurais pu lui faciliter les choses, mais, me souvenant de sa défection, lors du scandale de la maison John, j'avais durci mon cœur. Il lança enfin:

— Marions-nous, Émilie. Aussitôt que j'en serai capable.

«Sentant qu'il lui fallait ajouter quelque chose, mais ne sachant pas exactement quoi, il répéta: ...Aussitôt que j'en serai capable... et s'arrêta, bloqué.

— Pourquoi nous marierions-nous? ai-je demandé.

«Andrew en est resté tout pantois.

— Parce que... ça me plairait, a-t-il bégayé.

— Ça ne me plairait pas, ai-je dit.

«Il m'a fixée du regard un long moment, cherchant à comprendre comment il était possible qu'on pût refuser sa proposition.

— Pourquoi pas? a-t-il demandé, comme l'aurait fait tante Ruth.

— Parce que je ne t'aime pas.

«Andrew a rougi et m'a jugée sans scrupules.

— Je... je croyais... que ça plairait à tout le monde, a-t-il balbutié.

256

— Pas à moi, ai-je répété, sur un ton auquel il ne pouvait se méprendre.

«Il en fut si étonné qu'il en ressentit plus de surprise que de tristesse et ne sut alors plus que dire ni que faire. Un Murray ne s'abaissant pas à supplier, il est parti sans demander son reste et sans même claquer la porte. Le vent l'a fait pour lui. S'il avait au moins claqué la porte, j'en eus été moins frustrée.

«Le lendemain matin, tante Ruth, qui est tout sauf subtile et qui avait tiré ses propres conclusions de la brièveté de la visite d'Andrew, s'informa de ce qui s'était passé. Je lui ai répondu franchement.

— Mais qu'est-ce que tu lui reproches? a-t-elle interrogé, estomaquée.

— Il n'a pas de défauts, mais il est insignifiant, ai-je répondu, le nez en l'air. Il a peut-être toutes les vertus, mais il faudrait lui ajouter une pincée de sel.

— Tu pourrais faire beaucoup moins bien, sans aller loin, a-t-elle rétorqué, sous-entendant Stovepipe Town.

«J'aurais pu la rassurer: la semaine d'avant, Perry m'avait appris qu'il entrait à l'étude de Me Abel, à Charlottetown, occasion inespérée pour devenir avocat. Me Abel a entendu son discours au débat interscolaire et l'a gardé à l'œil, depuis. J'ai félicité Perry, ravie pour lui.

— Il me donnera assez pour payer ma pension, a dit Perry, et je me tirerai d'affaire pour m'habiller et pour les à-côtés. Ma tante Tom refuse de m'aider. *Tu* sais pourquoi.

— Désolée, Perry, ai-je dit, avec un petit rire.

— Tu ne veux vraiment pas m'épouser, Émilie? a-t-il quêté. J'aimerais que cette chose soit réglée.

— Elle l'est, ai-je dit.

— Tu trouves que je me conduis en parfait idiot avec toi.

— En effet, ai-je dit, riant plus fort.

«Je n'ai jamais pu le prendre au sérieux. J'ai toujours l'impression qu'il s'imagine qu'il est amoureux de moi.

— J'irai loin, Émilie, a-t-il insisté. Des hommes de mon calibre, tu n'en trouveras pas à la douzaine.

— J'en suis persuadée, ai-je dit, convaincue qu'il disait vrai. Nulle personne n'en sera plus charmée que ton amie, ici présente.

— Oh, les amis! a riposté Perry, déçu. Ce n'est pas une amie que je cherche en toi. Bon. Rien ne sert de cajoler les Murray pour en obtenir quoi que ce soit. Je n'en ferai donc rien, mais dis-moi au moins si tu vas épouser Andrew Murray, même si ce n'est pas moi que ça regarde.

— Ça ne te regarde pas, mais je te répondrai quand même: je ne l'épouse pas.

— Très bien, a conclu Perry, en me quittant. Si jamais tu changeais d'avis à mon sujet, préviens-moi. Si je n'ai pas changé d'avis moi non plus, on y verra.

«J'ai retranscrit cette conversation dans mon journal, mais j'en ai rédigé une autre version pour mon calepin-Jimmy. La version qui aurait dû être. J'apprends à laisser mes personnages parler d'amour avec naturel. Dans mon compte rendu imaginaire, Perry et moi nous nous exprimions comme dans les romans.

«Perry s'est senti, à ce qu'il m'a semblé, plus malheureux qu'Andrew de mon refus et j'en ai été peinée. Perry, c'est le camarade idéal. Je déteste le décevoir, mais il s'en remettra vite.

«Je serai donc la seule du quatuor à rester à Blair Water, l'année prochaine. Je trouverai sûrement le temps long. Peut-être qu'à trois heures du matin, je souhaiterai avoir suivi Mlle Royal, mais je vais m'atteler à ma tâche avec persévérance. J'ai une montagne à gravir pour atteindre la cime de mon sentier alpestre. Mais j'ai confiance en moi et j'irai de l'avant.»

«La Nouvelle Lune, 21 juin, 19-

«Ce soir, quand je suis entrée, j'ai deviné, à son air réprobateur, que tante Élisabeth savait tout à propos d'Andrew. Tante Laura paraissait peinée, mais ni l'une ni l'autre ne m'a rien dit. J'en ai parlé, au jardin, avec cousin Jimmy. Paraît-il qu'Andrew se sent mal en point depuis que l'effet de choc s'est dissipé. Il a perdu l'appétit, et tante Addie s'enquiert avec indignation si je m'attends à épouser un prince ou un millionnaire, puisque *son* fils n'est pas assez bon pour moi.»

«Je ne sais ce qui est pis: que quelqu'un qu'on n'aime pas vous demande votre main, ou que quelqu'un qu'on aime ne vous la demande pas. Les deux sont affreux.

«J'en suis venue à la conclusion que j'ai imaginé certaines des choses qui se sont passées dans la vieille maison John. Je crains bien que tante Ruth n'ait eu raison de dire que mon imagination a besoin d'être bridée. Ce soir, j'ai flâné dans le jardin. Bien que nous soyons en juin, c'était froid et humide et je me sentais un peu seule, découragée et à plat — peut-être parce que deux histoires dont j'espérais des étincelles m'étaient revenues dans le courrier. Soudain, j'ai entendu le signal de Teddy, son petit sifflement amical, au fond du verger. Je me suis précipitée. C'est toujours comme ça: il n'a qu'à me faire signe et j'accours, mais seul mon journal le sait.

«Dès que j'ai vu son visage, j'ai su qu'il avait de grandes nouvelles à communiquer.

«Il en avait. Il m'a tendu une lettre adressée à M. Frédéric Kent. J'oublie toujours que Frédéric est le nom de Teddy. Pour moi, il est et restera Teddy. Il a obtenu une bourse d'études de l'École des Beaux-Arts de Montréal: cinq cents dollars pour deux ans. Je suis devenue aussi emballée qu'il l'était, avec, derrière cet emballement, un étrange sentiment fait de crainte, d'espoir et d'expectative dont je ne savais ce qui prédominait.

— C'est épatant, ce qui t'arrive, Teddy, ai-je dit, la voix frémissante. J'en suis enchantée pour toi. Qu'est-ce que ta mère en pense?

— Elle m'autorise à partir. J'aurais voulu qu'elle m'accompagne, mais elle ne veut pas quitter le Trécarré. Elle y sera bien seule. Ça m'inquiète. Si elle avait eu de l'amitié pour toi, je serais parti rassuré: tu lui aurais été d'un grand réconfort.

«Et moi, Teddy, moi? ai-je pensé. Est-ce que je n'aurai pas aussi besoin de réconfort?

«Tout fut silence. Par le chemin de Demain, nous gagnâmes le pré de l'étang et nous restâmes appuyés à la clôture dans les ténèbres gris-vert des pins. Je me suis soudain sentie pénétrée de bonheur. Pendant quelques minutes, une partie de moi a planté un jardin, bâti d'amples penderies, acheté une douzaine de cuillers à thé en argent, modernisé un grenier et ourlé une nappe de damas double. L'autre partie *a attendu*.

«Et qu'a dit Teddy, à la fin, en regardant Blair Water, le firmament, les dunes et les vastes prairies verdoyantes et tout, sauf moi?

— Je vais travailler dur et tirer le maximum de ces deux années-là. Ensuite,... je me débrouillerai pour aller à Paris. J'ai soif depuis toujours de traverser l'océan et d'aller admirer les œuvres des grands maîtres, de voir les paysages que leur génie a immortalisés. Et, quand je reviendrai,...

«Teddy s'interrompit abruptement et se tourna vers moi. Il y avait une telle flamme dans son regard que j'ai cru qu'il allait m'embrasser. J'ai fermé les yeux.

— Quand je reviendrai, a-t-il répété...

«Il s'est de nouveau arrêté.

— Oui? ai-je soufflé, le cœur gonflé d'espoir.

— Je rendrai le nom de Frédéric Kent célèbre au Canada, a dit Teddy.

«J'ai ouvert les yeux.

«Sourcils froncés, Teddy regardait Blair Water, baigné dans l'or indistinct du couchant.

«L'air nocturne m'est néfaste, ai-je pensé, frissonnante. Sur un bonsoir poli, je les ai plantés là, lui et ses sourcils froncés. Teddy était-il trop timide pour m'embrasser? Ou, alors, peut-être ne le souhaitait-il pas?

«Je pourrais l'aimer éperdument, si je l'osais et s'il le souhaitait. Mais ça paraît évident que lui ne le souhaite pas. Il ne pense plus qu'au succès, qu'à sa carrière. Il a oublié le regard que nous avons échangé dans la vieille maison John. Il a oublié qu'il m'a dit, il y a trois ans, sur la tombe de George Horton, que j'étais la fille la plus délicieuse du monde. Des filles délicieuses, il va en connaître des centaines. Il m'oubliera.

«Je n'y peux rien.

«S'il ne veut pas de moi, je ne voudrai pas de lui. C'est une tradition, chez les Murray. Mais je ne suis une Murray qu'à moitié. La moitié Starr entre aussi en ligne de compte. C'est heureux que j'aie, comme Teddy, une carrière à laquelle me consacrer.

«Trois sentiments se disputent mon âme.

«Le premier, c'est de rester fidèle aux traditions de ma caste.

«Le second, c'est qu'il se glisse, là-dessous, quelque chose qui me ferait horriblement souffrir, si je me laissais aller à en prendre pleinement conscience.

«Et le troisième, dominant les deux autres, est un étrange sentiment de soulagement: je reste libre.»

«26 juin, 19-
«Ilse était furieuse que Perry ait présumé que je l'épouserais.

— Ce n'était pas de la présomption, ai-je dit en riant, c'était de la condescendance. Perry appartient à la noble maison des marquis de Carabas.

— Il fera son chemin dans la vie, c'est certain, mais il y aura toujours, dans son sillage, un relent de Stovepipe Town, a rétorqué Ilse.

— Pourquoi es-tu si dure envers lui? ai-je protesté.

— Je n'aime pas les Tit-Jos-Connaissants, a-t-elle répliqué, morose.

— Il est à l'âge où les garçons croient tout savoir, ai-je dit, me sentant vieille et sage. Avec le temps, il deviendra moins savant et plus supportable. Il s'est beaucoup amélioré depuis qu'il vit à Shrewsbury.

— Tu en parles comme d'un navet, a fulminé Ilse. Miséricorde, Émilie, cesse d'étaler ta supériorité et ta suffisance!

«J'avais mérité cette rebuffade. Ilse me ramène sur le plancher des vaches.»

«27 juin, 19-
La nuit dernière, j'ai rêvé que j'étais debout dans la cuisine d'été de la Nouvelle Lune et que le diamant perdu brillait sur le sol à mes pieds. Je m'en suis saisie avec ravissement. Il a reposé un moment dans ma main, puis il m'a échappé et s'est élancé dans l'air à la vitesse de l'éclair, laissant derrière lui un sillon étincelant. Il est devenu une étoile au-dessus du bout du monde. C'est mon étoile, il faut que je l'atteigne avant qu'elle ne s'efface, ai-je pensé, et je me suis lancée à sa poursuite. Soudain, Dean est apparu à mes côtés. Lui aussi suivait l'étoile. J'ai ralenti le pas parce qu'il boite, mais l'étoile, elle,

261

descendait de plus en plus rapidement. Je ne pouvais quand même pas abandonner Dean à son sort. Puis, tout aussi soudainement que Dean était venu, Teddy a surgi à mes côtés. Il me tendait les mains, avec, dans les yeux, le regard que j'y ai vu deux fois. J'ai mis mes mains dans les siennes. Il m'a attirée vers lui. J'ai relevé la figure. C'est alors que Dean a gémi : Mon étoile est disparue! J'ai tourné la tête pour vérifier, et je me suis éveillée sur un petit matin morne et pluvieux, un matin sans étoile, sans Teddy, sans baiser.

«Qu'est-ce que ce rêve peut bien signifier, si tant est que les rêves signifient quelque chose?»

«28 juin, 19-

C'est ma dernière nuit à Shrewsbury. Demain, cousin Jimmy viendra nous chercher, ma malle et moi, dans la charrette, et nous roulerons en grand apparat jusqu'à la Nouvelle Lune.

«Ces trois années à Shrewsbury me paraissaient interminables, quand je m'y suis engagée. En rétrospective, c'était hier. Et hier est derrière moi. J'y ai beaucoup appris : je n'emploie presque plus d'italiques, maintenant, dans mes textes. Je souris devant les lettres de rejet. Ça n'a pas été facile, mais j'y suis arrivée.

«Nous avons eu notre cérémonie de graduation, cet après-midi. J'avais mis ma nouvelle robe d'organdi crème, semée de violettes, et je portais un gros bouquet de pivoines roses. Dean, qui est à Montréal, où il s'est arrêté avant de rentrer, m'a fait télégraphier un bouquet de dix-sept roses, une pour chaque année de ma vie, et ce bouquet m'a été présenté quand je suis montée sur la scène chercher mon diplôme. Gentil.

«Perry, l'orateur de la classe, a prononcé un bon discours. Il a décroché la médaille d'excellence.

«J'ai rédigé les prédictions pour la classe. Et les ai lues. Le public a semblé apprécier. Celles que j'avais rédigées dans mon calepin-Jimmy étaient autrement plus divertissantes, mais il aurait été malséant de les livrer à cet auditoire.

«J'ai rédigé, ce soir, mon dernier carnet mondain pour M. Towers. Cette presse à sensation, je l'ai toujours détestée, mais j'avais besoin des sous qu'elle m'apportait.

«J'ai fait ma valise. Tante Ruth me regardait faire en silence. Silence déconcertant. Elle a finalement laissé tomber, en soupirant:

— Tu vas me manquer terriblement, Émilie.

«Voyez-vous ça! Était-ce bien tante Ruth qui parlait ainsi? J'avais peine à le croire. Déjà, elle s'était montrée étonnamment compréhensive, lors du scandale de la maison John. Je ne la voyais plus du même œil. Mais, de là à penser que je lui manquerais, il y avait un pas.

«Il fallait dire quelque chose.

— Je vous serai toujours reconnaissante, tante Ruth, ai-je dit, pour ce que vous avez fait pour moi, pendant ces trois années.

— Je n'ai fait que mon devoir, a-t-elle répondu, la mine vertueuse.»

* * *

«Ça m'étonne, mais je me rends compte que je suis triste de quitter cette petite chambre que je n'ai jamais aimée et qui ne m'a pas aimée, elle non plus, et la longue colline étoilée de lumières. J'ai connu ici de merveilleux moments. Le pauvre Byron agonisant y a participé, mais rien au monde ne me fera regretter le chromo de la reine Alexandra ou le vase de fleurs artificielles. La dame Giovanna me suit, bien sûr. Sa place est toute prête dans ma chambre, à la Nouvelle Lune. Ici, elle a toujours semblé en exil.

«Je n'entendrai plus le vent du soir, dans le pays du Bois Debout. Mais j'aurai mon vent à moi, dans le boisé du Grand Fendant.

«Tante Élisabeth a dit que j'aurais une lampe à kérosène pour écrire. Ma porte, à la Nouvelle Lune, ferme hermétiquement et je n'aurai plus à boire de cet insipide thé de fleur.

«Ce soir, au coucher du soleil, j'ai gagné le petit étang où j'ai toujours aimé m'attarder, les nuits de printemps. À travers les arbres qui le bordent, de délicates teintes de rose et de safran se faufilaient à l'ouest. Il n'y avait pas un souffle de vent et toutes les feuilles et les branches et les fougères et les brins d'herbe s'y reflétaient. J'ai vu mon visage réfléchi dans l'étang.

Par un bizarre caprice de la lumière, l'une des branches d'un arbre semblait me couronner de lauriers.

«Je me suis dit que c'était de bon augure.

«Après tout, Teddy n'était peut-être que timide?»

Émilie de la Nouvelle Lune 1
Extraits de critiques

...Émilie est une fée, à sa manière. Comme l'auteure qui l'a créée, elle sait d'un coup de plume traduire et transformer, ensorceler et exorciser le réel. Et comme par hasard, elle habite un petit coin d'univers magique et ravissant : la Nouvelle Lune.

(*Châtelaine,* décembre 1983)

...Lucy Maud Montgomery nous livre un texte d'une richesse et d'une complexité étonnantes, un texte ou fantasmes morbides, descriptions poétiques et innocence enchanteresse se chevauchent et s'enchevêtrent inextricablement, un texte où enfants et adultes peuvent trouver leur compte.

(Danielle Thaler, *Canadien Children's Literature/ Littérature canadienne pour la jeunesse,* n° 37 — 1985)

...Émilie enchante. Rien d'étonnant, puisqu'elle a les oreilles pointues des lutins et, comme les fées, le pouvoir magique de s'évader sur les ailes de la lune ou du vent. Un roman émouvant, chaleureux et parfois même éblouissant.

(Livres québécois pour enfants — *Sélection de Communication-Jeunesse,* 1986)

...Émilie est un personnage attachant... La traduction de Paule Daveluy est excellente. Celle-ci a non seulement retenu tout l'esprit, l'humour et la sensibilité du roman original, mais elle a décrit le milieu avec autant de réalisme et d'animation que Lucy Maud Montgomery.

(*Un choix de livres canadiens* — supplément 83 — Irène Aubrey)

265

Composition et mise en pages:
LES ATELIERS CHIORA INC.
Montréal

Achevé d'imprimer sur les presses de
Metrolitho Inc. — Sherbrooke
le quatrième trimestre mil neuf cent quatre-vingt-huit